THE FUTURE OF THE PACIFIC RIM

THE FUTURE OF THE PACIFIC RIM

Scenarios for Regional Cooperation

EDITED BY
Barbara K. Bundy, Stephen D. Burns, and Kimberly V. Weichel

Foreword by
Boutros Boutros-Ghali

Westport, Connecticut
London

Library of Congress Cataloging-in-Publication Data

The future of the Pacific rim : scenarios for regional cooperation / edited by
Barbara K. Bundy, Stephen D. Burns, and Kimberly V. Weichel ;
foreword by Boutros Boutros-Ghali.
p. cm.
Includes bibliographical references and index.
ISBN 0-275-94699-1 (alk. paper). ISBN 0-275-95088-3 (pbk.).
1. Pacific Area cooperation. 2. Pacific Area—Economic policy.
3. Pacific Area—Economic integration. 4. National security—
Pacific Area. 5. Asia—Economic policy. 6. Asia—Economic
integration. 7. National security—Asia. I. Bundy, Barbara K.
II. Burns, Stephen D. III. Weichel, Kimberly V.
HC681.P28295 1994
337.1'9—dc20 94-2982

British Library Cataloguing in Publication Data is available.

Library of Congress Catalog Card Number: 94-2982
ISBN 0-275-94699-1
ISBN 0-275-95088-3 (pbk.)

First published in 1994

Praeger Publishers, 88 Post Road West, Westport, CT 06881
An imprint of Greenwood Publishing Group, Inc.

Printed in the United States of America

The paper used in this book complies with the
Permanent Paper Standard issued by the National
Information Standards Organization (Z39.48-1984).

10 9 8 7 6 5 4 3 2 1

Contents

V
Emerging Players in Pacific Rim Regionalism

VI
New Directions for the Future

Foreword

In an era of rapid global change, when many old assumptions about the international system are being questioned, attention is rightly focusing on parts of the world where change seems to be particularly rapid. The Pacific Rim — an area that extends from the ancient kingdoms of Southeast Asia to the emerging nations of the Pacific Islands and includes the dynamic economies of Northeast Asia — is one such region.

This volume, bringing together scholars and practitioners of international relations in an expert survey of international relations in the region, is, therefore, particularly welcome at this time.

One theme of this book is the role of regional organizations. The importance of regional cooperation, and of regional organizations, in supporting and reinforcing the work of the international organizations, has never been as great as it is today. In a region like the Pacific Rim, where levels of development are uneven, regional cooperation takes on a special significance. It will, therefore, be particularly interesting to see how the work of regional organizations is coordinated with the work of the United Nations, which has already been called on to carry out a variety of tasks in the region.

The United Nations has played a major role in a number of countries of the region. The international community has invested substantial human and financial resources in support of peace and progress in Southeast Asia. In Cambodia, for example, the United Nations undertook one of the greatest commitments in history.

What of the region's place in the world of the future? In many ways, this is a region of outstanding promise. Yet, prophecy in international relations is a hazardous undertaking. Many of the elements in the global world of the future remain unpredictable.

One element that is now clearly emerging is the question of information. The Age of Information has begun. Global commerce is now linked by communication technology, which compresses time and space into a new, unified world system in which information is the key resource. This new fact of global life has vast implications, especially for the Pacific Rim. It puts a new focus on human rights and development.

In the post–Cold War era, a new and broader vision of peace and international security is emerging. It is a vision that recognizes that the three great tasks given to the United Nations by its Charter — the maintenance of international peace and security, the promotion of economic and social progress, and the protection of human rights — are interlocking and indivisible. Development, peace, and democratization, in other words, are mutually self-supporting.

The work of the United Nations in fulfilling its Charter mandate has already moved far beyond the limited peacekeeping operations of the past. The international community has convened major international conferences to consider such issues as the environment and sustainable development, human rights, the role of women, and economic and social development.

In the Pacific Rim, as in the world in general, lasting peace and sustainable development will come through the successful blending of these different elements. The United Nations will, for its part, proclaim international standards and do all it can to support member states in their efforts to abide by those standards.

I congratulate the editors and contributors on their initiative in bringing out this book, which I know will provide stimulating material for debate and discussion of many key issues in the region.

Boutros Boutros-Ghali

Acknowledgments

We have many colleagues and friends to thank for their help on this book. We thank each of them who cannot be mentioned here individually. Above all, we thank our contributors, who come literally from around the Pacific Rim, for giving generously of their knowledge and experience to make this book possible.

We especially thank Dr. Antonius D. J. Brantenaar, visiting scholar at the Hoover Institution on War, Peace and Revolution at Stanford University, for his commitment to this book from its very beginning and his valuable suggestions along the way. Mark Borthwick, executive director of the U.S. Pacific Economic Cooperation Council Committee, was also encouraging and helpful. The late Mark Earle, Jr., deserves special mention for his invaluable assistance in the early stages of this volume.

We owe great thanks to Krysten Cogswell Elbers of the University of San Francisco Center for the Pacific Rim for her exceptional organizational and editing assistance on the project. We also acknowledge the University of San Francisco Center for the Pacific Rim for serving as the secretariat for the project and Mark Mir of the Ricci Institute at the University of San Francisco for his research assistance and cartography.

Finally, we are most grateful to Praeger Publishers for their support along the way and for making this publication possible.

Acronyms

ADB	Asian Development Bank
AFTA	ASEAN Free Trade Association, ASEAN Free Trade Area, ASEAN Free Trade Agreement (in process)
ANZCERTA	Australia-New Zealand Closer Economic Relations Trade Agreement
APEC	Asia Pacific Economic Cooperation / Asia Pacific Economic Conference
ARATS	Association for Relations Across the Taiwan Straits
ASA	Association of Southeast Asia
ASEAN	Association of Southeast Asian Nations (Brunei, Indonesia, Malaysia, Philippines, Thailand, Singapore)
ASEAN-PMC	ASEAN Post-Ministerial Conference
ASSW	Anti-Strategic Submarine Warfare
ASW	Antisubmarine Warfare
CAP	Common Agricultural Policy
CCC	Customs Cooperation Council
CEPT	Common Effective Preferential Tariff
CER	Closer Economic Region
CNN	Cable News Network
CSCA	Conference on Security and Cooperation in Asia
CSCAP	Council for Security Cooperation in the Asia Pacific
CSCE	Conference on Security and Cooperation in Europe
CUSTA	Canada-U.S. Trade Agreement
DAC	Development Assistance Committee
DPP	Democratic Progressive Party (Taiwan)
DPRK	Democratic People's Republic of Korea (North Korea)

EAEG/EAEC	East Asia Economic Grouping / East Asia Economic Caucus
EAI	Enterprise for the Americas Initiative
EC	European Community
ECSC	European Coal and Steel Community
EDI	Electronic Data Interchange
EEA	European Economic Area
EEC	European Economic Community
EFTA	European Free Trade Association
EMS	European Monetary System
EPG	Eminent Persons Group (of APEC)
FDI	Foreign Direct Investment
FTA	Free Trade Agreement
G-7	Group of 7 Nations
GATT	General Agreement on Tariffs and Trade
GBN	Global Business Network
GDP	Gross Domestic Product
GNP	Gross National Product
HRD	Human Resource Development
IAEA	International Atomic Energy Agency
IGO	Intergovernmental Organization
IMF	International Monetary Fund
JERC	Japan Economic Research Center
JIIA	Japan Institute of International Affairs
LDC	Less Developed Country
LLDC	Least Developed Country
LDP	Liberal Democratic Party
MFN	Most Favored Nation
MITI	Ministry of International Trade and Industry
MNE	Multinational Enterprise
MTO	Multilateral Trade Organization
NAFTA	North American Free Trade Agreement
NET	National Economic Territories
NGO	Nongovernmental Organization
NIC	Newly Industrialized Country
NIEs	Newly Industrialized Economies
NPCSD	North Pacific Cooperative Security Dialogue
NPNWFZ	North Pacific Nuclear-Weapon-Free Zone
NPT	Nonproliferation Treaty
NTB	Nontariff Barriers
ODA	Official Development Assistance
OECD	Organization for Economic Cooperation and Development
OPTAD	Organization for Pacific Trade and Development
PAFTA	Pacific Free Trade Area
PAFTAD	Pacific Trade and Development Conference

PBEC	Pacific Basin Economic Council
PCC	Pacific Cooperation Committee
PEC	Pacific Economic Cooperation
PECC	Pacific Economic Cooperation Council
PRC	People's Republic of China
PRK	People's Republic of Kampuchea
PSA	Pacific Science Association
PTC	Pacific Telecommunications Council
RIC	Regionally Industrializing Core
ROC	Republic of China (Taiwan)
ROK	Republic of Korea (South Korea)
RTL	Regional Trade Liberalization
SEATO	Southeast Asia Treaty Organization
SEF	Straits Exchange Foundation
SEM	Single European Market
SEZ	Special Economic Zones
SII	Structural Impediments Initiatives (United States-Japan)
SLBM	Sea-launched Ballistic Missile
SOC	State of Cambodia
SRTA	Subregional Trade Arrangements
SSBN	Fleet Ballistic Nuclear Submarine
UMAP	University Mobility in the Asia Pacific
UNDP	United Nations Development Program
UNTAC	UN Transitional Authority in Cambodia
VER	Voluntary Export Restraint
ZOPAN	Zone of Peace, Freedom, and Neutrality

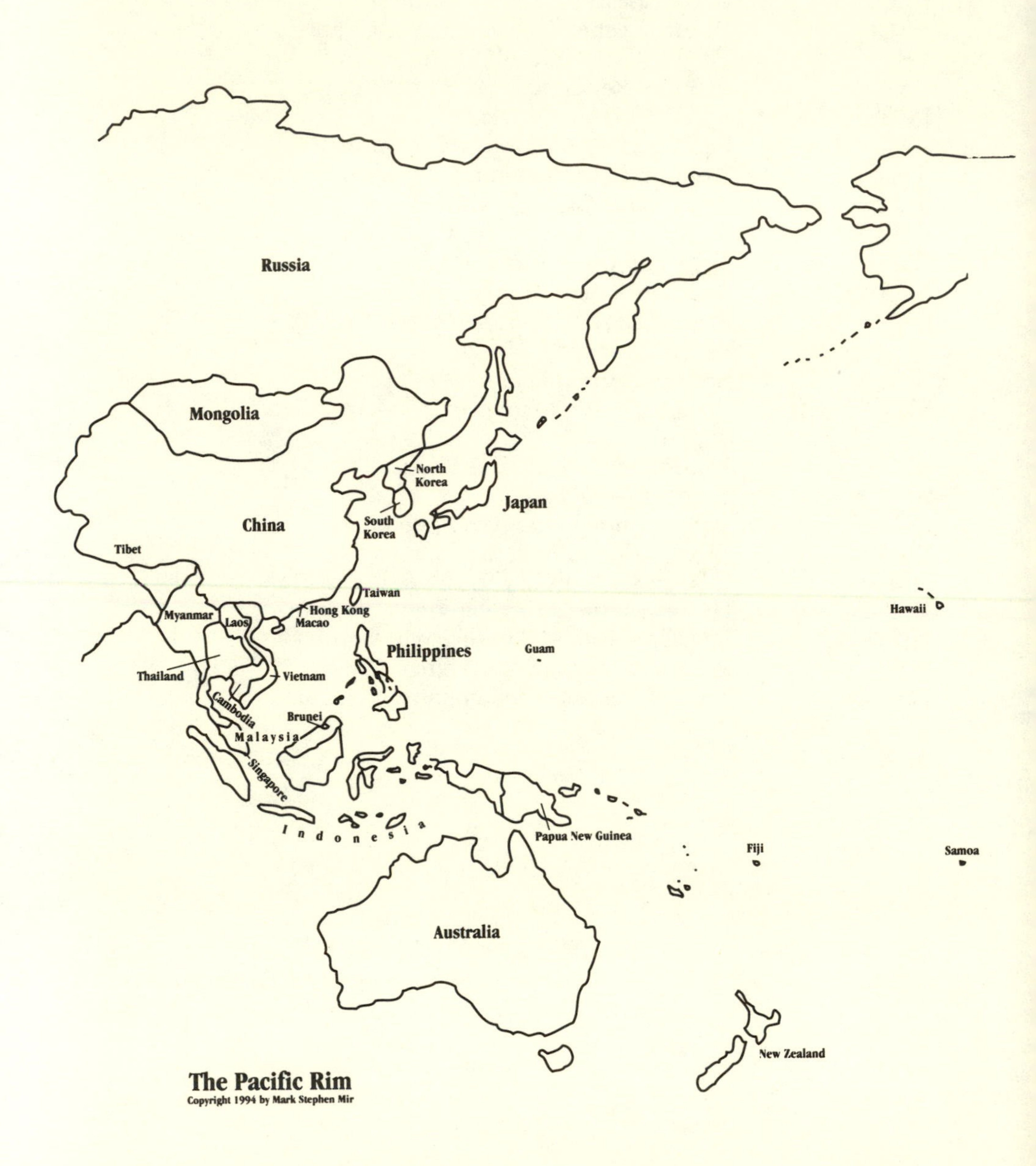
Russia
Mongolia
North Korea
South Korea
Japan
China
Tibet
Taiwan
Hong Kong
Macao
Myanmar
Laos
Thailand
Vietnam
Cambodia
Philippines
Guam
Hawaii
Brunei
Malaysia
Singapore
Indonesia
Papua New Guinea
Fiji
Samoa
Australia
New Zealand
The Pacific Rim
Copyright 1994 by Mark Stephen Mir

Canada
United States
Mexico
Honduras
Nicaragua
Guatemala
Panama
El Salvador
Costa Rica
Columbia
Ecuador
Peru
Chile

I

OVERVIEW OF REGIONAL COOPERATION IN THE PACIFIC REGION

1

Introduction

Barbara K. Bundy, Stephen D. Burns,
and Kimberly V. Weichel

THE WIDENING CIRCLE OF THE PACIFIC RIM

The focus of this volume is on the future of regional cooperation in the widening circle of the Pacific Rim. The chapters presented here focus on the Pacific Rim in the most inclusive sense of the term and represent diverse perspectives and voices from around the rim: the eastern, western, northern, and southern shores of the Pacific. The Pacific Rim has come to include the countries and economies of four distinct subregions:

the North Pacific, made up of East Asia (Greater China — the People's Republic of China, Hong Kong, and Taiwan — Japan, North and South Korea) and Russia;

Southeast Asia, which includes the six Association of Southeast Asian Nations (ASEAN) — Brunei, Indonesia, Malaysia, the Philippines, Singapore, and Thailand plus Indochina and Myanmar;

the Southwest Pacific, which includes Australia, New Zealand, Papua New Guinea and the diverse states and territories of Micronesia, Melanesia, and Polynesia; and

the Americas, including North America (Canada, Mexico, and the United States) and the western Pacific countries of Latin America.

Omitted from this operational concept of the Pacific Rim are contiguous geographical areas such as South Asia (Afghanistan, Bangladesh, India, Pakistan, and Sri Lanka) and the countries of Southwest Asia (Turkey, Iraq, Iran, the Arabian Peninsula, and the West Asian former Soviet republics of the Commonwealth of Independent States). The concept of the Pacific Rim, however, is undergoing redefinition at a quick pace in the evolving new world order. It is becoming defined less by geographic considerations and increasingly on a functional basis, by emerging Pan-Pacific interactions and influences that are determining the parameters of this dynamic geoeconomic and geopolitical concept.[1]

Randolph maintains that the success of Pacific economic regionalism in the 1990s will require a reconsideration of what constitutes "the Pacific" due to an expansion in the membership of what he calls the "Pacific club" and by the advent of a host of bilateral and subregional trade agreements and arrangements within the Pacific region. In this regard, we can look for a number of countries presently not included in the Pacific Rim concept to be included in the 1990s and beyond.

Meanwhile, the idea of a Pacific community remains controversial. Although President Clinton referred in his speech delivered at the July 1993 Group of 7 Summit to a "new Pacific Community," others, like Malaysian Prime Minister Mahathir, view the concept as an exaggeration, if not an impossibility. Mahathir maintains that economic imperatives alone are not enough: the ocean is too wide, with social, demographic, and political differences too extreme for a viable Pacific Rim community to emerge.

GLOBAL CHALLENGES IN THE POST–COLD WAR ERA

For the past 20 years the Asia Pacific region has easily outstripped all other regions of the world in terms of economic growth. In a 1993 study, "The East Asian Miracle," the World Bank estimates that over the next decade, East Asia alone will continue to outperform the rest of the world by a margin of at least two to one. According to the bank's report, the economies of eight East Asian superstars — Hong Kong, Indonesia, Japan, Malaysia, Singapore, South Korea, Taiwan, and Thailand — have together grown at an annual rate of 5.5 percent, more than twice as fast as the rest of East Asia and three times as fast as Latin America.

With the circle of subregions and countries included under the Pacific Rim concept continuing to expand and the prospect of a more powerful Pacific community on the horizon, it is clear that the Asia Pacific region will be driving future world economic growth. Frequent reference to the last two decades of this century as the Pacific era has forced upon public consciousness a different perspective of the world — as multipolar, with several centers of economic and political power, in contrast to the Washington-Moscow bipolar axis of the Cold War era. Because over half of the world's population lives in the Pacific, it is critically important to determine whether it is possible to restructure regional relations along more cooperative, transnational lines. This will serve the purpose of strengthening multilateral decision making and nonviolent dispute resolution mechanisms, as well as collective security agreements that emphasize nonproliferation of nuclear weapons and demilitarization. Democratization, sustainable development, and the protection of the environment and human rights are now issues included on international policy agendas — a marked change from the Cold War era, when military and economic security and the containment of communism were the primary goals of foreign policy.

As the post–World War II generation of leaders in the Asia Pacific begins to pass away, a new generation of leaders is emerging, with little or no memory of the war and the political rivalries that caused it. These new leaders understand the economic basis of the Asia Pacific's power, they recognize the debilitating effects of political infighting and conflict in the former Eastern bloc and Soviet Union, and they realize that regional cooperation and economic growth are the keys to greater prominence in global affairs.

We live in a world where boundaries are generally no longer clear. Geographic boundaries alone have undergone unimagined changes since the revolutions in Eastern Europe that began in 1989 and culminated in the collapse of the Soviet Union and the formal end of the Cold War on July 1, 1991, when the former Soviet Union abrogated the Warsaw Pact. These epoch-making events have ushered in a period of considerable global instability in the 1990s. International policy is changing, and ethnic and trade frictions among former allies have begun to escalate. Although the Asia Pacific today is more prosperous and stable than at any time in its history, new security concerns have arisen for the Pacific Rim. Controversies over borders on land and at sea, subregional disputes left over from the Cold War, increases in military procurements and deployments, and such transnational issues as emigration, drug trafficking, environmental pollution, and human rights all could lead to increased tensions and perhaps even the use of armed force between nations in the region.

Moreover, the growing national power of some regional actors (such as Japan, China, and India), coupled with the retrenchment of the two superpowers (Russia and the United States), produces a fluid, and potentially imbalanced, international strategic environment. As Harding points out, the governments of the Asia Pacific region tend to view cooperative mechanisms for dealing with these issues with considerable skepticism, on the one hand, and growing interest, on the other. There is "increasing awareness that many unconventional threats to national security can be effectively addressed through cooperative measures" such that it may be feasible eventually to create a single, regionwide security organization.

Importantly, the nation-state is no longer the sacrosanct building block it once was, as independent sovereign states have been transformed by information and knowledge, trade, capital flows, ethnic migration and overseas diasporas, disease, environmental degradation and the globalization process. Although the nation-state is likely to remain powerful in world affairs in the short term, sovereign states have lost their power to prosper in isolation and to work toward viable solutions to the global challenges facing us.

Instead, we face the prospect of a tripolar world shaped by regional blocs comprised of the European Community, the Americas, and the Asia Pacific region. Regional cooperation itself is also at a crossroads: it can take the shape of rigid trading blocs where protectionism is the norm, which can only weaken the world economy, or it can develop along the lines of recognizing that "closed," that is, discriminatory, regions are not viable in today's world. Therefore, we must strive to keep regions "open" as we seek to strengthen cooperative ties within and among regions as one step toward an acceptable globalism. "Globalism," notes Okita, "refers to the principle of nondiscriminatory and multilateral free trade promoting the unimpeded movement of goods, services, and the factors of production so as to contribute to global economic development and global economic integration."

As the sun sets on the twentieth century — an era dominated by Western powers and influences — global politics and economics enter a new phase. Perhaps the greatest single challenge confronting us as a world civilization in the future is to balance the tensions and conflicts among the forces of nationalism, regionalism, and globalism in a multipolar environment. We have come to realize that we cannot resort to using yesterday's mechanisms and structures to meet the challenges of a highly interdependent, global economy and that regional organizations and other multilateral institutions must work together to preserve and enhance economic openness and the national security of member states.

Unilateral actions have become dangerous, bilateral arrangements alone are limited in their effectiveness and inadequate to the collective realities we face, and multilateral cooperation is increasingly seen as essential to human survival, conflict resolution, and peacekeeping. The perception of the potential effectiveness of regional multilateral agreements and organizations in dealing with certain types of conflicts among member states cooperatively or collectively is increasing rather than diminishing in the post–Cold War international political order. In this context, "multigeopolicity," to use Olloqui's term, and "multilateralization," in Choate's words, are perceived to offer more viable alternatives to bipolarity or tripolarity for the future.

As a major Pacific power, the United States must concentrate on becoming a more serious partner in the Pacific Rim, not only in economic cooperation but also in comprehensive security matters (an area of highest priority) and in seeking multilateral policy solutions to the overwhelming problems related to environmentally sustainable development. Loss of U.S. political influence in Asia, not as a hegemony but as a stabilizer in neutralizing the negative aspects of potential trade blocs and economic wars and in security matters, means that more decisions will be made in Asian capitals without reference to U.S. wishes or interests. Revising this trend requires greater U.S. attention to the Asia Pacific region and new, more constructive U.S. policies. For perhaps the first time in history, the political, economic, social, and environmental state of the planet demands the creative leadership of persons, nations, and regions in dealing with transnational issues in wholly new ways.

CHALLENGES AHEAD

Economic regionalism and its mechanisms and structures will be seriously challenged in the remainder of the 1990s to accommodate new subregional systems and trade arrangements and increasing security concerns. In order to respond to the challenges ahead, a new paradigm clearly will be required that redefines the Pacific as a geoeconomic zone and articulates a rationale for how and why nations participating in subregional agreements can also benefit from participation in a wider regional framework.

As Kim, Choate, and Evans argue, the Asia Pacific Economic Cooperation forum is perhaps the key organizational mechanism for governmental involvement in future regional cooperation in the Pacific. Unlike the integration of the European Community, which was government led from the start, integration in the Asia Pacific and the broader Pacific Rim is market driven. Governments have been very reticent either to institutionalize or even to officially condone and fully support the movement. This tendency can be explained as due partly to lingering memories of World War II, partly to fears of Japanese or U.S. economic hegemony, and partly because it has been roughly 15 years since the cessation of large-scale conflicts in the region has allowed for renewed concentration on the building of trade and economic relationships. All of these factors notwithstanding, the Pacific Rim is home to incredibly disparate political and economic structures, religions, and cultures. To organize the Pacific is to overcome enormous historical and political barriers. Comparisons with the European integration experiment are, therefore, largely moot.

The authors in this book share a free trade-based vision of Open Regionalism for the Pacific of the future. They support public and private practices that encourage regional economies to become increasingly open to flows of goods, investment, services, information, and technology and to comply with the principles, disciplines, and practices developed by the world community through the General Agreement on Tariffs and Trade (GATT). The coeditors and many of the authors represented here endorse Open Regionalism in the Pacific Rim as a means of fostering global economic cooperation as set forth in the San Francisco Declaration adopted by the Pacific Economic Cooperation Council at its Ninth General Meeting in San Francisco in September 1992. This endorsement includes, above all, expanding existing cooperative efforts, such as Asia Pacific Economic Cooperation, developing new subregional arrangements and agreements consistent with GATT principles, continuing support for the GATT in light of the successful conclusion of the Uruguay Round in December 1993, and enhancing growing economic linkages between Asia and North America. As Emmerson notes, the GATT agreement will reinvigorate global free trade and reduce temptation to seek regional protection in a tripolar world of Asian, American, and European blocs.

A major challenge to regionalism is the promotion of continuing global integration. Integration differs from the regional cooperation process in that it takes cooperation a step further in forging linkages and ties uniting diverse cultures, nations, and economies. As Okita notes, the integration process has both breadth and depth, and both cooperation and integration should be fostered as part of Open Regionalism, consistent with the internationalization process. Although regional cooperation is achieved, or driven, primarily by trade, integration is driven more by investment than by trade. Integration is primarily a geoeconomic concept and applies to all realms of foreign policy, from military security to the environment, with economic issues in the lead. The dominant role in the integration process is played by the private sector, especially by multinational enterprises.

In this context, the successful conclusion of the Uruguay Round of the GATT is insufficient to support continued regional and global integration processes, partly because the GATT does not currently include investment principles and it has failed in its mechanism for dispute resolution. Finally, frameworks for cooperation in the Pacific Rim and other regions will need to be open in terms of trade and investment and also with respect to security, human rights, and environmental issues. The challenge to regionalism for the remainder of the twentieth century and into the next millennium may indeed be to support integration in all of these areas, to adapt the GATT model to continue preserving the free trade system in the post–Cold War order, and to strengthen the role of the United Nations in fostering regional cooperation in the Pacific region. It is in the search for continued growth, integration, sustainable peace, and global stability that the following chapters were compiled in order to share the perspectives, hopes, and predictions for the future of the Pacific Rim from leaders throughout the region.

NOTES

1. Bundy, Barbara K., Stephen D. Burns, and Kimberly V. Weichel, eds., *The Pacific Century: Scenarios for Regional Cooperation* (Westport, Conn.: Praeger, 1994), pp. 90–109, 116–22, 197–208, 209–22, 223–31.

2

The Pan-Pacific Movement: An Interpretative History

M. Hadi Soesastro

Interests in the Pacific Basin as a region have found their expression in ideas about organizing the region through a variety of institutional arrangements. Over the years, the ideas have evolved either in response to changing circumstances and different perceived needs or as a result of critical evaluations of the concepts themselves.

It is not easy to pinpoint the origin of the idea for organizing the Pacific region. Over the past two to three decades a number of proposals have been made to create various Asian regional organizations. These will be examined by employing different frames of reference or approaches. For example, a concept-oriented approach would recognize that the Pan-Pacific idea that is of relevance today is derived from the fact and implications of regional economic interdependence. Such ideas began to emerge only in the mid-1960s and found their more elaborate expressions in the 1970s. The rationale given for an institutionalized arrangement in the Pacific rested on the realization that the growing economic interdependence of the region requires new mechanisms for more effective communication and association and the recognition that "bilateralism is no longer adequate while regional rather than global considerations are more suited to the circumstances."[1]

An event-oriented frame of reference can be employed to identify the origin of an idea. However, because a concept might emerge as a response to a particular event, this approach often would converge with a concept-oriented approach. For example, it was pointed out that the early concerns in post-war Japan with schemes for broader regional economic cooperation occurred at the time when the Japanese were far from sure that Japan would achieve its so-called economic miracle.[2] However, a different view suggested that "the notion that the Pacific

Basin can be made a world economic center by promoting freer flow of trade and capital among the nations on its periphery did not come into fashion until the rise of Japan as a major economic world power."[3]

A third orientation focuses on the factors involved. Actors can be nations, institutions, or individuals, depending on the preferred level of analysis. The role played by Robert Schuman and Jean Monet in the formation of the European Coal and Steel Community definitely was a decisive one, although other factors also contributed favorably to that end. With such actors in mind, Han Sung-joo observed that "in the Pacific region today, it is simply very difficult to find leaders who carry much weight either among the developing or developed countries, let alone among countries in both of the groups, and who are committed to the idea of Pacific Community."[4] Nonetheless, a person such as the late Saburo Okita clearly comes to mind as one of the most important actors in the Pan-Pacific movement. Individual actors are important because they develop ideas or modify concepts to changing circumstances by virtue of their ability to interpret or foresee events.

However, ideas on cooperation in the Pacific often are scrutinized not on the basis of the soundness of the concept itself but with reference to the originators or actors involved. Because of historical factors, ideas for a broader regional cooperation that originate from Japan tend to arouse a great deal of suspicion. It is unfortunate that Japan often finds itself in such a situation.

Since the early 1960s the Japanese have been in the vanguard of the development of Pan-Pacific ideas. Japanese proposals to form regional cooperation arrangements certainly were made with a view to promoting Japan's national interest. In fact, each nation must clearly see its interests in its pursuit of a particular objective. The various Pan-Pacific ideas, of Japanese or of other origin, must be assessed by all the respective countries on that same basis. Discussions on Pan-Pacific ideas, especially in the late 1970s and early 1980s, were not free from misperceptions and were often motivated by a search for hidden motives. Perhaps the lack of a proper perspective on the historical evolution of the idea has contributed greatly to the widespread misunderstanding.

The history of the ideas for regional economic cooperation in the Pacific has not yet been well-researched. Evolution of the concepts has been written mainly to demonstrate the growth of interest in Pan-Pacific ideas, especially Pacific Economic Cooperation (PEC).[5] This examination of the evolution of Pan-Pacific ideas is an attempt to describe the various proposals and the circumstances in which they were presented and to identify the main actors that influenced the developments of the concepts and the efforts to translate them into action.[6] It identifies three consecutive periods in the development of PEC ideas. The first is the period from the early 1960s to around 1967, which was marked by efforts that were almost exclusively taken in Japan to initiate and develop ideas of and schemes for PEC. The second period, from 1968 to 1977, saw a process of "internationalization" of the idea, in which persons and institutions from many other countries became actively involved, but these activities were still confined mainly to the academic and business circles. The third period, starting in 1978, was marked by the beginning of serious attempts to translate ideas into action. This process saw an increased involvement of governments. The period also witnessed the emergence of a regional consensus, albeit still weak, on the main principles for organizing PEC. This process may be followed by a fourth period, perhaps starting in the early 1990s, in which the region is faced by a more urgent task to further consolidate the process of cooperation in a changed international political economic environment.

THE PERIOD 1960–67

In the first period, three different developments of the idea of Asia Pacific regional cooperation can be identified in Japan. The first idea can be viewed as a concept of cooperation for promoting regional cohesion, an idea that originated with Morinosuke Kajima, a businessman and Liberal Democratic Party politician, who raised the question in 1960 in the Upper House of the Diet about the possibility of creating a Pan-Pacific organization. Kajima's proposal was based on the idea of Pan-Asianism rather than on a Pan-Pacific concept, and the proposal could have been motivated by Japan's broader regional interests that became apparent as Japan vigorously pursued its economic development. Kajima saw the importance of a Japanese role in promoting regional consolidation, namely, the improvement of the political and economic situation in Asia. He, therefore, proposed a Marshall Plan-type Asia Development Fund that would provide grants, rather than credits, that were deemed necessary for development. He took great pains to explain that his proposed scheme of cooperation was based on an entirely different concept than that of the Greater East Asia Co-Prosperity Sphere. This suggests his clear understanding of the sensitivities involved. Nonetheless, Kajima's Pan-Asianism was not free from charges of being another form of Japanese hegemonism.[7]

The second idea developed independently of Kajima's proposal and was manifested in a series of studies and research on regional economic cooperation undertaken by leading Japanese economists such as Saburo Okita and Kiyoshi Kojima. The underlying concept was the promotion of regional economic integration that began to develop in the early 1960s. Although Morinosuke Kajima's proposals seem to have gotten nowhere, the works by Okita and Kojima have contributed significantly to the subsequent developments of PEC ideas.

In the early 1960s, the establishment of the Japan Economic Research Center provided an institutional vehicle in Japan for studies on PEC by leading Japanese economists. This proved to be of great importance to subsequent developments of the PEC idea. The center's first report, entitled "Economic Cooperation in the Pacific Area," proposed that annual meetings be held among representatives from the five developed Pacific nations — Australia, Canada, Japan, New Zealand, and the United States — to discuss issues of common interest in the fields of economic relations and transportation and communication, as well as cultural exchanges. The questions of the status of representatives — whether they should be ministers, government officials, or private business — was left open.[8] In November 1965, at JERC's first international conference on Measures for Trade Expansion of Developing Countries, Kiyoshi Kojima and Hiroshi Kuimoto of Hitotsubashi University presented a paper entitled "A Pacific Economic Community and Asian Developing Countries," in which the idea of a Pacific Free Trade Area (PAFTA) was proposed.[9] In their proposal, Kojima and Kurimoto argued that a PAFTA, comprising the five developed Pacific countries, possessed the conditions necessary for effective regional integration. Moreover, if they would welcome developing countries that would wish to join as associate members with preferential treatment, the result would be a vast Pacific trade expansion.

This led to the third development in May 1967, when the idea of regional consultations was first espoused by the Japanese at an official level. With Prime Minister Sato's encouragement, Foreign Minister Miki formally endorsed the notion of an Asia Pacific Policy for Japan. This foreign policy initiative could be seen as the first attempt by Japan to play a greater role in Asia in the post-war era. Miki's policy focused on the fact that the central issue for all Asian nations was the problem of poverty and suggested that any solution to this problem must be predicated upon a combined effort of both the developed Pacific nations and the developing countries of Asia.

Another quite notable development during the period of 1960–67 occurred in the business world. In April 1967 at a meeting of the Japan-Australia Joint Economic Committee, the respective business groups established the Pacific Basin Economic Council (PBEC), a private organization with five national committees (Australia, Canada, Japan, New Zealand, and the United States). PBEC's objectives were to promote the study and discussion of issues raised in regional trade and investment and greater cooperation between public and private interests.

THE PERIOD 1968–77

During the second period of the development of PEC ideas, one of the most important changes was the process of internationalization of the idea, although this was largely confined to academic circles. With the support of Foreign Minister Miki, a Pacific Trade and Development Conference (PAFTAD) was convened by Kiyoshi Kojima in January 1968 in Tokyo under the auspices of the Japan Economic Research

Center, headed by Saburo Okita. This gathering of academics and the next PAFTAD of the following year actively discussed the pros and cons of a PAFTA among the five developed Pacific countries. These conferences involved an ever-increasing number of policy-oriented economists in the discussion of regional foreign economic policy issues and became an important vehicle for the development of PEC ideas. Discussions in PAFTAD, however, showed in the end that the idea of a PAFTA was not acceptable (Kojima later withdrew his support for the idea).

In Japan, no new ideas on PEC were developed in the late 1960s and early 1970s, but a number of commissioned studies were undertaken. In 1970 the Japan Institute of International Affairs, a Foreign Ministry-related research organization, commissioned Okita and Kojima to study the prospects for Pacific economic cooperation. In the same year, the Institute of Developing Economies, which is related to the Ministry of International Trade and Industry, published a collection of studies on the Pacific economic region.[10] The second wave of public interest in PEC ideas in Japan came with the publication of studies conducted by the Nomura Research Institute beginning in 1977, one of which was on "International Environment and Japan's Grand Strategy for the 21st Century." The report proposed that Japan's future security interests lay within the framework of a Pacific regional organization. It put forward plans for a $20 billion Pacific Cooperation Fund, an expanded program of personnel exchanges, and a regular series of ministerial or summit meetings.[11]

Outside Japan, studies on PEC were initially very sporadic, with the majority being undertaken in the United States. These included studies at the Brookings Institution, the Hudson Institute, the Asia Society, the Pacific Forum, the East-West Center, and various universities.[12] In addition, the end of this period saw the beginning of a series of international meetings and conferences that were specifically convened to examine the PEC idea. Such meetings brought about a greater awareness on the part of policy makers in the region on the development of the idea.

In addition to the unofficial international meetings, there were also important developments at the official level, primarily initiated by Japan. In May 1968, following his Asian Pacific Policy of the previous year, Foreign Minister Miki outlined a four-point Asian Pacific Bloc Establishment Plan when he called home all Japanese ambassadors to the Asia Pacific area for a four-day conference. As described by Gordon, "one of its points is the critical role which he hopes Japan will play as a bridge between the developed Pacific nations . . . and the States of Southeast Asia. Miki hoped to press for a greater Japanese role as the Vietnam war subsided."[13] Miki's plan manifested the gradual revival of Japanese interests in Southeast Asia.

However, the Japanese leaders were not quite sure at the time as to how they should promote relations with Southeast Asia. In the second and last ministerial conferences in Manila in 1967, the Japanese discerned the fears and resentment in the thrust of some Southeast Asian nations' comments on Japan's role. Analyzing this relationship, Gordon perhaps rightly observed that

> These apprehensions . . . and latent resentments growing from the wartime experiences cannot be erased altogether, but a greater degree of collaboration among Southeast Asian states is expected to better enable these small states to stand up to Japan. Lacking some degree of cohesion, the developing states of Southeast Asia must otherwise remain too easily susceptible to Japan's sheer weight in Asian affairs. Southeast Asian leaders are indeed the first to stress this, and their recognition acts as an additional incentive towards regional cooperation. For they too believe (as do many Americans) that the objective factors of location and Japan's economic interest will lead her inexorably to more involvement in Southeast Asia; regionalism among the weaker and smaller Southeast Asian nations appears to them as one more way by which to be better able to deal with the Japanese.[14]

Apparently, Japanese leaders also came to the same appreciation. With the Association of Southeast Asian Nations' (ASEAN) successful conclusion of its first summit in Bali in 1976, it appeared to have definitely proved itself in Japan's eyes. It was reported that Miki, who became Japan's prime minister in December 1974, sought to attend that meeting. This was "an unusually assertive act, but the ASEAN group made clear that the meeting was for members only."[15]

However, as ASEAN became better organized, the group sought greater cooperation from Japan. This was met by a Japanese initiative in the summer of 1977. Only several months after his inauguration as prime minister, Fukuda undertook a major tour of ASEAN and announced in Manila the so-called Fukuda Doctrine, or "heart-to-heart" diplomacy. Fukuda pledged to contribute to projects that would strengthen ASEAN cooperation. In addition, this initiative also was to put to rest Southeast Asian fear of Japan's possible domination. Seen from the point of view of relations within the Asia Pacific community, Fukuda's diplomacy was a significant step. In fact, this period can be regarded as an important one from a political-diplomatic perspective, namely, in which attempts were made to develop one of the most crucial relations in Pacific regional building, that is, the relationship between Japan and the ASEAN countries.

Up to this point, perhaps the most significant achievement in the development of the PEC idea was with regard to the evolution of the concept of cooperation and its institutional arrangements. Kojima's original PAFTA proposal, which involved institutional integration as in the case of the European Economic Community, was abandoned and modified (initially by Kojima himself), and the concept of cooperation evolved into a more loosely structured type of arrangement, similar to the Organization for Economic Cooperation and Development (OECD). However, up to 1977, no prominent elements in the bureaucracies or governments of the countries in which PEC ideas have been actively pursued, namely, Japan, Australia, or the United States, were associated with the public advocacy of the Organization for Pacific Trade and Development or other regional cooperation proposals.

THE PERIOD SINCE 1978

The year 1978 saw the beginning of a new era in the development of PEC ideas, marked by greater interests and activities at the official and policy levels in a number of countries. Two important events took place in that year. The first was the request made in April 1978 by Senator John Glenn, chairman of the Subcommittee on East Asian and Pacific Affairs, Committee on Foreign Relations of the U.S. Senate, to the Congressional Research Service of the Library of Congress to examine the feasibility of a regional economic organization.

The importance of this event is twofold. First, the idea was taken up by the United States and given serious consideration at the policy level. As discussed elsewhere, interest in the United States in the PEC idea has for a long time been confined to groups and individuals and has had a very limited audience.[16] In fact, without the interest and participation of the United States — the largest economy in the region — a Pacific regional economic association of any form would be less meaningful. Second, the examination of the idea at the policy level made use of intellectual input of considerable credibility.

The second important event in 1978 was the official support in Japan for a Pan Pacific Association, announced — and, in fact, initiated — by the then newly elected Prime Minister Masayoshi Ohira in December. Ohira formed the Pacific Basin Cooperation Study Group, an advisory group to Prime Minister Ohira to study ways to enhance regional cooperation and harmonious relations among Pacific countries as well as to construct a regional community within the Pacific Basin region.

There occurred in the late 1970s an unprecedented upsurge of international seminars and study projects and other activities relating specifically to the PEC idea. The Ohira study group took note of the upsurge of international seminars on the idea, and in its report, it assigned an important role to be assumed by a forthcoming seminar at the Australian National University in a continuing series of international conferences. The study group proposed a step-by-step approach and recommended the setting up of a committee as a first step in building the machinery for Pacific Basin cooperation. The recommendations of the Japanese study group were, indeed, examined in the Pacific Community Seminar organized in Canberra by the Australian National University, September 15–17, 1980.

The seminar in Canberra was an important initiative. In some respects, this seminar was different from earlier international seminars that were organized to discuss PEC ideas. First, this seminar was directly government sponsored. The prime minister of Australia, Malcolm Fraser, expressed his support for the PEC idea, and the Australian government agreed to sponsor the meeting. Second, the seminar was action oriented. Discussions in the seminar were focused not only on the forces promoting the Pacific Community idea or the issues for substantive cooperation and the interest of countries in participating but also, as explicitly placed in the agenda, on the next steps that might be taken. Deliberations at the seminar led to the recommendation to establish a standing committee, which was named the Pacific Cooperation Committee (PCC), with the task to coordinate an expansion of the information exchange within the region and to set up task forces to undertake major studies of a number of issues for regional cooperation.

Soon it became apparent that the PCC could not get off the ground because other governments were reluctant to endorse it and to make the necessary commitments — financial or otherwise. Although the PCC was proposed to be unofficial, private, and informal, in a way, its establishment was made conditional upon the endorsement by governments. Governments of the ASEAN countries were very reserved with respect to the idea and did not respond positively. However, they were not the only ones. Questions began to be raised as to whether it was wise to bring in governments at that stage. To some governments, the idea was too new. In addition, it should also be noted that some governments were hesitant to involve themselves in the act of exploring the idea because this could be mistaken for a commitment to the idea. In Japan itself, the lack of a concrete agenda and the unexpected death in June 1980 of Ohira caused public interest to wane.[17]

Although for a short period following the seminar in Canberra there appeared to have been a setback, the attempt at translating the idea into action was a valuable one. For example, discussions at the Canberra meeting noted the desirability of a tripartite involvement of academics, businesspeople and other professionals, and government officials from both the developed and the developing countries, not only in the efforts to realize the PEC idea but also in the merging (and ultimate) structure of Pacific cooperation itself. Indeed, the period since 1978 witnessed a much greater interest and involvement in the development of the PEC idea by a much larger and diversified group of people and institutions.

As a consequence, discussions on PEC were no longer confined to issues of desirability and the designing of neatly structured technocratic blueprints. They had to confront the issues of feasibility. Political scientists and practitioners — including government officials in their private capacity — who joined in the discussion strongly argued for greater understanding of the political aspects of cooperation and the political conditions and sensitivities involved in community building.[18] Since then, a greater realism has been introduced in the examination of the PEC idea. The Canberra seminar showed that although there was increasing support for the idea of PEC, no consensus had emerged on the actions that should follow. The years following saw a gradual emergence of a regional consensus on the principles of cooperation and the direction of its development. They also witnessed a slow but gradual involvement of governments in the process. The most important vehicle for this consensus building and for involvement of governments in the process became known as the Pacific Economic Cooperation Conference (PECC).

Members of the PECC are so-called national committees, or representatives of countries or regional institutions. At present, PECC has 20 committees representing the economies of its members: Australia, Brunei Darussalam, Canada, Chile, China, Hong Kong, Indonesia, Japan, Korea, Malaysia, Mexico, New Zealand, Peru, the Philippines, Russia, Singapore, Chinese Taipei, Thailand, the United States, and the Pacific Island nations. In addition, two international organizations — PBEC and PAFTAD — are "institutional members" of PECC. As such, they participate in all PECC activities but have no vote on the standing committee.

It is also widely believed that the unofficial PEC process, which started at Canberra, has survived primarily because of subsequent official initiatives taken by ASEAN countries, Thailand and Indonesia in particular.[19] In July 1984, the first initiative was undertaken at the official level and is known today as the so-called 6 plus 5 meeting of ASEAN-Post Ministerial Conference. The cooperation formula calls for the foreign ministers of the five developed Pacific countries to join their ASEAN counterparts at the time of the regular ASEAN foreign ministers' meeting for an exchange of views on the subject of Pacific economic developments and cooperation. Its importance as a means to increase ASEAN's confidence rests on the fact that the terms of the exercise are set by ASEAN itself. Although there were some apprehensions about this formula, the 6 plus 5 scheme was seen then as the only viable one at the official level.

The series of meetings of the PECC and the many task force activities and other regional study groups and fora under its auspices are often criticized for their lack of real actions, but they must be seen as a necessary part of the process of getting to know each other, which must be immensely time and energy consuming in view of the region's diversity. As perhaps well stated by two thoughtful German observers, PECC's influence on the progress of efforts toward Pacific economic cooperation "is ambivalent: they have destroyed many illusions concerning any kind of rapid formation of a Pacific cooperation organization, but on the other hand — and this may be due to the mere fact of their existence — they have indeed been able to reinforce the feeling of solidarity among the Pacific nations."[20]

In 1989 the PECC was strengthened and the PEC process extended to the ministerial level by the formation of an intergovernmental forum called "Asia Pacific Economic Cooperation" (APEC), led by then-Prime Minister Robert Hawke of Australia. Initially a response to Australia's need for deeper integration intraregionally into the dynamic Asia Pacific, APEC soon captured the interest of eastern Pacific countries, including Canada and the United States. This, in turn, led to the formation of a 12-nation forum comprising the 6 plus 5 ASEAN countries and Australia, Canada, Japan, Korea, New Zealand, and the United States. Since then, the membership has been enlarged to include China, Hong Kong, and Taiwan (under a formula like the one used to determine their membership in PECC).

In June 1989, then-Secretary of State James Baker announced his agreement with Hawke's APEC initiative, and at the Group of 7 (G-7) Summit in July 1993, President Clinton announced his administration's support of the APEC Ministerial Meeting in Seattle in November 1993, emphasizing the importance of APEC principles to U.S. policy in the Asia Pacific and referring to a "new Pacific community."

APEC has, thus, emerged in the aftermath of the epoch-making events in Eastern Europe, the former Soviet Union, and the Persian Gulf since 1989 as the leading policy-making group to move economic regional cooperation forward in the Asia Pacific and encourage regional institution-building, including Japan and the United States, to avert subregional trade wars and protectionism and stimulate trade creation. As noted by Mark Borthwick, APEC may be the first stage in a long-term process that will eventually create a formal Pacific cooperative institution resembling the information-oriented OECD rather than the trade-oriented European Community (EC).

APEC is a manifestation of the "multilateralization" process that has occurred gradually in the region, rather than by the wrenching changes produced by political upheaval in Europe and the former Soviet Union. It represents increasing awareness on the part of Pacific nations other than the US and Japan of their growing dependence on a stable Japan-US relationship in the 1990s and into the 21st century. One thing is clear: the pre–Cold War old visions of Japan's dominance in the Asia Pacific region and of US global dominance based on a policy of containment of communism will no longer work in the present and future. It reflects a growing awareness on the part of governments and heads of state that integration, regional cooperation, and regional coalition-building are increasingly effective means to assure world stability and prosperity in the post–Cold War era.[21]

APEC was created out of a perceived need for a more comprehensive regional dialogue than that afforded by the PECC. It has been guided by the same principles that have enabled the PECC to succeed in its objectives: openness, equality, and gradual evolution. So far, a positive and interdependent relationship has evolved between APEC and the PECC: PECC can generate issues based on the practical problems of the private sector in the Asia Pacific region on which APEC can make policy decisions at the ministerial level. The work projects undertaken by APEC have already produced benefits for the member economies and for the region as a whole. The work projects cover areas ranging from trade promotion, expansion of investment and technology transfer, human resources development, energy cooperation, marine resources conservation, and fisheries to telecommunications.

APEC and PECC have become, perhaps by default, the most important "actors" in the development and realization of the PECC idea. They are a substitute for the individual (or individuals), like Monet in the case of the EC or perhaps Cohn, for a country (or countries) that would be expected to take the lead.

FUTURE PROSPECTS

For the future, APEC and PECC should cooperate and coordinate fully to avoid duplication of their work and fractiousness, building upon each other's research and work. At the same time, they should reinforce one another by identifying an agenda of complementary activities to promote regional economic cooperation. As Ambassador Vejjajiva, chair of the APEC Senior Officials Meeting in 1992 in Thailand, noted,

> This will lead to an effective interweaving of informal relationships between PECC and APEC and will in turn strengthen multilateral cooperation among the economies in the region. This suggestion is put forward in earnest, and in no way is it an attempt to integrate APEC and PECC. Far from it, both fora in fact should maintain their own separate identities.[22]

It is hoped that APEC and PECC working together can be effective in the future in dealing with the North-South problems emerging in the Asia Pacific region, as well as with other issues relating to East-West relations in the expanding Pacific Rim region. With respect to problems of a North-South nature in the region, the main manifestation is in the relationship between the ASEAN countries and Japan. In terms of East-West relations in the region, there is continued uneasiness about the security implications of the movement. Are these concerns still valid when the region is currently experiencing a shift from alliances to alignments? The genesis of the new Pacific regionalism is the development of regional economic interdependence; the problem is that such development has led to the emergence of a functional region rather than a geographic region. In essence, this defines who would be included and who would be excluded. APEC and PECC advocate the principle of openness or nonexclusiveness.

Yet another issue for the future is the trend toward subregional arrangements. This may be a natural tendency in view of the vastness and diversity of the Pacific region. The U.S.-Canada Free Trade Agreement and the North American Free Trade Agreement can be seen as a special case. By the same token, the Closer Economic Region between Australia and New Zealand also is a special case, as is ASEAN and the recent proliferation of subregional special economic development zones involving several countries. A case in point is the three-nation "growth triangle" project that aims to promote trade and economic development by Thailand, Malaysia, and Indonesia. It is not clear how these subregional agreements affect the realization of the PEC idea and the principles of APEC and the PECC. They can become building blocks for PEC, but they could also lead to regional fragmentation. An increased concern about the possibility of such fragmentation has led to increased pressures upon APEC and PECC to move more rapidly toward greater institutional integration.

Whether countries opt for a subregional or for a broader regional framework in approaching international economic issues depends upon their individual conviction about the ways by which those issues could be better handled. PECC's and APEC's most difficult task is to demonstrate the efficacy of regional-multilateral solutions. This, indeed, is of much greater relevance today compared with the recent past in view of the great uncertainties in the development of the international political economy. As Borthwick suggested, "progress toward regional cooperation will respond to more than just an internal Pacific Basin dynamic. Global economic and political forces will play an equal if not greater role in determining the pace of future direction of any cooperative arrangements."[23] However, the ability of governments and other sociopolitical forces in the various countries to properly assess the importance of their ability to anticipate and meet such challenges and to see the merit of a Pacific focus in their responses starts at home. Therefore, the agendas of APEC and PECC in the years to come will need to emphasize the importance of strengthening the national or local committees that are the real focal points in the region. A systematic regional effort to undertake this task must be based on a continuous identification and examination of the basic interests, positions, and conditions of all the respective countries.

NOTES

1. Russel H. Fifield, "ASEAN and the Pacific Community," *Asia Pacific Community* 11 (Winter 1981): 14–22.

2. Bernard K. Gordon, "Japan and the Pacific Basin Proposal," *Korea & World Affairs*, Summer 1981, pp. 268–88.

3. Hoon-mok Chung, "Economic Integration in the Pacific Basin: A Historical Review," in Han Sung-joo, ed., *Community Building in the Pacific Region: Issues and Opportunities* (Seoul: Asiatic Research Center, Korea University, 1981), p. 4.

4. Han Sung-joo, "Political Conditions of Pacific Regional Cooperation: Theoretical and Practical Considerations," in Hadi Soesastro and Han Sung-joo, eds., *Pacific Economic Cooperation: The Next Phase* (Jakarta: Centre for Strategic and International Studies, 1983), p. 65.

5. Peter Dysdale, "An Organization for Pacific Trade, Aid and Development: Regional Arrangements and the Resource Trade," in Lawrence Krause and Hugh Patrick, eds., *Mineral Resources in the Pacific Area* (San Francisco, Calif.: Federal Reserve Bank of San Francisco, 1978).

6. For earlier attempts, see Hadi Soesastro, "Institutional Aspects of Pacific Economic Cooperation," in Hadi Soesastro and Han Sung-joo, eds., *Pacific Economic Cooperation: The Next Phase* (Jakarta: Centre for Strategic and International Studies, 1983); James W. Morley, "The Pacific Basin Movement and Japan," Roundtable Reports No. 7, East Asian Institute, Columbia University, 1983.

7. Y. Bandura, "The Pacific Community — A Brain-Child of Imperialist Diplomacy," *Moscow International Affairs: A Monthly Journal of Political Analysis* (Distributed from Cambridge), 6(6) (June 1980): 63–70.

8. Tessa Morris-Suzuki, "Japan and the Pacific Basin Community," *The World Today* 37 (December 1981): 454–61.

9. In *Measures for Trade Expansion of Developing Countries*, Proceedings of the November 1965 Conference, Tokyo, Japan Economic Research Center, October 1966, pp. 93–134.

10. Morley, "The Pacific Basin Movement and Japan," p. 29.

11. Ibid., p. 34.

12. Ibid., p. 35.

13. Bernard K. Gordon, *Towards Disengagement in Asia* (Englewood Cliffs, N.J.: Prentice-Hall, 1969), p. 6.

14. Ibid., pp. 66–67.

15. Gordon, "Japan and the Pacific Basin Proposal," p. 277.

16. Charles E. Morrison, "American Interest in the Pacific Community Concept," in *The Pacific Community Concept: Views from Eight Nations*, JCIE Papers No. 1 (Tokyo: Japan Center for International Exchange, 1980), pp. 17–31.

17. Kumao Kaneko, "A New Pacific Initiative: Strengthening the PECC Process," *Japan Review of International Affairs* 2(2) (Spring/Summer 1988): 73.

18. Sung-joo, "Political Considerations of Pacific Regional Cooperation."

19. See Kaneko, "A New Pacific Initiative," p. 73.

20. Willy Kraus and Wilfried Luetkenhorst, *The Economic Development in the Pacific Basin* (New York: St. Martin's Press, 1986), p. 109.

21. Mark Borthwick, "Pacific Basin Institutions: Current Directions and Future Possibilities," in *Pacific Basin: Concept and Challenges*, Alternatives for the 1980s, No. 20 (Washington, D.C.: Center for National Policy, 1986), p. 54.

22. Vitthya Vejjajiva, "The Evolving APEC/PECC Relationship," remarks delivered at the PECC IX General Meeting, September 1992, San Francisco, in *PECC IX Executive Summary* (Washington, D.C.: U.S. National Committee for Pacific Economic Cooperation, 1992), p. 19.

23. Yasuhiro Nakasone, "Japan-U.S. Coop for Peace and Prosperity in the Asia Pacific Region — Toward a Pacific Initiative," Ellsworth Bunker Memorial Lecture, San Francisco, March 11, 1988.

II

ECONOMIC STRUCTURES AND RELATIONSHIPS

3

Economic Blocs or Open Regionalism: A Japanese View

Nobuo Matsunaga

Two broad views about the prospects of Asia Pacific regionalism once prevailed. One perspective held that the Asia Pacific region is an area of substantial political, social, cultural, and linguistic diversity that limits the development of a thoroughly defined sense of common identity. The other view granted this huge region's diversity but argued that because of its economic dynamism and its relatively complex internal economic linkages, the region has the potential of becoming a significant economic area for interactive cooperation. Reality has shown that these views are not irreconcilable.

The bridge, or, more appropriately, bridges, between the Asia Pacific region's diversity and its growing interaction have already been or begun to be built. The basis for this development has been the region's economic successes. The central issue now confronting the Asia Pacific region is how it can ensure that its economic dynamism and regional economic cooperation remain an integral part of the global economic network. This goal is at the heart of the concept of "open regionalism." The concept must be the foundation for any future economic structures involving the Asia Pacific.

The issue of open regionalism has taken on a practical urgency. At the end of the Cold War, the world faces complex and seemingly contradictory trends toward growing international economic interdependence on the one hand and regionalism on the other. The latter trend is most visible in the moves toward regionally based economic

The author acknowledges the valuable assistance of Japan Institute of International Affairs Visiting Research Fellow Satu P. Limaye in the research and compilation of this chapter.

organizations in North America and Europe. Two other factors have also made open regionalism a cutting-edge topic. First, the remarkable economic growth of countries in the Asia Pacific has attracted worldwide attention, and naturally there is an interest in understanding the future direction of this dynamism. Second, the end of the Cold War has diverted attention (perhaps too much) from security-strategic issues to matters concerning political economy. Against this background, several questions will be addressed in this chapter. What are the "structures" for economic cooperation in the Asia Pacific region? How can these prevailing structures ensure that the region remains open to the rest of the world? What is the role of Japan in Asia Pacific economic relationships? Finally, what is the connection between Asia Pacific economic cooperation and regional political stability?

ECONOMIC STRUCTURES AND RELATIONSHIPS IN THE ASIA PACIFIC

Any discussion of structures and, indeed, even the Asia Pacific as a region must admit some definitional problems. Structures can be formal or informal, governmental or nongovernmental. The Asia Pacific region itself, given its size and diversity, comprises many parts. Hence, it is best to approach the matter in a broad-minded way.

Economic structures in the Asia Pacific region currently reflect the diversity of the region and efforts to increase interaction among its countries and economies. Various metaphors or descriptions have been used to explain the nature of these structures. For example, one leading scholar on the issue has referred to "concentric circles" of economic cooperation.[1] Whatever descriptive terms we employ, it is evident that several types of regional economic structures exist or are being contemplated. The origins, aims, and implications of these various structures inevitably differ, but they must all be identified briefly in order to fully appreciate the nature of economic relationships in the region.

At the bilateral level, a host of economic interactions obviously exist. At the subregional level, for example, we have the Growth Triangle involving Singapore, Jahor in Malaysia, and Riau in Indonesia. Other natural economic territories could emerge in the future. At the Southeast Asian regional level, the Association of Southeast Asian Nations (ASEAN) Free Trade Area was implemented on January 1, 1993. The formation agreement for the ASEAN Free Trade Area, signed in 1992 at the Fourth ASEAN Summit in Singapore, calls on members of ASEAN to reduce tariffs on all manufactured goods to between 0 percent and 5 percent over a period of 15 years. The process of tariff reduction has begun on an incremental basis. Observers have pointed out that the potential ASEAN market has some 300 million consumers. At the broadest level of the Asia Pacific region, there is the Asia Pacific Economic Cooperation (APEC) forum. Though young, this grouping is an important basis for cooperation — especially because it reaches across the Pacific Ocean to include Canada and the United States. Finally, there have been and continue to be discussions in the region about a proposal for an East Asian Economic Grouping. An original version of this idea was proposed by Malaysian Prime Minister Mahathir bin Mohamad. The acceptability of such a grouping and its form will in part be shaped by broader international economic developments, including the fate of the Uruguay Round of GATT.

The various approaches to regional economic relationships in the Asia Pacific indicate the complexity of the situation. Hence, efforts to create a single or inflexible structure for economic cooperation in the region cannot hope to succeed. This factor makes it all the more important that rather than seeking to create something entirely new, the focus should be on retaining the bilateral, multilateral, and global connections that have contributed to the region's economic success thus far. Japan has taken precisely such an approach.

JAPAN AND ASIA PACIFIC ECONOMIC COOPERATION

Although the successful completion of the Uruguay Round of the GATT negotiations remains the most pressing challenge in the trade policy of Japan, national interests have also been advanced over the past few years through an initiative aimed at greater cooperation with regional economies in the APEC process.[2] APEC was initiated originally by Australia, which foresaw in 1989 that continued economic growth in the Asia Pacific region would be advanced by wider and more structured regional cooperation. Today the APEC region accounts for nearly 50 percent of global output of goods and services and one-third of the world's trade. The purpose of APEC is to secure open economic intercourse in the region, ranging from trade and services to technology transfers. APEC holds annual ministerial meetings, its working groups meet regularly, and it has its own secretariat and budget designed to achieve these objectives. Membership has expanded to include 16 economies, and Chile will soon be included.

The key word descriptive of the Asia Pacific region is "openness," and Japan has much to do with ensuring that this goal is met. Japan firmly believes that any regional economic cooperation should forestall trade protectionism while remaining open to participation from outside the region. As Japan's former Prime Minister Kiichi Miyazawa made clear in his January 1993 speech in Bangkok, "[a] scenario we must avoid at all costs is a replay of the 1930s, in which the vicious spiral of mutual distrust and egoism led to a narrow-sighted protectionism and the formulation of trade blocs." In this context, it should be noted that Japan strongly supported the inclusion of the United States and Canada in APEC.[3] This position testifies to Japan's and the region's interest in retaining close ties between Pacific Asia and North America.

This becomes all the more important as the North American Free Trade Agreement (NAFTA) proceeds.

Indeed, a suggestion has been made on previous occasions that the United States and Japan discuss the creation of an open economic association of free-trade association that would include all other countries and territories of Asia and the Pacific Rim for purposes of consultation and participation.[4] The intent of such a U.S.-Japanese free-trade arrangement, it should be emphasized, would be neither to exclude nor to discriminate against other countries and territories. It would not be an economic super bloc designed to challenge Europe or check Southeast Asia but would complement the workings of the GATT system and welcome new partners who would recognize that their economic interests continue to be served by the expansion of world trade and not by its contraction.

Such an association could also be melded to the free-trade areas now being created in the Western Hemisphere or combined with the various efforts underway in Asia and the Pacific to expand regional economic cooperation. Despite the barriers, no community of nations is more committed to an open trading system than are the Pacific Rim countries. Again, such proposals reflect the reality that economic relationships in the Asia Pacific have already developed distinctive structures. The goal, therefore, should be to make certain that these relationships and structures are not removed in the future from the wider, more stable anchor of the international economic system.

Japan participates in Asia Pacific economic cooperation in other major ways. These are often overlooked because of the attention given to actual or potential regional groupings. First, Japan has extensive bilateral economic dealings with the countries of the region. As former Prime Minister Miyazawa explained during a speech in Bangkok:

> Between Japan and the ASEAN countries, trade has been expanding, for the past few years, at an annual rate of approximately 20 percent. In particular, exports of manufactured products from the ASEAN countries to Japan have grown remarkably, about 4.6 times from 1986 to 1991. Japanese direct investment to the ASEAN countries since the Plaza Accord in 1985 amounts to roughly 20 billion dollars. It is evident that these actors have contributed greatly to the economic development of the ASEAN countries.[5]

In the same speech, Miyazawa also reiterated Japan's intention to make further efforts to cooperate with countries of the region, especially regarding future investment flows and technology transfers.

Another way in which Japan plays a role in regional economic relations is in its strong support for the role of the Asian Development Bank. Japan also contributes to economic cooperation through its Official Development Assistance (ODA) program. Although ODA itself is largely bilateral, it is helpful to the overall improvement of the investment and trade climate in the region. Asia will remain a priority area for Japan's ODA. Finally, Japan will maintain its present course of fiscal and monetary policy aimed at restructuring its economy and further opening its markets to foreign goods and services. A comprehensive package of economic measures was recently approved by the Japanese government in order to provide for the sound expansion of the domestic economy. An emphasis was given to promoting domestic demand-led growth. The good health of the Japanese economy will naturally have a beneficial impact on the entire region.

Japan, in essence, approaches economic relationships on a bilateral, multilateral (which includes regional groupings), and global basis. During this time of profound international change, nations will inevitably be compelled to assess various approaches to assure prosperity and development. However, the most important consideration in assessing structures should be the extent to which they promote regional cooperation while retaining their openness to the world economic and trading system.

SECURITY AND DIALOGUE IN THE ASIA PACIFIC REGION

It is important to realize that economic cooperation must go hand in hand with political stability in the Asia Pacific region. As is characteristic of many other areas of the world, the Asia Pacific region is experiencing profound change. Thus far, developments in the region have been generally favorable, and it will require continued cooperation and vigilance to ensure that they remain so.

As an example of the most recent positive events, one can point to the democratic and almost wholly peaceful elections in South Korea, the Philippines, and Indonesia, as well as the restoration of democracy in Thailand. Positive moves toward reconciliation between countries have occurred also. The rapprochement between the People's Republic of China and Vietnam is welcomed. Although changes will inevitably come to the region in the years ahead, we face certain key issues in terms of regional political stability and security.

A crucial element in the security of the region is the presence of the United States, whose significance for the region has only been heightened in the aftermath of the Gulf Crisis and dissolution of the Soviet Union. The U.S. withdrawal from the Subic Bay naval base in the Philippines in late 1992 does not detract from the importance of the role of the United States in the region. Continued U.S. involvement and leadership are indispensable to efforts aimed at reducing tension and enhancing political stability in the region. The U.S.-Japanese alliance is one of the most important bilateral relationships in the region, providing an essential basis for security assurances and a framework for foreign policy cooperation, which is essential for economic development and political stability.

It is also becoming increasingly important for both Japan and its fellow Asia Pacific nations to maintain opportunities for close communications on a constant basis. In this regard, the ASEAN Post-Ministerial Conference (ASEAN-PMC) — the annual meeting of the foreign ministers of the six members of ASEAN and the seven "dialogue partners": Australia, Canada, the European Community, Japan, Korea, New Zealand, and the United States — remains one of the most appropriate bases for addressing the regional peace and security issues and providing a forum for such necessary communication. The security dialogue that has already begun through the ASEAN-PMC offers a forum for the members of the region to deal with the issues in a manner that minimizes potential for misunderstandings.

In the interest of ensuring long-term stability in Northeast Asia, Japan intends to continue its policies regarding the Korean Peninsula by maintaining contacts with the Republic of Korea, the United States, and the People's Republic of China. However, the issue of nuclear proliferation remains a matter of serious concern, especially in view of North Korea's stated intention to withdraw from the Nuclear Non-Proliferation Treaty (at the time of this writing). A realistic attitude on the part of North Korea is critical if stability and peace are to be ensured in this vital area of the Asia Pacific.

The achievement of overall stability and development in the region hinges largely on the inclusion of Indochina into the framework of economic development in the Asia Pacific region. This goal has been at the center of Japan's policy in the region since it was articulated by Prime Minister Fukuda in the mid-1970s. A first step in the development of Indochina is the establishment of peace in Cambodia. It is commonly known that Japan has contributed to the Cambodian peace process in financial, political, and personnel terms in accordance with United Nations resolutions and the Paris Peace Agreements on Cambodia. Obviously, many difficulties still must be overcome in this area, but Japan is committed to assuring the smooth implementation of the peace process. Simultaneously, Japan will seek economic reconstruction and development of Cambodia and Vietnam, a process that is already underway.

The stability and development of the Asia Pacific region also depend greatly on the promotion of active cooperation for economic and political reform and openness in China. An isolated and inward-looking China runs counter to the region's strategic and economic interests. Regional stability will be influenced also by China's key role in such issues as the Cambodian peace process and by its economic modernization reforms. Given China's population of 1.2 billion people, the direction and pace of reform in the next few years may have profound consequences for the stability and prosperity of the region.

Viewing these developments in their entirety, a conceptualization developed by Japan's Foreign Ministry suggests that a multiplex mechanism for stability and security is becoming firmly entrenched in the Asia Pacific region. This mechanism is composed of bilateral and multilateral frameworks of cooperation designed to enhance regional stability and security in a comprehensive manner.

JAPAN AND OPEN REGIONALISM: CONCLUSIONS

Despite the potential productivity inherent in the Asia Pacific region's diversity, it is also a reality that such differences can be destabilizing, especially if too much is attempted too quickly. This word of caution is not intended to discourage the progress toward regional multilateralism, which holds great hope for our future. Rather, it is merely to advocate an incremental approach that utilizes a series of already established bilateral and global relations as the building blocks of the Asia Pacific region's economic and political stability in the future.

Japan will, of course, assume a major role in shaping this incremental approach that bridges regional initiatives with existing structures of bilateral and global interaction. It is important that Japan cooperate for mutual benefit and foster both bilateral and multilateral frameworks in its approach to political, economic, and global issues relevant to regional stability and development. In addition to its bilateral ties, Japan's active participation in the ASEAN-PMC with the dialogue partners, the ministerial meetings for APEC, the Pacific Economic Cooperation Council, and other multilateral fora for cooperation is essential in strengthening the level of mutual trust between Japan and the other nations of the Pacific Rim.

These Asia Pacific organizations are already functioning as a stimulus to regional cooperation and policy coordination. Their economic and political structures, combined with existing bilateral and global relationships, offer the basis for peace and prosperity in the future. This is the basis for political and economic open regionalism that Japan strongly supports.

NOTES

1. See Hadi Soesastro, "ASEAN Economic Cooperation," paper presented to the Asia Pacific Forum on "ASEAN Internal and External Cooperation in the 1990s and Beyond," Manila, January 13–15, 1993.

2. This section relies heavily on Ambassador Nobuo Matsunaga, "A Japanese Perspective on the Pacific Rim in the 1990s," *Japan Review of International Affairs* 6 (1992): 67–73.

3. See Takashi Inoguchi, "Japan's Foreign Policy in East Asia," *Current History* 91(59) (December 1992): 407–12.

4. This suggestion and the subsequent discussion in this chapter are taken from the article by Stephen J. Solarz and Nobuo Matsunaga, "Open a Freeway for Pacific Trade," *Los Angeles Times*, June 24, 1992.

5. Prime Minister Miyazawa, "The New Era of the Asia-Pacific and Japan-ASEAN Cooperation," an address delivered to the Foreign Correspondents' Club of Thailand, January 16, 1993.

4

Economic Structures and Relationships in the Pacific Rim

Walter E. Hoadley

The economic potential of the Pacific Rim nations is widely acclaimed, but full realization will depend heavily upon avoidance of serious economic conflicts. Unfortunately, the dangers of economic warfare cannot be minimized. Some troublesome clouds may be forming on the horizon.

In the foreground lie Pacific Rim dynamic markets, massive investments, high productivity, product quality enhancements, manufacturing process innovations, aggressive merchandising, and vast creativity. Lurking in the background, however, are forces capable of breeding economic tension: abusive power, unrelenting drives for market share, trade and investment restrictions, "only within the family" business relations, stalled or failed international negotiations, retaliation policies, cultural differences, and ethical breakdowns.

Generalizations about the large and complex Pacific region obviously can be misleading and, at times, even dangerous. Variety in races, religions, languages, traditions, and cultures abounds. Geography and climate differ widely. Moreover, information about the economies of the Pacific and their interrelations too often is deficient.

Yet, the economies around the rim of the Pacific have much in common besides location. Even a casual observer can note a strong sense of destiny, determination, anxiety to learn and achieve, and dedication to family. Resources — human and natural — seem to be available if not abundant.

Together, the Pacific Rim nations have established a distinctly better than global average real economic growth rate, particularly in recent years. This, of course, has attracted considerable global attention and interest. Business is growing faster within the region than between the Asia Pacific and the rest of the world.

The Pacific Economic Cooperation Council conference (PECC IX) held in September 1992 in San Francisco echoed the prowess of the Pacific economies, especially the 20 nations whose representatives from business, academe, and government participated. However, the shadow of concern about future economic relations was evident throughout the deliberations. The theme of the conference was "open regionalism." It was chosen because of increasing fears that economic policies of Pacific nations could be moving toward more protectionism or "closed" regionalism. Unchecked, such a trend could cause economic turmoil.

The election of Bill Clinton to the presidency of the United States shortly after PECC IX intensified overseas concerns about U.S. future foreign economic policies in the light of perceived protectionist rhetoric during the campaign. The United States is being watched intensively to confirm or deny whether the new leadership leans inward toward greater nationalism at a time when closer global linkages are needed and are occurring elsewhere.

In appraising economic and related prospects for Pacific nations during the coming decade, serious consideration must be given to at least the following challenges:

limited public understanding of the importance of keeping international trade and investment channels open,

the sluggish rate of global real economic growth,

the need for more shared leadership,

the availability and cost of capital as well as the effective functioning of the financial system,

widely varying government-business relationships, and

the need to update Western capitalism.

PUBLIC UNDERSTANDING OF OPEN REGIONALISM

Public opinion is usually preoccupied with near-term issues and readiness to support quick defensive measures against offshore economic threats. Not surprisingly, history is almost continuously marked by economic attacks and counterattacks. Far more attention needs to be given on all sides to the likely consequences of contemplated policy decisions and actions designed to resolve international economic disputes.

Increased public understanding of the longer range importance of preserving and strengthening open regionalism is not easy to generate. Interest in the subject rises only when attention-getting information becomes readily and repeatedly available to demonstrate the adverse personal and practical results of a breakdown in the freedom of goods, services, and investments to move more or less uninhibitedly across international borders.

Comments about jobs being lost to "unfair" foreign competitors can always be expected to prompt political responses with protectionist overtones. Media reports tend to emphasize the most sensitive economic transgressions of other nations and, less frequently, home country protectionist measures. The overall significance of foreign trade and investment for the U.S. economy as a whole is seldom mentioned. For example, much-publicized "net" trade imbalance data in particular fan the flames of potential retaliation, as if the massive two-way, that is, "gross," flows were unimportant. Trade gaps cannot be ignored, but they commonly represent a small fraction of total trade volume.

In the real day-to-day world of commerce, "open," that is, totally free, unrestricted, anti-protectionist, movement of goods, services, and investments among nations seems very theoretical and even naive. No country is "pure" nor ever will be. Every nation in the Pacific Rim imposes some direct or indirect limitations, and this condition cannot be expected to change completely. There are always special situations that must be dealt with politically. However, there is a substantial difference between restriction mainly by exception and restriction by ongoing vendetta policy to keep others from achieving their legitimate economic goals.

What is too often overlooked in discussions of openness is that protectionist policies, laws, and regulations inevitably bring retaliation. To minimize the dangers of economic warfare requires reasonable general acceptance of such basic international principles as fairness, a "level playing field," and national treatment. Otherwise, restrictive measures can set in motion an escalation process that in due course will limit, prevent, or divert trade and investment to the detriment of all concerned. This consequence is difficult for most people to grasp firsthand and even more so in advance. Only after jobs are lost, prices rise, and the supply of wanted goods and services becomes limited does the hurtful impact of protectionism become clear. Then it is often too late for a politically face-saving retreat on all sides. Shooting wars may not be far behind.

Substantial efforts are continually required to correct the widely accepted view that international trade and investment are part of a zero sum game, that is, when one nation wins, another automatically loses. This belief ignores the enormous synergy that arises from the compounding interplay of markets, companies, suppliers, buyers, transport firms, governments, and others.

Comparative advantage (generic superiority) remains one of the key international economic principles that impacts the whole range of openness issues. In a free world, nations are expected to benefit from their natural advantages, for example, human and other resources, location, traditions. Gains should accrue to those who have advantages such as lower costs, superior quality, and state of the art technology, which provide the basis for strong economic competitiveness. Over time, economic forces are more powerful than political forces. Currently, economic globalization is overriding political boundaries to an ever-increasing degree. However, in the real world, there is never-ending need for politically sensitive negotiation and compromise to keep international transactions flowing. When political positions harden and agreements become unobtainable, economic confrontation is virtually certain.

Any analysis of openness also confronts the emotional matter of richly-developed versus poorly-developed nations. The latter commonly contend (with varying degrees of rationality) that they really have few, if any, comparative advantages and, therefore, ask for or demand preferences that discriminate against others. Citizens in wealthier countries must come to appreciate their stake in achieving and preserving world peace by helping poorer nations accelerate their economic progress. More than compassion is involved.

Improved living conditions in developing countries throughout the Pacific region and elsewhere are absolutely necessary to open up new markets, build alliances, temper social unrest, reduce incentives to migrate, and limit the rise of refugees in a world that has an annual population growth of 100 million persons.

In summary, the public must increase its understanding of the value of economic openness across the Pacific and globally in promoting higher living standards generally as well as in increasing personal well-being. Unless economic advancement occurs with some consistency, it will be more and more difficult for political leaders to resist new protectionism, which can only make the situation progressively worse. The dire consequences of a closing or closed Pacific region on the peoples and economies involved must be fully appreciated so that proper foreign economic policies will keep them from becoming a reality.

THE RATE OF REAL ECONOMIC GROWTH

Growth is the economic lubricant for change. Yet, growth is often resisted by those who emphasize only the negative dimensions of growth, for example, congestion and pollution. Without growth, economic stagnation distorts, disrupts, or prohibits change. Without change, improvements in living standards are limited or nonexistent. Without economic gains, social unrest rises.

Global real growth of at least 3 percent annually has been shown repeatedly to be prerequisite to vigorous and healthy international trade and investment. In recent years, global growth has lagged well below 3 percent (1 percent in 1991; 1.5 percent in 1992 and 1993), and economic problems have risen in number.

Fortunately, real growth among Pacific Rim countries has increased noticeably faster than the world average. The record is even better if the United States and Japan are not included.

Real Gross Domestic Product
(annual rate of change)

	1991	*1992*	1993 *(estimated)*
World	1.0	1.5	1.5
Pacific Rim nations	2.7	3.3	4.0
Pacific Rim nations exclusive of United States and Japan	4.0	4.9	5.5

Most Pacific nations individually have exceeded the 3 percent minimum annual growth standard. The overall growth trend has provided a positive economic climate for trade and investment and the basis for compromise and agreement in negotiations. Australia, Canada, New Zealand, the Philippines, along with Japan and the United States, however, are current subpar performers. In each case, trade and investment problems have been aggravated. Economic peace in the Pacific region generally would be in jeopardy should real growth slow significantly.

Despite some earlier views to the contrary, the United States has proved again in recession and recovery that it still remains the primary engine influencing the course of the world's economy. For the Pacific region, the United States provides a major market outlet and a vital economic role generally. At times this tends to be taken for granted by many Pacific leaders. Therefore, they often are shocked and distressed whenever U.S. business and governmental leaders raise questions about fairness and restrictions to openness. The Clinton administration is definitely asking more quid pro quo trade and investment questions.

Solid U.S. real economic growth will be needed all the more in the years just ahead, but this may prove difficult to achieve if sluggishness persists in Europe and Japan. Prospects are reasonably encouraging, but a rolling recovery of intermittent surges and setbacks in the U.S. economy is now anticipated. This will give some new ongoing general economic support to Pacific Rim nations. Whether it will be sufficient to remove tensions related to openness is doubtful.

THE NEED FOR GREATER SHARED LEADERSHIP

The United States has provided the principal overall leadership for the Pacific region through the post–World War II years. Although the U.S. role is widely perceived to be diminishing by circumstance and choice, it is commonly acknowledged that political stability and a supportive climate for business across the Pacific will still depend heavily for some time to come upon the strong presence of the United States.

However, U.S. voters, among others, seem widely convinced that our nation has neither the capability nor the desire to assert as much international leadership in the future as in the past. Obviously this poses a major threat to the Pacific Rim if the United States loses status and a political and economic leadership vacuum emerges. Which nation will take over? Japan often has been cited as the successor to the United States. However, Japan's many domestic problems, defense constraints, and diminishing leadership image minimize any such near-term possibility. The People's Republic of China has many long-term aspirations but, again, has no practical chance of accepted regional leadership soon. China, of course, can always influence the leadership of other nations by its size and rising economic and military power. Russia is too preoccupied with domestic problems to lead in the Pacific.

Meanwhile, incipient economic nationalism and synergy are increasingly evident in the ongoing grouping of many Pacific Rim nations into varying clusters of countries determined to find added strength through economic alliances. There has been no tendency, however, to follow the political and economic pattern of the European Community or to form a broad-based free-trade area. Yet, the movement toward economic blocs seems unstoppable.

The six-country Association of Southeast Asian Nations (ASEAN) has progressed the furthest, announcing its own free-trade system, the ASEAN Free Trade Area. The North American Free Trade Area (NAFTA) links Canada, Mexico, and the United States. NAFTA will have an impact on the future of the global trade and investment negotiation process, essential to economic peace.

The Japanese complain that they expect to be injured by enactment of NAFTA. However, the stated NAFTA intent is to invite other nations in due course to participate. Meanwhile, there is concern throughout Asia that Japan will form some alliances of its own, for example, in Northeast Asia.

The necessity of Pacific Rim nations to share leadership soon is certain to be recognized, if indeed it has not already been recognized. The challenge is to find practical ways to make shared leadership work. How can leadership within different sectors be established and pursued? Informal acknowledgement of the comparative advantages and noteworthy superiority of individual Pacific countries no doubt is known in the marketplace. All participant nations at the table obviously must have voting rights, but it would be helpful if each country could be ready and accepted to play some sectoral leadership role for a reasonable period or, perhaps, on a rotational basis. Which nation can effectively accept above-average responsibility, for example, for security, environment, human resource development, technological improvements, agricultural productivity and marketing, energy, trade, and investment? It is far from clear whether Pacific Rim countries are now prepared to move ahead on some shared leadership basis, but the alternative is likely to be more conflict and less cooperation.

AVAILABILITY AND COST OF CAPITAL: EFFECTIVE FUNCTIONING FINANCIAL SYSTEM

Adequate financial resources and a well-functioning financial system are critical to future Pacific Rim growth and development. Developed nations, of course, require large ongoing amounts of capital to restructure industrial and financial institutions as well as manage debt. For developing nations, the need is more acute; they face a nearly hopeless outlook without infusions of capital for infrastructure and widespread development of competitive industrial, agricultural, and service enterprises.

Given the enormous projected financial needs of Pacific Rim nations, capital can be expected to remain tight and relatively expensive in the years just ahead. During the 1980s, Japanese capital flowed substantially throughout most parts of the Pacific, but this is not likely to continue, certainly not on the same scale. Japanese, in fact, are repatriating funds from overseas in response to deteriorating financial conditions at home. In the process, conversion of dollars and other hard currencies to yen has temporarily increased the demand for, and value of, yen.

The flow of U.S. capital into most Pacific Rim countries has fallen behind that of other nations during the 1980s and early 1990s. This trend diminishes the future economic potential of the United States in Asia particularly, a matter that alarms many leaders and investors. Apparently, Americans have not visualized profitable opportunities as quickly or convincingly as Asians and Europeans, no doubt in large part because of necessity and higher priority being given to corporate restructuring, downsizing, and debt reduction at home.

To complicate financial developments across the Pacific, almost the entire banking and related money-credit system has been undergoing major change and correction in structure, capital requirements, technology, product and market modification, competition, market share, currency and other asset values, and much more. Moreover, the correction process can be expected to persist throughout the remainder of the 1990s. All this obviously intensifies uncertainty and provokes tensions across economic and political boundaries of the Pacific and elsewhere.

GOVERNMENT-BUSINESS RELATIONSHIPS

The triumph of the market system over authoritarian rule in recent years has caused a surge in privatization and entrepreneurship across the world and, to a considerable but uneven degree, within the Pacific region. This has been widely welcomed as a powerful and positive force leading to greater prosperity and peace among nations. There is little to challenge these expectations so long as it is deeply appreciated that satisfactory results will come forth by sustained good working relations between the private and public sectors.

Democracy is the way of the future, but its achievement and sustainability depend upon a firm base of economic living standards together with reasonable expectations for a better tomorrow. The market system functions well only with private entrepreneurs owning property and other assets at reasonable risk, with the opportunity to earn a profitable return on investments, and a positive supporting government climate. These conditions are evident to a varying degree but far from automatic or consistently well-rooted around the Pacific Rim.

On balance and despite the new global emphasis on market orientation in economic policy, governments currently exert more powerful influences upon markets than private business in most Pacific nations. Yet, there are innumerable strong entrepreneurial organizations in place and more to come, commonly reaching well beyond national borders. Very close relationships frequently prevail between government and business, almost to the point where it is often difficult to distinguish between the public and private sector leadership.

This, of course, is not the case in the United States. The United States has a long-standing traditional cleavage, if not animosity, between business and government. Business generally has little confidence in government and resents regulatory interference. Government, in turn, is marked by officials who feel a strong sense of duty to protect the public from the profit-making strategies and tactics of many entrepreneurs. It is hoped that this cleavage will be reduced in the years ahead, at least to the extent of promoting neutral versus negative relations. The present system, in theory, preserves the ideology of private sector freedom and "hands-off" government but at a cost in lost productivity through bureaucratic delays and private sector antagonism amid endless legislative hearings and litigation.

The Clinton administration is getting more, rather than less, directly involved in issues of U.S. competitiveness. This brings a new sense of business-government cooperation but also sends up Pacific and global alarms that new protectionism is on the march in the United States. A reasonable goal would clearly be for the United States to explore more and better ways for government and business to work together in the national interest and Pacific Rim nations to explore more and better ways for government and business to work more independently. Carefully explained movements in these directions would help stimulate economic growth and stability across the Pacific in the years ahead.

NEEDED: UPDATE OF WESTERN CAPITALISM

The collapse of communism resulted from the inherent weaknesses of the system and the inability or refusal of leadership to recognize the ongoing economic, political, and ethnic-moral decay. It is now time for the Western world to reexamine its capitalistic system to insure against its own decay and potential breakdown.

The challenges that lie ahead for the Pacific Rim are staggering and well-known by thoughtful people. The difficulties facing former Communist nations trying to pursue democratic market-oriented principles should teach Western leaders that there is no all-perfect transferable form and style of capitalism. Accordingly, it would be wise to update the system to meet the challenges ahead. In particular, where does the middle ground between rich and poor lie? What answers are there to charges that human beings are being treated much the same as any other resource, to be exploited and discarded at will? What has happened to the ethical and moral foundations of capitalism? How can trust and discipline be taught or learned? What answers does our system have in facing a world or region of increasing population explosion and diversity?

Many more questions can and should be raised about the future of Western capitalism. Some modifications certainly are needed to win continuing popular support. No one is suggesting major deviation from time-honored principles, but ideals and institutions that have served well in the past can hardly be expected to thrive precisely in a vastly different and changing environment. Economic peace in the Pacific will depend to a large extent on the manner in which Western and U.S. capitalism can adapt to and resolve the profound challenges certain to come in the decade ahead.

CONCLUDING OBSERVATIONS

No region in the world now has greater promise than the Pacific Rim nations. The essentials for healthy growth and improved living standards are available or obtainable, but the seeds of conflict are also being sown, as indicated here.

Much will depend upon the sustainable growth rate of the overall economy, which will condition thinking on near-term and longer-range issues. The accurate flow of understandable economic and other information to the public in all nations will be critically important. A monitoring process to evaluate the changing degree of openness that prevails will be particularly important. Not forgotten must be the commitment toward openness that was signed at PECC IX by the representatives of 20 Pacific nations in September 1992. Where openness falters, a collective effort must be made promptly to address the causes and seek correction. Above all, leaders in business must accept more responsibility to help in the monitoring and resolution process, in its own interest as well as humankind's, because only business can really build the economic base for enduring peace in the Pacific.

5

East Asian Economics: Development, Cooperation Prospects, and China's Strategy

Huang Fan-zhang

Since the 1980s, every country in the world, whether developed or developing, has focused on the Asia Pacific region, especially on the countries of the western Pacific. Economic institutional reforms, industrial structural adjustments, and political system reforms have created great economic vitality in this region during the 1980s and into the 1990s. In its annual report for 1990, the World Bank said that the economic growth rate of East Asia had increased from 6.6 percent in the 1970s to 8.5 percent in the late 1980s, making the 1980s "the economic miracle period of East Asia." The growth of the East Asian economies has not slowed in the early 1990s and is distinctive in the context of a depressed world economy. This momentum will certainly exert profound and significant influences on the pattern and direction of the regionalized development of Asia Pacific economies and will become a vital factor to be considered by all nations, especially those of the Asia Pacific region, in drawing up their foreign economic strategies for the 1990s and the early twenty-first century.

THE RAPID GROWTH OF THE EAST ASIAN (WESTERN PACIFIC) ECONOMIES IN THE 1980S

In the 1980s the East Asian economies grew rapidly, particularly the Asian "four dragons" (Korea, Singapore, Taiwan, and Hong Kong). These four economies achieved an annual average growth rate of 7–8 percent after adjusting their economic strategies in the early 1960s from one based on import substitution to one based on bold and determined export orientation. They further refined their export-oriented strategies in the 1980s (see Table 5.1). The four dragons then became recognized as newly industrialized economies (NIEs).

It is praiseworthy that rapid economic growth had been recovered in the Association of Southeast Asian Nations (ASEAN) countries (Indonesia, Malaysia, Thailand, the Philippines, Singapore, and Brunei) after 1986, even though the economies of these countries had not been very stable due to shocks from the economic recessions of other developed countries in the early 1980s. This rapid economic growth recovery resulted from making full use of advantageous opportunities provided by the exchange rate fluctuations in the international market and by the industrial structure adjustments achieved by the four dragons. Thailand and Malaysia, in particular, achieved high-speed economic growth by actively using foreign funds and making enormous efforts to develop their export-oriented processing and service industries. The economic growth rates in Thailand had been in double digits for three years in the late 1980s (1988–90).

During the 1980s, the economic growth rate in Japan was the highest among the Western industrialized countries, with an annual gross national product average of about 4.3 percent. After Japan experienced two structural shocks of "Yen appreciation" and "structural change from outward oriented to domestic demand-leading," it became the biggest supplier of funds and the largest capital exporter in the world.

The success of China's reforms and open-door economic policies resulted in 9 percent annual average growth rate in the 1980s. By the end of 1987, the gross national product had doubled in comparison with 1980. Clearly, China brings distinctive forces to the vigorous East Asian economic growth patterns.

The rapid development of internal trade and economic relationships within East Asia and the Asia Pacific region is closely related to the long-term industrial structural adjustment of the region. Through long-term structural adjustment and industrial transfer, the situation of multilevel linkage of industry, trade, technology, and finance within this region has been firmly established. Japan is the super economic power in the region and has become the major supplier of funds, technology, and advanced products in the Asia Pacific, as well as a significant market for energy, raw material, and consumer goods. The four dragons have become an important base for industry, finance, and trade in the region, an important supplier of production equipment, intermediate products, and spare parts, and a major consumer of energy and raw material in the Asia Pacific. The ASEAN countries have become the processing base of components, spare parts, and necessary accessory equipment and an important supplier of raw materials and labor-intensive products for Japan and the four dragons. The formation of this kind of economic linkage is the result of internal mutual exchange of capital, trade, and technology within the region and promotes the

TABLE 5.1
Economic Growth 1981–92: Four Dragons and Four Association of Southeast Asian Nations

Region	*1981*	*1982*	*1983*	*1984*	*1985*	*1986*	*1987*	*1988*	*1989*	*1990*	*1991*	*1992*
South Korea	6.7	7.3	11.8	9.4	6.9	12.4	12.0	11.5	6.2	9.2	8.4	6.0
Singapore	9.6	6.9	8.2	8.3	–1.6	1.8	9.4	11.1	9.2	8.3	6.7	5.5
Taiwan	6.2	3.6	8.4	10.6	4.9	11.6	12.3	7.3	7.6	4.9	7.2	6.4
Hong Kong	9.4	2.0	6.5	9.5	–0.1	11.9	13.9	8.3	2.8	3.8	4.2	5.3
Indonesia	7.9	2.2	4.2	6.7	2.5	5.9	4.9	5.8	7.5	7.1	6.6	6.1
Thailand	6.3	4.1	7.3	7.1	3.5	4.5	9.5	13.3	12.3	11.5	7.9	7.5
Philippines	3.9	2.9	0.9	–6.0	–4.3	1.4	4.7	6.3	5.9	2.5	–1.0	0.5
Malaysia	6.9	5.9	6.3	7.8	–1.0	1.2	5.2	8.9	9.2	9.7	8.7	8.3

continued development of various levels of trade and economic linkages.

Strategies for Economic Cooperation

Encouraged by the rapid development of trade and economic linkages within East Asia and the Pacific Rim and faced with challenges from the European Community and the North American Free Trade Area, people in the Asia Pacific region have been actively exploring ways for greater regional economic cooperation during the 1980s and early 1990s. In the Asia Pacific region, differences in development levels and social and political systems among countries are great. Japan, the United States, Australia, Malaysia, and other countries have their own considerations and provide their respective strategy suggestions for economic cooperation in the region. Among these strategies, the most important are the "flying geese" strategy suggested by Japan and the open regionalism strategy suggested by the United States.

Japan's Flying Geese Strategy

Japan's flying geese strategy includes the following:

1. Taking Japan as the head of the geese and the four dragons and the ASEAN countries as the two wings of the geese, the countries can be arranged according to different economic development levels.
2. The development of the members of the geese led by the head of the flock is mainly based on industrial transfer, that is, some matured industries are transferred from Japan to the four dragons first and then transferred from the four dragons to the ASEAN countries. During the 1960s and 1970s, the textile industry was transferred through this strategy. Since the 1980s, the home electrical appliance industry and the chemical industry have been transferred and the auto industry is beginning to be transferred along the geese strategy lines.
3. There are several ways to transfer these industries: first, through local firms able to accept the technologies, and second, through Japanese multinational enterprises, which is much more common and likely. If the products of the industries are export oriented, the country that accepts the transferred industries is likely to depend on Japanese multinational enterprises that know the international market well.

With respect to the other countries of the East Asian region, this strategy is significant in two ways: it may be helpful for driving the development of the Asia Pacific region, and the four dragons and the ASEAN countries have gained economic development benefits from the industrial transfers. However, Japan maintains its technological advantage and economic leadership by fixing the orders of industrial transfer and often retains the dependence of these countries on Japan by transferring industry but not critical technology. This strategy is essentially predicated on Japan's leadership in East Asia and the Western Pacific region, which Japan is intent on establishing.

The flying geese strategy was suggested by Japanese scholars in the mid-1960s and has been criticized as a second edition of the "Greater Co-Prosperity Sphere for the East Asian Economy." Although Japan concealed its true intentions to reconstruct this "Common Prosperity Rim" at a time when it was not urgent to build up the economic community, Japan has reinforced its policy of economic infiltration in the four dragons and the ASEAN countries. According to statistics, Japan's direct investment in the four dragons and the ASEAN countries increased by 68.5 percent and 86.3 percent from 1986 to 1987, respectively, and increased by 26.5 percent and 90.9 percent from 1987 to 1988, respectively. Although Japan's direct investment overseas was reduced, Japan nevertheless carried out its flying geese strategy actively and seemed to choose it as a basic national strategy, presenting it as part of its official report to Asia Pacific Economic Cooperation. Japan's attempts and practices to establish its East Asian new order have attracted the widespread attention of other countries.

The Open Regionalism Strategy of the United States

The United States has been very sensitive to Japan's actions in the Asia Pacific. Many Americans advocate the strategy of open regionalism. They not only recognize that economic regionalization would be helpful to promoting specialized production and economic cooperation but also emphasize that this kind of regionalism should be open to the outside world and should support the principles of free trade and fair competition without fostering protectionism and various barriers and discrimination. The United States believes that the policies of the European Community are discriminatory against foreign trade, that Japan has adopted various measures to protect its domestic market, and that only the North American Free Trade Area is open to the outside world. In the Pacific region, the spearhead of open regionalism is pointed first at Japan.

Naturally, the United States is concerned about its own economic interests in the Asia Pacific, especially in the East Asia region. The high-speed growth of the East Asian economy provides a vast market and investment site with huge potential for the United States. In his speech on the topic of "New Partner Relations in the Pacific Region: Framework for the Future," delivered in June 1989, former U.S. Secretary of State James Baker stressed the following three points: the need to maintain the central role of the United States in the economic and political affairs of the Pacific region; the need to put regional cooperation on the agenda of U.S. interests; and the need for partners in the Asia Pacific region to lend their economic force in support of the leadership of the United States in the region and globally.

Although the economic ability of the United States currently falls short of its desired objectives, it has, nevertheless, actively penetrated the East Asia region. For example, U.S. direct investment in the four dragons increased from $7.8 billion in 1980 to $14.8 billion in 1990, and its direct investment in four of the ASEAN countries (Thailand, Indonesia, Malaysia, and the Philippines) increased from $6.6 billion in 1980 to $8.4 billion in 1990. The United States intends to expand its economic performance and interests in East Asia, and Japan insists on carrying out its flying geese strategy. A report issued by the World Bank in February 1993 noted that Japan is "quietly becoming the major partner in the development of the East Asia region instead of the US." A future scenario suggests that if Russia does not become a threat to the United States and Japan, the conflicts between these powers will accelerate daily. The East Asia region and even the entire Pacific Rim will become the major battlefield for trade and economic conflicts between the United States and Japan.

Some Considerations Regarding China's Strategy

China's economic reforms and open policies of the past decade have prompted greater economic cooperation between it and the countries of the Asia Pacific region in trade matters. According to statistics, the proportions of China's total exports to and imports from the Asia Pacific region are more than 60–70 percent and 50 percent, respectively. Since the 1980s, China's major trade partners — Hong Kong and Macao, Japan, the United States, Taiwan, Korea, and others — are all located in the Asia Pacific. Foreign direct investments are basically from this region also, especially from East Asia. According to statistics for total contracted investments in 1991, Hong Kong and Macao show the largest proportion (62.6 percent), Taiwan shows the second largest (11.58 percent), Japan ranks third (6.77 percent), Germany is fourth (4.65 percent), the United States is fifth (4.57 percent), and Singapore ranks sixth (1.29 percent) (Table 5.2). The development of the trade and economic relationships between China and the Asia Pacific region has contributed to the great economic success of China since 1980, and China's future economic development will still depend on economic cooperation with the Asia Pacific, especially with the East Asia region.

It must also be emphasized that economic cooperation in East Asia or in the Pacific Rim as a whole should not exclude China's participation. China is a huge market and investment site and is a neighbor of the East Asian countries, thus, facilitating transnational economic cooperation. With an integrated industrial production system, a powerful technological force, and rich labor resource, China can cooperate widely at different industrial and technological levels with the countries in the region that are at different states of development. This

TABLE 5.2
Main Sources of Foreign Direct Investment to China in 1991
(in billion dollars)

Country or Region	*Investment Agreed*	*Percentage of Total Investment*
Hong Kong and Macao	7.51	62.60
Taiwan	1.38	11.58
Japan	0.81	6.77
Germany	0.56	4.66
United States	0.55	4.57
Singapore	0.16	1.29

point should be acknowledged by all countries in their trade and economic relationships with China.

China has always been enthusiastic about economic cooperation within East Asia and the Asia Pacific region. Regional cooperation is beneficial not only to the economic development of China and the region but also to maintaining peace and stability in the Asia Pacific. At present and in the near future, though, China faces an economic situation and structure in East Asia and the Asia Pacific characterized by triangles at three levels: the big triangle (China, Japan, and the United States); the medium triangle (China, the ASEAN countries, and the four dragons); and the small triangle (China, Taiwan, and Hong Kong). The basic relationships of the three levels are naturally the major reference points for China to develop its economic strategy in the region.

The trade and economic relationships among the economies of the small triangle have developed rapidly in recent years, reflecting a trend of sharing common prosperity and depression. China needs the funds, technology, and management expertise of Taiwan and Hong Kong. Taiwan and Hong Kong need the market and resources of mainland China to enhance international competitiveness. Furthermore, Taiwan's comprehensive level of science and technology is relatively low, and outside support is needed for developing new technologies and technology-intensive industries and for renewing the present technological equipment. Therefore, economic integration of the small triangle has become a desirable trend.

Within the medium triangle we see both complementary and competitive developments between China, the ASEAN countries and the four dragons. At the present, all have carried out their own long-term development programs for the next five to ten years, especially the construction of infrastructure. The four dragons and Thailand, Malaysia and Indonesia have decided to invest $450 billion in these construction projects. Naturally, these countries will be competitive in seeking the funds. With a multilevel industrial structure, China can both accept transfers of matured industries and technologies from the four dragons and transfer some matured industries and technologies to the ASEAN countries. At the same time, China will be competitive with these countries because of economic competition with the four dragons in steel, machinery, chemical, and shipbuilding industries and with the ASEAN countries in labor-intensive industries such as textiles, clothing, and construction materials.

Thus, due to the nature of their trade and economic relationships with China, the four dragons are more complementary than competitive, and the ASEAN countries are more competitive than complementary. However, no major conflicts of interest exist between China and the four dragons or the ASEAN countries, and there are common basic interests in maintaining economic independence and sovereignty and in promoting common economic prosperity. Competitive relations can promote internal horizontal divisions of industry, which, in turn, stimulate production.

In the big triangle, trade and economic relationships will consist of both alliances and differences (or conflicts), because both the United States and Japan seek to assume leadership in trade and economic cooperation in the Asia Pacific region. China will remain independent and develop bilateral or multilateral trade relationships, furthering economic cooperation among the Asia Pacific countries and regions.

Economic cooperation between China and Japan is beneficial to both nations. However, some points should be highlighted:

Japan is sensitive about China's development from a "great political nation" and a "great armed nation" to a "great economic nation." Japan would like to see that China remains at the end of the flying geese and does not want to see China emerge as a future competitor.

The private direct investment of Japan will flow mainly to the ASEAN countries and to the four dragons, not to China.

Japan expects Chinese economic development to provide it with a huge market but does not favor the flow of Chinese goods, capital, and technology into the South Asian and East Asian markets, due to its own interests in the region.

Japan's close relations with Taiwan and Hong Kong through enhancement of trade and economic opportunities may influence the south coastal regions of China. Some factions in Japan might even promote ideas of independent deviations in Taiwan and Hong Kong after 1997, ideas that may be supported by some Western countries.

In general, as the Chinese economy continues to develop at a high speed, economic conflicts between China and Japan will tend to increase.

In the trade and economic fields, the Chinese-U.S. relationship is more complementary than competitive. In the fields of political ideas and social ideology, however, conflicts between the two countries will continue for a long period and will, in turn, both fluctuate and affect trade and economic relations. However, because both the United States and China wish to curb the economic expansionism of Japan, the two countries have similar long-term strategic interests. This has been recognized by persons of vision in both countries.

Therefore, the trade and economic relationships between China and Japan in the short term will be more harmonious than those between China and the United States. The Chinese-U.S. trade and economic relationship will fluctuate and at times reach serious levels but will not reach the breaking point.

In analyzing the general structure of the large, medium, and small triangle relationships in the Asia Pacific economy, the best strategic choice for China is to rely on the small triangle, to win over the medium triangle, and to contend among the large triangle, that is, China should develop the trade and economic relationships with Hong Kong and Taiwan, reinforce bilateral or multilateral local cooperation with the ASEAN countries and Korea and Singapore, and enhance the economic "complementarity" and open up the far overseas markets (the Americas, Australia, and Europe) by leading the Asia Pacific region as a "gangplank." China should contend with the developed countries such as the United States, Japan, Canada, and Australia by making full use of favorable outside environments to assist with furthering the prosperity of the Chinese economy and to promote the unification of the country.

Finally, it is worth mentioning that as a member of the Asia Pacific region, Russia will play an important role. Throughout most of the 1990s, Russia will be limited by its domestic economic and political difficulties, which will not allow it to participate extensively in Pacific economic affairs. As the Russian economy recovers, however, Russia will naturally increase its influence in the region's trade and economic relationships, as well as increase its participation in regional economic cooperation. This will undoubtedly bring change and important influences to bear on the structure of East Asia and the Asia Pacific region.

6

Pacific Economic Cooperation: Outlook and Agenda for the 1990s

Kim Kihwan

Until recently, the idea of economic cooperation among countries in the Asia Pacific region has been promoted for the most part by the private sector. For quite some time, it seemed as if the governments of the countries concerned had been disinterested in the subject, but in 1989 a significant breakthrough occurred. The governments of 12 countries in the Asia Pacific region joined together to form the Asia Pacific Economic Cooperation (APEC) forum. At its third annual meeting in Seoul in 1991, the membership of APEC expanded by admitting China, Hong Kong, and Taiwan as additional members. However, even after APEC came into being, it was not clear whether it would be anything more than an intergovernmental forum where ministers of the member countries exchange their views but take no binding action on behalf of their countries.

Most recently, however, another significant breakthrough took place. U.S. President Clinton hosted the heads of state of the APEC member countries or economies in Seattle for the fifth annual APEC Ministerial Conference in November 1993. The meeting was a major turning point for Pacific economic cooperation because it was the first time that the heads of state of Asia Pacific countries met to discuss economic cooperation.

It is most appropriate to define some of the key issues and challenges facing Asia Pacific countries. Such a task, however, should be preceded by an examination of the major historical developments taking place in the world today, because they are the very reasons that give rise to the issues and challenges. In any case, once the issues and challenges have been defined, there is a need to formulate strategies for dealing with those challenges.

The purpose of this chapter is to address these tasks, and accordingly, the chapter has four parts: major historical developments and their implications, major issues and challenges, strategies, and actions to be taken.

MAJOR HISTORICAL DEVELOPMENTS AND THEIR IMPLICATIONS

One of the major historical developments that has occurred in recent years is, of course, the end of the Cold War. During the Cold War, the military threat from the former Soviet bloc served as a strong bond that held the Western alliance together. With such a bond in place, consensus was relatively easy to achieve on many global issues, including the development and maintenance of the world trade system. However, now that this bond has dissolved, it is difficult to reach a consensus on any issue.

With the military threat present, the United States has not only a strong incentive but also a greater capacity to provide strong leadership for the development and maintenance of the multilateral trading system based on the principles of the General Agreement on Tariffs and Trade (GATT). Now that the military threat has disappeared, the United States has less incentive and less capacity to provide such leadership.

Furthermore, with the disintegration of the Soviet military bloc, the world no longer places as high a premium on military strength as before. In fact, a high premium is now placed on economic strength, a factor which has greatly raised the relative position of countries such as Japan vis-à-vis the United States. Usually, a country whose international position has gained greater prominence would readily assume the leadership corresponding to its new position. In the case of Japan, however, this does not seem to have happened so far. As a result, the world is lacking the kind of leadership that had previously sustained the multilateral trade system.

The second major historical development concerns the accelerated globalization of economic activities and the increasing interdependence among economies in the world. Propelled primarily by technological revolutions in information processing, communication, and transportation, globalization is progressing at an unprecedented pace. There is little question that in the long run the world economy will benefit from this development. However, in the short run, this same development continues to create issues and problems far beyond the capacity of the present GATT system.

The third important development relates to the strong desire of many countries to make fundamental shifts in their economic policy orientation. The best examples are the Eastern European countries and former Soviet republics that want to transform their centrally planned economies into market-oriented economies. Another group of countries in this category are those that were previously committed to import substitution and that now want to adopt an outward-looking strategy. In order to make their policy orientation shifts successfully, these countries will require not only capital and technology but also markets for their exports. It remains to be seen whether these requirements will be met.

The fourth important development concerns the emergence of regionalism both inside and outside the Asia Pacific region. Despite the difficulties in making the European Monetary System work, there is little question that the European Community (EC) has become a more integrated economic bloc. Even within the Asia Pacific region, the regional approach is also becoming a trend, especially with the conclusion of the North American Free Trade Agreement (NAFTA) between the United States, Canada, and Mexico. Although NAFTA claims that it has no intention of being an exclusive trading bloc, there is concern about the possibility that trade diversion effects may outweigh trade creation effects.

MAJOR ISSUES AND CHALLENGES

Based on the foregoing discussion, four major challenges facing Pacific cooperation can be readily identified. First, there is a critical need to keep the multilateral trading system safe from many dangers, including the lack of political leadership. This need is more critical in the Asia Pacific region than elsewhere, because this region has benefitted from the multilateral system more than other regions over the past 40 years or more.

Second, there is a need to strengthen and to improve fundamentally the multilateral world trading system itself. This is true even with the successful conclusion of the Uruguay Round in December 1993. To be sure, the round has already produced highly significant results in such cases as improved surveillance procedures, a proposed multilateral trade organization, integration of textiles into GATT, and improved rules on safeguards. However, many issues in areas such as tariff reduction, investment and trade in services, sectoral derogations, and intellectual property rights were not adequately addressed in the Uruguay Round. What is more, such vital issues as trade-environment linkages have not been addressed at all.

Third, it is necessary to accommodate countries adopting an outward-looking strategy in an attempt to integrate their economies into the world economy. Given the degree of interdependence among countries in the "shrinking" world today, leaving them frustrated in their efforts will be not only undesirable but also very dangerous for the peace and stability of the world.

Fourth, ways must be found to reconcile the inherent conflict between regional and multilateral approaches to trade. Even if a regional arrangement is not inward looking, there is always the possibility that trade creation effects may not be sufficient to offset trade diversion effects. However, even if trade creation is large enough to offset trade diversion in a particular case, the arrangement, after all, may not be an optimal one from a global point of view.

STRATEGIES

It is difficult to outline a comprehensive strategy that can deal with all these issues and challenges at once; however, suggestions may be offered for tackling each challenge individually. With regard to the threats to the multilateral trading system, it was most desirable to have a successful conclusion of the Uruguay Round. Nonetheless, fundamental differences of views still remain on issues such as agriculture, tariffs, and services between the United States, Japan, and the EC. Fundamental improvements are needed in many areas, including tariffs, services, sectoral derogations, contingency trade measures, and voluntary export restraints. In addition, some creative thinking is required regarding the application of the principle of reciprocity. As long as countries make concessions on a reciprocal basis, they tend to hold onto existing market barriers to use them as future bargaining chips, which overall slows down the pace of liberalization. As the U.S.-Japan Structural Impediments Initiative negotiations have demonstrated, elimination of border barriers alone is seldom sufficient to avoid trade friction. A critical need also exists to do something about the rights of individual citizens in international transactions.[1]

This last point deserves further elaboration. It should be remembered that the rights and obligations derived from key principals of the GATT, such as multilateralism, nondiscrimination, national treatment, and transparency, are currently applicable between governments but not so between a government and individuals. In other words, individual citizens do not enjoy the rights to buy and sell goods and services freely anywhere in the world, that is, within and beyond national borders. If an individual citizen had these rights, the citizen could sue the government if and when these rights were violated. Given the rapid pace of globalization, it will not be very long before many citizens will demand such rights. Incorporating such rights in the GATT General Agreement itself and in domestic legislation of the contracting parties would not only help strengthen protrade constituencies in every country but also increase world trade dramatically.

It is a truism that countries adopting an outward-looking strategy will go nowhere unless they have access to markets for their exports. By the same token, they will achieve little without access to capital, technology, and know-how from abroad. For their own part, these countries need to adopt a sound macroeconomic policy and a progressive policy on direct foreign investment. In addition, they must build an efficient banking system to increase domestic savings and to allocate investments efficiently. To facilitate all these tasks, it is imperative that these countries be permitted to join GATT and other multilateral organizations, such as the International Monetary Fund and the World Bank, without further delay.

With respect to the emergence of many regional arrangements within the Asia Pacific area, the key lies in ensuring that trade creation effects are greater than trade diversion effects. Article XXIV of GATT was designed for this purpose. The article, however, does not go far enough. By merely prohibiting new barriers against outsiders, one cannot guarantee that trade creation outweighs trade diversion. Chances for trade creation to exceed trade diversion will be improved greatly if countries entering a new regional arrangement are required also to reduce barriers against outsiders. In short, the proper policy for Asia Pacific countries toward subregional arrangements should be one that permits arrangements only if discriminations against nonmembers are also reduced within a certain time frame.

The most important trade bloc outside the Asia Pacific region in the foreseeable future is, of course, the EC. Therefore, the policy of Asia Pacific countries toward trading blocs outside the region amounts to some kind of policy toward the EC. Hence, the question to be raised is, what policy should Asia Pacific countries have toward the EC?

The policy of Asia Pacific countries toward the EC should depend on the nature of the EC as a trading bloc. If the EC is going to be as outward looking as it has claimed, it makes no sense for Asia Pacific countries to apply any pressure on the EC. However, it is unclear as to whether the EC will remain outward looking in the future. As the EC expands its membership and establishes special relationships with neighboring countries, it is likely to give preference to the new members as well as to its close neighbors. In addition, as internal barriers are removed and preference is extended to neighbors, competition among EC firms will intensify. This will result in the strong demand for protection. The EC commission will most likely accommodate these demands by pooling national quotas into community-wide restrictions and by applying the more stringent use of antidumping and countervailing provisions and safeguards.[2]

If this inference regarding the future evolution of the EC is correct, then there will surely come a time when Asia Pacific countries will have to exert their influence on the EC to make sure that it will not pursue policies detrimental to the interests of the Asia Pacific region.

It should, therefore, be asked how such an outcome can be deterred. Two alternatives are available. First is for the Northeast Asian economies to join North America, forming a large NAFTA. This is possible because membership in NAFTA is open-ended. If Southeast Asian countries join Northeast Asian countries in this move, NAFTA will, in effect, encompass all countries represented in APEC. As such it may be called the Asia Pacific Free Trade Area. One way to trigger this process is for Taiwan, Korea, or Japan to join NAFTA first. If any one of these three countries joins, say Taiwan, which currently has every incentive to join an international arrangement such as NAFTA, Korea will be compelled to join, given the fact that the two economies are competitors in the North American market. If Taiwan and Korea join, Japan will have no choice but to join. If these three countries join NAFTA, it is most likely that the ASEAN nations, Australia, and New Zealand will join NAFTA as well.

The other alternative would be for Asia Pacific countries to make special efforts to strengthen APEC. One way to do so is to elevate the annual ministerial meetings to official summit meetings. This may indeed be what President Clinton had in mind when he invited all the heads of state of APEC members to Seattle. In any event, a strengthened APEC can serve as an umbrella organization for all subregional arrangements in the APEC region, including NAFTA and the ASEAN Free Trade Area. As an umbrella organization, one of the responsibilities of APEC will be to ensure that all subregional organizations result in more trade creation than trade diversion. To ensure this outcome, the preferential benefits afforded to member countries should be extended also to nonmember countries within a certain time frame after a regional arrangement has come into being. The group of Asia Pacific economies closely coordinated either through a strengthened APEC or an enlarged NAFTA will be in an excellent position to apply pressure on the EC. The combined gross domestic product of all countries in APEC accounts for more than one-half of the world's gross domestic product, while combined trade accounts account for almost 40 percent of world trade.

Some might worry that applying pressure on the EC in this manner would jeopardize world peace and stability. It should be remembered, however, that confrontations are less likely to occur in a bipolar world than in a tripolar world. A tripolar world will emerge if East Asia forms an exclusive trade bloc in opposition to NAFTA. As Singapore's Senior Minister Lee Kuan Yew has pointed out, a tripolar world will create a situation where each bloc will be discordant internally and aggressive externally — a situation quite similar to that which led to World War II.[3]

ACTIONS TO BE TAKEN

With regard to the efforts to strengthen and to reform the GATT fundamentally, it would be most desirable if the heads of state of Asia Pacific nations undertake a commitment to launching another round of global trade negotiations within a year or two following the conclusion of the current Uruguay Round. Such a commitment will serve to maintain the momentum of progress toward the ultimate goal of achieving a full-fledged liberal world trade system.

As for the effort to help countries trying to make the transition from centrally planned to market-oriented economies, it would be most desirable if the heads of state join forces in preparing a comprehensive aid package for those countries. In doing so, the heads of state would do well to remember that the enormity of the task involved in restructuring centrally planned economies into well-functioning market economies is in many ways comparable to that which the Western countries faced in the reconstruction of their war-torn economies at the end of World War II.

As to the need to deal with the rise of regionalism within the Asia Pacific region, the heads of state should adopt a new trade and investment code that incorporates the idea of reducing discrimination against nonmembers within a certain time frame.

With regard to the relationship between Asia Pacific countries and the rest of the world, particularly the EC, it will, of course, be necessary to discuss the relative merits of the two options discussed above and to choose one over the other. If they do so, chances are that they will come out in favor of strengthening the APEC. Although the NAFTA extension option has a number of practical advantages, it has some serious drawbacks. For one thing, it would create new discriminations within the region, at least during the transition period. For another, it would be divisive, particularly between the countries that want to join readily an expanded NAFTA and the countries that have serious reservations about doing so.

Since these policy decisions relate to the Uruguay Round, the reform of the GATT, and the APEC's relations to the NAFTA and other regional arrangements, including the EC, they will have enormous consequences for the future of the world economy. One hopes that the heads of state will have both the courage and wisdom to make proper decisions not only for the well-being of their people but also for the peace and prosperity of the world.

POSTSCRIPT

Since this chapter was written, at least two important developments have taken place: the de facto first APEC "summit" and the more or less successful conclusion of the Uruguay Round of trade negotiations, both of which are not unrelated to each other.

At the APEC meeting in Seattle, it is true that the heads of state did not take all the actions recommended in the chapter. However, it is important to note that the most critical actions were in fact taken, thus ensuring the continued development of APEC in the manner envisioned. At the meeting, heads of state not only called for a timely conclusion of the Uruguay Round but also ensured its success by making several significant concessions, including tariff reductions on several key products. They also agreed to hold a second heads of state meeting next year in Indonesia, which amounts to the first step toward not only holding regular meetings but also elevating the annual Ministerial meeting to the summit level. In order to maximize trade creation and minimize trade diversion resulting from any regional arrangements, the Seattle meeting adopted the APEC Trade and Investment Framework and launched the Trade and Investment Committee to implement the agreement in a way suggested by the chapter.

The Seattle meeting, however, failed to bring about the explicit commitment of APEC members to launch a new round of trade negotiations soon, as suggested in the chapter. The meeting also failed to give explicit attention to problems of integrating former socialist countries with the liberal world trade system. However, with regard to the first shortcoming, a sub-cabinet senior officials' meeting was requested to study the question of a Pacific initiative for a new round. As for the need to pay attention to the problems facing former socialist countries, now that the heads of states have acquired major personal stakes in the successful development of APEC, they are most likely to take this development into account when making decisions on related matters. For instance, when the president of the United States makes a decision on whether to maintain most favored nation status for China, he must consider the impact of such a decision on the future development of APEC,[4] thus bringing the central issue, as it were, through the back door.

In sum, although the first APEC "summit" in Seattle came somewhat short of meeting all the challenges identified in the chapter, it did go quite far toward laying the foundation for the resolution of all key issues in the time to come.

NOTES

1. For this point, see John Whalley, "The Uruguay Round and GATT: Whither the Global System?" paper presented at the 20th Pacific Trade and Development Conference, Washington, D.C., September 10–12, 1992, p. 25.

2. Soogil Young, "East Asia as a Regional Force for Globalism," paper presented at the Workshop on Regionalism and the Global Trading System, Geneva, September 3–5, 1992, p. 28.

3. For a fuller exposition on this view, see Kuan Yew Lee, "Asia Pacific: A Bullish Scenario Relies on Partnership," *International Herald Tribune*, June 24, 1991.

4. C. Fred Bergsten, "Sunrise in Seattle," *Interational Economic Insights*, 5(1) (January/February 1994): 19.

7

The Importance of the Asia Pacific Region for California's Economic Vitality

Tapan Munroe

> The Mediterranean is the ocean of the past, the Atlantic the ocean of the present, and the Pacific the ocean of the future.
>
> — John Hay, Secretary of State, 1898

More than 90 years ago, John Hay, Secretary of State, made his visionary statement — and he appears to have been right. The Pacific is not only bigger than the Atlantic, it carries more trade and the volume is growing faster than trans-Atlantic trade. Today the fastest growing economies in the world include China, Singapore, South Korea, Hong Kong, and Malaysia (Table 7.1). China is the leader in economic growth in the region, with real gross domestic product growth averaging over 10 percent annually from 1988 to 1993. China's record growth has been due to commitment to economic reform and to a large influx of foreign investment from Taiwan and Hong Kong.

For the past 20 years (1973–1993) Asian countries have outperformed the rest of the world in economic growth. The performance of Asia Pacific countries has been particularly remarkable: 7 percent average growth, compared with 2.5 percent for western Europe and the United States, 3 percent for Latin America, and 2 percent for Africa. The World Bank forecast for the next decade suggests that Asia Pacific countries will continue to outperform the rest of the world by a margin of two to one. It is estimated that in the 1990s, the region will contribute twice as much to world output as North America or the European Community.

The phenomenal economic growth of the Asia Pacific economies is to a considerable degree a result of investment in plant and equipment technology. Between 1988 and 1992, Asia Pacific countries far

TABLE 7.1
Economic and Demographic Data for Selected Pacific Basin Countries, 1992

	Gross Domestic Product Growth	*Rank*	*Personal Consumption*	*Rank*	*Gross Private Domestic Investment*	*Population Growth*	*Rank*
Australia	3.0	10	1.4	12	0.8	1.5	7
Canada	2.3	14	0.9	14	1.3	1.3	9
Chile	6.5	5	4.1	3	2.7	1.6	5
Hong Kong	5.4	8	3.2	6	3.1	0.8	14
Indonesia	6.4	6	2.4	8	4.3	1.6	6
Japan	2.5	11	1.9	10	–0.3	0.3	15
Korea	7.5	3	5.1	1	2.4	0.9	12
Malaysia	8.5	2	4.0	4	3.0	2.3	3
New Zealand	2.4	13	0.2	15	2.8	1.1	10
Peru	3.5	9	3.0	7	5.0	2.4	1
Philippines	2.5	12	1.8	11	0.5	2.4	2
Singapore	6.0	7	2.2	9	6.3	1.8	4
Taiwan	6.8	4	3.4	5	27	1	11
Thailand	8.6	1	4.6	2	4.1	1.4	8
United States	1.6	15	1.2	13	0.5	0.9	13

Source: Pacific Economic Outlook 1992–93, Pacific Economic Cooperation Council.

surpassed the investment in Europe and the United States (Figure 7.1). However, that is not the entire story. The quality of human resources in Asia Pacific countries continues to improve and is comparable to that of many Western industrial nations (Table 7.2).

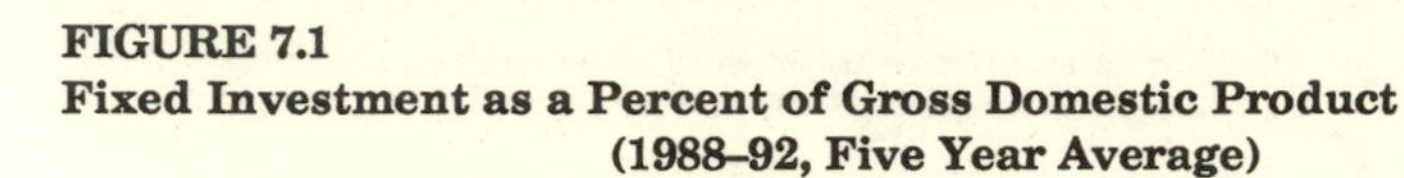

FIGURE 7.1
Fixed Investment as a Percent of Gross Domestic Product (1988–92, Five Year Average)

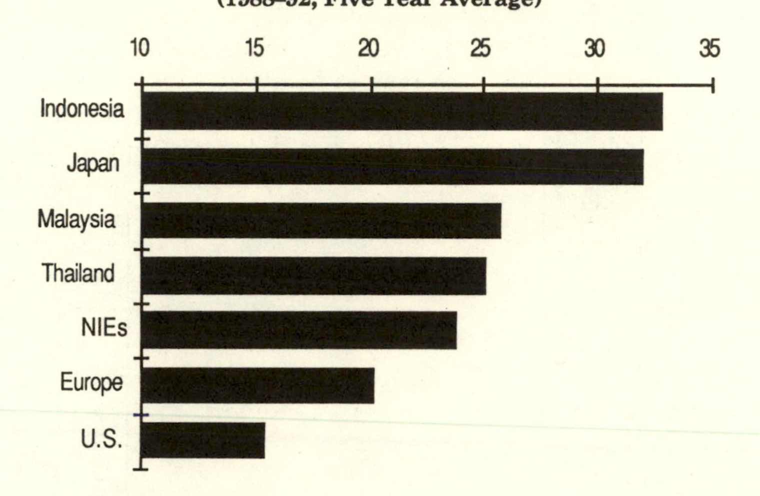

Source: The WEFA Economic Database, The WEFA Group, Bala Cynwid, Pennsylvania, 1993.

TABLE 7.2
Literacy and Education in Asia Pacific Nations

Country	*Literacy Rate (%)*	*University Students per 100,000 Persons*
Japan	99	1,971
South Korea	92	3,671
China	70	190
Taiwan	90	2,346
Hong Kong	88	1,410
Philippines	88	3,580
Thailand	89	1,990
Malaysia	80	680
Singapore	87	1,718
Indonesia	72	600
Australia	99	2,444

Source: *Fortune* (Special Issue), Fall 1989, pp. 74–84.

These trends clearly point to one conclusion: the Asia Pacific region will be the place of greatest business opportunity for the next decade. Specifically, opportunities in the Asian markets will be greatest in two areas: consumer goods and infrastructure needs.

The first — consumer goods — is a result of 20 years of rapid economic growth, growing population, rising household formation, a shift from rural to urban settlement, and increasing participation of women in the labor force. Rising prosperity has spread broadly enough to create a middle class that is serious about raising their standard of living. A 1988 McKinsey and Company study estimate showed that in 1988, nearly 72 million people (excluding Japan) lived in households with incomes greater than $10,000. By the year 2000, the same study suggests, the number could exceed 110 million. By then, Korea and Taiwan — with populations over 42 million and 20 million, respectively — will have higher per capita income levels than Ireland and Spain.

What do these trends mean for business opportunities in the Asia Pacific region? They mean more housing, which in turn means more telephones, appliances, televisions, light bulbs, furniture, other household goods, and building supplies. Similarly, the trend of more women staying in school longer, marrying later, having fewer children, and entering the workforce in large numbers means rising demand for apparel, shoes, cosmetics, accessories, and office supplies and equipment.

Nowhere is the demand greater than in infrastructure development, the second opportunity area. In order to support growing middle class consumption, Asia Pacific economies need to expand public infrastructure such as roads, bridges, ports, power plants, and telecommunications. China is likely to be one of the largest markets for telecommunications equipment in the remainder of the 1990s and into the next century. Between now and the year 2000, Asia Pacific economies are likely to spend nearly $1 trillion on infrastructure and development.

Given the end of the Soviet empire, a stagnant Europe, and a lackluster U.S. economy, Asia Pacific economies offer the greatest opportunities for dynamic consumer and infrastructure-related markets for the 1990s. With California in the fifth year of a painful recession, the worst since the Great Depression (Figure 7.2), the Asia Pacific economies are particularly alluring as an export market. In light of California's severe structural problems that range from defense cutbacks and base closures to surplus commercial space and business retention problems, expansion of exports to Asia Pacific countries offers an important avenue for reinvigorating the economy. Export development to the Asia Pacific could be an important reconversion strategy for the state.

FIGURE 7.2
California Total Nonagriculture Employment
(January 1990–July 1993)

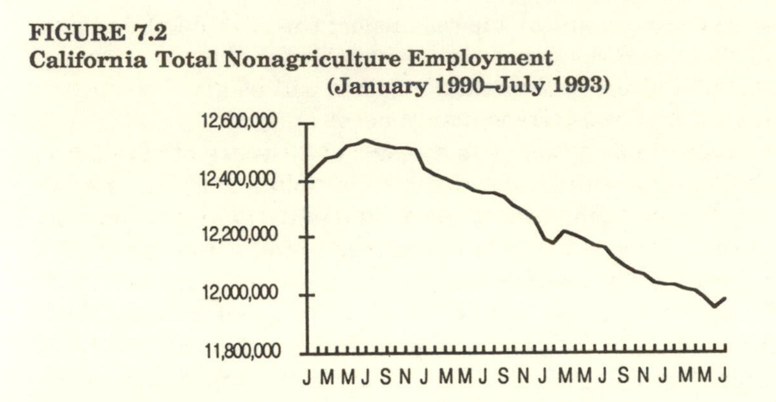

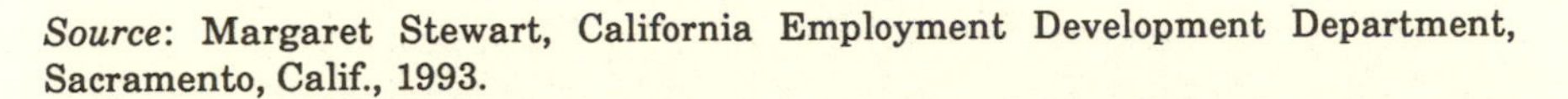

Source: Margaret Stewart, California Employment Development Department, Sacramento, Calif., 1993.

International trade has always been important for California. In 1991, trade via California ports (sea, air, and land) amounted to nearly $175 billion — $75 billion in exports and $100 billion in imports (Figure 7.3). From 1983 through 1993 the dollar volume of California trade has tripled, with imports growing slightly faster than exports. Trade creates a large number of jobs in the state. Exports create nearly 200,000 direct jobs, mostly in manufacturing (87 percent) and a majority of the remainder in agriculture (12 percent). If we include indirect job creation via exports, the total number of jobs created would be in the 650,000–670,000 range. Imports also create a significant number of jobs in areas such as handling of cargo, processing, distribution, and

FIGURE 7.3
California's Foreign Trade, 1980–91

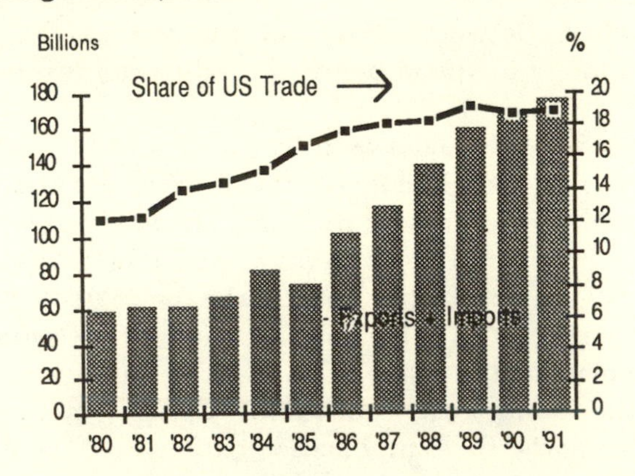

Source: Special Report on the California Economy (Palo Alto, Calif.: Center for Continuing Study of the California Economy, 1991), p. 18.

sales. These jobs are primarily located in port areas such as the San Francisco Bay area and the Los Angeles–Long Beach area.

A majority of California's foreign trade is with the Pacific Rim, namely, the East Asian countries and Mexico. In 1991, 62 percent of exports were to Asian countries, and nearly 81 percent of imports were from Asian sources (Figure 7.4). Europe is a distant second. California's top ten trade partners in 1991 were Japan, Taiwan, South Korea, Singapore, China, Mexico, Hong Kong, Germany, Malaysia, and Australia (for additional detail, see Figure 7.5). Seven of the ten countries belong to the Asia Pacific group. Japan is undoubtedly California's largest trading partner, with $37 billion in imports and $18 billion in exports.

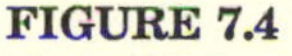
FIGURE 7.4
Exports from and Imports into California Ports by World Region, 1991

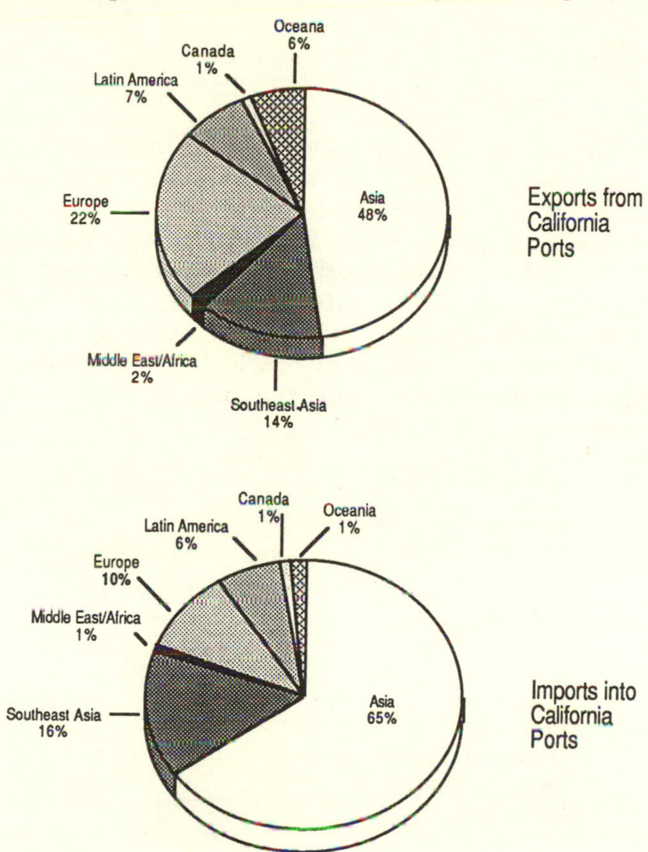

Source: Economic Report of the Governor, June 5, 1992, California, p. 13.

FIGURE 7.5
California Trade by Major Country, 1991
(Exports and Imports, $ millions)

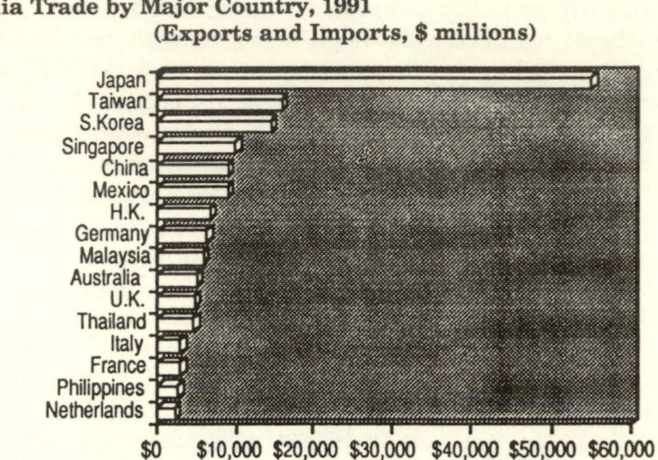

Source: Economic Report of the Governor, 1992, California.

The principal goods in trade between Japan and California include automobiles and auto parts, high-tech equipment and components, and foods. Except for autos, similar patterns of trade exist with Taiwan, South Korea, Singapore, Hong Kong, Malaysia, Thailand, and the Philippines. There is a considerable amount of two-way trade in high-tech products and components that depicts the true Pacific Rim character of the state's electronic industry. An examination of U.S. trade with Asia Pacific countries, most of which passes through U.S. west coast ports, reinforces the California pattern (Table 7.3). Although

TABLE 7.3
U.S. Trade with Asia Pacific Nations

Country	*Principal Export*	*Principal Import*
Japan	Office machines	Autos and parts
South Korea	Hides and skins	Apparel and electronic appliances
China	Wheat	Apparel
Taiwan	Autos	Footwear
Hong Kong	Electronic integrated circuits	Apparel
Philippines	Electronic integrated circuits	Apparel
Thailand	Electronic integrated circuits	Data processing machines
Malaysia	Electronic integrated circuits	Electronic integrated circuits
Singapore	Electronic integrated circuits	Data processing machines
Indonesia	Cotton	Petroleum
Australia	Aircraft and related products	Aluminum oxide

Source: U.S. Department of Commerce.

many of the countries are competitors with California high-tech industries, they are also important suppliers to California high-tech industries. Thailand, Malaysia, and Singapore are good examples of such supplier/competitor relationships.

Opportunities for development of exports to the Asia Pacific in light of the region's economic strength, promise, and demographic changes are very significant. The areas of strength include telecommunications, energy technologies, infrastructure development, aircraft and parts, environmental clean-up technologies, entertainment, biotechnology, food and agricultural products, and tourism. California can obtain a large share of the fast-growing Asia Pacific market because of its location, strength in aerospace, telecommunications, high technology, and a strong agricultural base. In addition, the state possesses world-class universities, a highly educated workforce, several venture capital centers, and a strong high-tech research and development base.

California's economic ties with the Asia Pacific region extend well beyond trade. Five of California's 10 major banks are Japanese owned, and nearly 30 of the smaller banks have Chinese origins. The majority of Japanese cars are designed in California. Nearly 700 of the 1,400 Taiwanese companies in the United States are located in California. Many significant Asian family businesses are truly Pacific Rim businesses: the parents live in Taiwan or Hong Kong, with factories in Thailand or Singapore, but research and development, marketing, and the younger members of the family are located in San Francisco or Los Angeles. Investment and cultural and family ties with Asia Pacific countries are an enormous advantage for California if it chooses to expand trade further with Asia Pacific countries.

California needs to reinvent its economy in light of its serious problems. Business as usual policies will result in a stagnant state economy even after the state recovers from the current prolonged recession sometime in 1995. Economic conversion of California requires many initiatives. They include development of new industry clusters such as combining education, high technology, and communication; investment in critical infrastructure needs; investment in worker training and retraining; conversion of military bases; and export development. Most of the attention is currently being focused on defense reconversion. We need to pay much greater attention to California's international economic relations, particularly with the Asia Pacific countries.

California's economic future can be shaped to a significant degree by its relationships with the Asia Pacific now that its umbilical cord of defense dollars is being cut. California's ties to countries such as Japan, Korea, Taiwan, and Mexico are strong in terms of immigration, capital flows, trade, and culture. We should make the best of this situation.

The principles of open regionalism are essential to California's success in enhancing its trade potential with the Asia Pacific. Given the fact that intra-Asian trade and investment flows are becoming much greater than trans-Pacific flows, California's opportunities may diminish if we allow our relations to languish and protectionism to increase. Open regionalism is not inevitable, however. If the Pacific region does not remain open, we will move toward closed regions and an era of greater economic conflict. The chances of a regional bloc centered around Japan is very likely if other regional blocs veer toward protectionism, and this would hurt California's chances of developing a strong export-based economy.

III

GOVERNMENTAL MECHANISMS FOR REGIONAL COOPERATION AND INTEGRATION

8

Regionalism and the Asia Pacific Development Outlook

Saburo Okita

The international community is increasingly aware that the twenty-first century is likely to be the century of Asia and the Pacific, and with this realization has come increasing interest in the Asia Pacific region. For some time after World War II, it was an Atlantic Era, with Europe and North America being the main theaters of world economic recovery and development. Yet, this has gradually changed with Japan's rapid economic growth starting in the 1960s, the rise of the newly industrialized economies of Hong Kong, Korea, Singapore, and Taiwan in the 1970s and the emergence of the rest of the Association of Southeast Asian Nations (ASEAN) countries and China in the 1980s. With these three overlapping waves of growth, development has come to the Asia Pacific as well. Achieving dynamic development, the Asia Pacific region has become increasingly important to world trade and has taken its place as a global economic center.

With the expansion of intraregional trade and investment capitalizing on both the tremendous advances in transportation and telecommunications technologies and the heightened multinationalization of corporations world-wide, the Asia Pacific region has attained increasing interdependence and converted the broad Pacific to the size of an inland sea. Awash in economic dynamism, the Asia Pacific region is expected to be a major locomotive force for the world economy in the twenty-first century, and study is, thus, being given to ways to establish more strongly cooperative arrangements that will enable the region to realize its full potential.

SALIENT PROBLEMS IN GLOBAL AND REGIONAL DEVELOPMENT

In looking at the institutions for cooperation in the Asia Pacific region, it is instructive to examine this issue in terms of regionalism versus globalism, outward-looking policies versus inward-looking policies, free trade versus managed trade, trade creation versus trade diversion, market integration versus discriminatory integration, and widening versus deepening.

Regionalism versus Globalism

Globalism refers to the principle of nondiscriminatory and multilateral free trade promoting the unimpeded movement of goods, services, and the factors of production so as to contribute to global economic development and global economic integration. By contrast, regionalism is frequently used but seldom defined. For the sake of discussion, it seems useful to postulate two types of regionalism. One is regionalism with firm trading blocs where protectionism is the norm. This is a regionalism that can only weaken the world economy. The other kind of regionalism is one that, recognizing that closed regions are not viable in today's world, strives to keep the region open even as it seeks to strengthen the cooperative ties among the region's members as one step toward globalism.

Outward-looking Policies versus Inward-looking Policies

The global economic expansion engendered by the recent advances in transportation, telecommunication, and information processing technologies has sharply reduced transaction costs internationally and created conditions more conducive to the multinational companies' activities. It has created what has been termed the "borderless economy." In the Asia Pacific region, foreign direct investment and in-company trade by these multinational companies has done much to stimulate intraregional trade and the development of intraregional interdependence, and it has also contributed to the success achieved by export-oriented development strategies. As a result, the region has industrialized rapidly, with the industrial structure moving rapidly upscale and exports of manufactures increasing sharply. Growing global integration and complementary policies have combined to feed the region's economic dynamism, and this has been an outward-looking dynamism.

Free Trade versus Managed Trade

A basic proposition in free-trade theory is that the principle of comparative advantage will enable each country to benefit from an international division of labor if it specializes in what it does best. However, comparative advantage is not a static state but is constantly changing with dynamic economic development and the developing countries' catch-up efforts. As a result, it sometimes happens that countries suffer unemployment and economic weakening as their industries lose comparative advantage and they face international balance of payments difficulties, and this can easily turn into protectionist pressures. It is, thus, imperative that we have effective international arrangements on rules, negotiations, remedies, and dispute settlement procedures to promote global free trade, and that is why the Uruguay Round is so important to the quelling of protectionism.

There are four basic approaches to international trade negotiations: multilateral trade negotiations, regional agreements, bilateral agreements, and the unilateral approach. These involve progressively fewer countries in the decision-making process. The problem is that, even as countries recognize the benefits of global free trade and multilateral trade negotiations, there is an increasing tendency to bilateral and even unilateral management approaches for their supposed efficiency.

Even bilateral arrangements are of two types. The first is to use voluntary export restraints and other means to restrict trade running against most favored nation (MFN) treatment. However, such arrangements tend to prolong the problems in the importing country — problems that cannot be solved except by industrial restructuring and technological innovation to create new comparative advantage. The second type of bilateral arrangements are those negotiated on the MFN principle. Because the benefits of these bilateral agreements are also extended to third countries, they have the potential for generating trade breakthroughs. However, they are not an appropriate way to deal with intellectual property rights and other standards, issues that are better left to multilateral negotiations.

Unilateralism has very little to redeem it. Not only does its unilateral determination of what is and is not "fair" and its unilateral imposition of penalties quickly exacerbate protectionism, by its very nature, it poses a threat to the international system. In addition, the results-oriented approach that seeks to achieve predetermined quantitative targets is incompatible with the dynamic workings of a market economy. Finally, because managed trade results in monopolistic profits for the protected industry, it actually leads to further deterioration in that industry's international competitiveness.

Trade Creation versus Trade Diversion

With the conclusion of the U.S.-Canada Free Trade Agreement, these two countries ought to reduce and eliminate their tariffs on a reciprocal basis. This tariff-reduction process is expected to be further enhanced with the North American Free Trade Agreement (NAFTA). In Asia, ASEAN has proposed the ASEAN Free Trade Association (AFTA) to reduce tariffs among its member countries. The only problem with these agreements is that they may easily lead to regional protectionism — economic blocs that are open on the inside and closed to the outside. The test here is whether or not the trade creation is greater than the trade diversion. Trade creation, of course, refers to the increase in imports from extraregional economies and trade diversion to when trade within the region crowds out imports from without the region. It is also worth looking at whether it is investment diverting, as when U.S. investment to East Asia might be diverted to Mexico as a result of NAFTA.

NAFTA is reported to be basically development oriented with the hope being that it will open a vast domestic market to domestic producers by limiting imports from outside the region and harmonizing standards within the region, and it is expected that the greater mobility for the factors of production will enhance the three countries' international competitiveness. Although there is some question how compatible this is with MFN principles and what will finally happen in the Uruguay Round, the possibility exists that the long-term trade creation may complement the short-term trade and investment diversion as NAFTA expedites development within the region by taking advantage of geographical proximity and the diversity of countries at different stages of development.

Market Integration versus Discriminatory Integration

There are three main differences between the Asia Pacific region and the European Community (EC). First, although the Asia Pacific region is rich in diversity and includes nations at all stages of development, the EC is premised upon its member countries' relative political and economic homogeneity. Second, although the increasing intraregional economic activity in the Asia Pacific has been driven largely by commercial concerns responding to market forces, the EC has been driven largely by government policies and treaties. Third, although the cooperative relations in the Asia Pacific are intended to be open regionalism promoting growth based upon nondiscriminatory and self-initiated liberalization in line with MFN principles, the EC is working for economic integration discriminating against non-EC partners for economic reasons, such as the need to regain industrial competitiveness. The EC is a highly political process, which is evident as it moves ultimately to integrated security arrangements for Europe, sustained by deep financial and political integration.

In effect, it may be said that the Asia Pacific is striving for market integration and that the EC is striving for exclusionary integration and institutional integration. Because intraregional economic development and the expansion of intraregional trade inevitably heighten the need for policy coordination and because it is the track record of policy coordination that leads to institutional integration, institutional integration is also important to the Asia Pacific region and should not necessarily be seen as inherently discriminatory. The Pacific Economic Cooperation Council (PECC) held its ninth general meeting in September 1992, at which its 20 member committees adopted the San Francisco Declaration "Open Regionalism: A Model for Global Economic Cooperation." It noted that Asia Pacific economic dynamism is grounded in openness and suggested that this experience should enable the region to make an even greater contribution to the strengthening and opening of international economic institutions. As such, it said that the five principles that should govern Asia Pacific open regionalism are the unimpeded movement of goods, services, information, and technology; compatibility with the General Agreement on Tariffs and Trade principles; intraregional agreements for trade creation; enhanced trade with extraregional partners; and the promotion of greater economic openness both within the region and world-wide.

Widening versus Deepening

Looking at the membership question, because Asia Pacific Economic Cooperation (APEC) is of a practical bent and emphasizes policy dialogues and other means for the harmonization of intraregional trade policies, it has been able to promote economic cooperation transcending the members' various political differences. This has included admitting China, Hong Kong, and Chinese Taipei to membership and offering a forum for discussion between China and Korea before they normalized diplomatic relations and between Korea and Taiwan even after the rupture in their relations. PECC has an even broader membership than does the ministerial-level meeting on APEC, and it functions largely as a think tank–like source of analysis and ideas for APEC, collecting and collating data from throughout the region, drafting joint policy recommendations by the region's industrialists and academics, and compiling a regional economic outlook so as to give the APEC members a common basis for their policy discussions. It is, thus, hoped that PECC and APEC will move increasingly for wider and deeper cooperation.

Free Globalism

Because the Asia Pacific region includes both the Americas and Asia, promoting Pacific economic cooperation centered on PECC and mportant for what it can do to prevent the formation of on either side of the Pacific. In 1990, Japan accounted f the total GNP of Asia, including India and China, and tes accounted for 79 percent of the total GNP of the he same year, 70 percent of Japan's two-way trade was partners, and 74 percent of the United States' two-way trade was with non-American partners. It should be clear from these numbers alone that neither Japan nor the United States can prosper or even survive without a global free-trading system.

THE FUTURE OF ASIA PACIFIC COOPERATION

Even if the western Pacific were to form a trade bloc, there would be a sharp deterioration in economic efficiency within the region, there could be a high dependence on Japan, and west Pacific economies would find their access to North American and other markets much more difficult. Just in terms of the member countries' interests alone, it is clear that the Asia Pacific economies should work to further enhance the multilateral free-trading regime and should strive to ensure that their economic structures are all the more open to their extraregional partners. At the same time, even the subregional groupings that are showing up and the various organizations that are working for economic integration, be they governmental organizations such as APEC or quasi-governmental organizations such as PECC, should work to promote closer economic cooperation, not to shut other economies out but rather to lessen the disparities among and within their own economies.

9

Regionalism and Cooperation in the Asia Pacific: The Role of Asia Pacific Economic Cooperation Governments

Gareth Evans

The major challenge confronting the international economic system in the 1990s is whether emerging changes in global economic power bases can be accommodated positively in the framework of an open set of economic rules, or whether countries will retreat into inward-looking, defensive postures. Stresses in the international economic system are already apparent, as evidenced by increasing resort to protectionism and unilateral measures that circumvent the multilateral "rules of the game," as well as the growing popularity of bilateral or subregional trade groupings. Although the latter may be consistent with the letter of the General Agreement on Tariffs and Trade (GATT), they may not be in full accord with the GATT spirit. Overshadowing these considerations are still unresolved issues related to the Uruguay Round of multilateral trade negotiations.

With the coming of the post–Cold War world, two diametrically opposed trends have come to dominate the international scene: the revival of nationalism and interethnic conflict, with their consequent disintegrative effect, and the trend to global economic integration. Europe probably provides the best illustration of this. The nationalist revival has been most evident in Eastern and Central Europe, with the dissolution of the former Soviet Union and the radical reorganization of Eastern Europe, and has been apparent to a lesser degree in the reservations toward Maastricht. All of this bears witness to the strength of nationalism in perhaps the most economically integrated continent of the world.

I am indebted to Lynne Pezzullo of the Australian Department of Foreign Affairs and Trade for her assistance in writing this chapter.

MOTIVATION FOR REGIONALISM

It is not surprising that with the absence of the unifying tendencies of the Cold War (where strategic considerations papered over economic tensions between friends and allies) and the revival of nationalism, some fragmentation in the fabric of the international economic order is occurring, despite the overwhelming economic arguments in favor of internationalism. At the same time, trends to internationalism are also apparent, as evidenced in phenomena such as globalization or borderlessness. These latter phenomena derive from natural economic complementarities in resource endowments and a variety of other factors that induce firms to locate production facilities offshore and to integrate their production processes across national borders. The more liberal the regulations of countries with respect to trade and investment, the greater the extent to which these integrative transfers are possible. Moreover, as economies become increasingly more efficient in new industries, the rationale for old forms of protectionism become less important and the motives for liberalization increase, creating a cycle of free trade, investment, and wealth.

In East Asia and the western Pacific, the payoffs from this cycle of liberalization are clearly evident, and this situation has helped to change political perceptions about international economic issues. There is growing recognition that enhanced national economic performance gains outweigh, and can be used to compensate for, the income distribution effects associated with trade and investment liberalization. However, some concerns remain regarding the pace of liberalization and pockets of protectionism that persist, although, on the whole, protection is falling in Asia (in contrast with the Americas and Europe, where protection is on the rise[1]).

The complementarities associated with structural transformation and globalization explain greater internationalization of economies over time, but, strictly speaking on the economic side, it is primarily the lower transaction costs of geographic proximity that lead to regionalism. Although transport costs have been falling in real terms over time, other transaction costs exist that are possibly quite strongly negatively correlated with distance (such as business management costs). Social, cultural, and political affinities also contribute to closer regional economic linkages. These affinities tend to be more pronounced intraregionally, although even in Europe, the Middle East, and North or Latin America, political factors often arise from ethnic differences, and this can retard cooperation. Asia is perhaps the least homogeneous continent in this regard, but there are, arguably, many similarities in ways of doing business in Asia that are quite foreign to a good many Europeans or Americans. Noneconomic affinities can also support extraregional linkages, for example, with the U.K.'s geographically disproportionate relations with its former colonies or the U.S. trade agreement with Israel.

The politics of regionalism are based, to some extent, on the popular imperative that governments must deliver policies that stimulate economic growth for the sake of enhancing living standards at home and on the fact that growth is perceived to underlie national security and stability. To secure growth, the emerging trends are for nation states to identify with like-minded others to form cooperative economic partnerships or coalitions as a counter to the uncertainties of the global economic environment. The Cairns Group is a nonregionalized example (a 14-country, 5-continent coalition of agricultural exporters committed to the reform of agricultural trade policies in the context of the Uruguay Round). Moreover, plurilateral agreements with strategic partners can enable a nation to achieve its primary objectives while being less costly and time-consuming to negotiate than multilateral agreements and not incurring the negotiation, compromise, and maintenance costs of a series of nonuniform bilateral agreements. The days of going it alone through autarkic or strongly protectionist economic and trade policies are, in the main, over, due to the long-run economic costs of such policies. The trade wars that culminated in the Great Depression are not easily forgotten for the lessons they imparted regarding the necessity of economic cooperation for growth and, indeed, peace.

Yet, at the same time, doubts prevail about the ability of the multilateral economic system established at Bretton Woods in the wake of World War II to resolve, in the time frame of current national political imperatives, fundamental issues at the top of the agenda for many governments and the business sectors they represent. Government-driven regionalism can, thus, result from policies designed to minimize damage in a world where neither unilateralism nor multilateralism seems able to achieve the economic objectives of nations. This is particularly likely where such "spoke" nations are economically (and often geographically) close to larger economic "hubs" and the question becomes not one of what is to be gained from closer integration but, rather, what is to be lost by being "out" rather than "in." This is possibly a significant factor behind the queues for membership in the North American Free Trade Agreement (NAFTA).

The emergence of regionalism has been influenced by both economic and political factors. The balance of these factors in each case will determine the type of regionalism to emerge, what is loosely termed the openness of the regional arrangement. Market-driven regionalism generally cannot be assessed in these terms. Rather, it is government involvement in regionalism that can develop it as either open or in the direction of a trade bloc.

OPEN REGIONALISM VERSUS TRADE BLOCS

Genuine openness goes further than simple adherence to GATT rules and, in particular, to the oft-cited Article XXIV of the GATT. Article XXIV of the GATT was an attempt to enshrine, as a guiding principle, the imperative that regional integration should not be at the expense of third parties. It recognizes that, provided the implementation of regional agreements is matched by a strong degree of shared commitment to open economic integration, there is no reason why such agreements should not, on balance, provide gains for members and nonmembers alike (although not necessarily in the same quantities). Of course, our experience with such agreements over the years has not been without examples of problems in the application of this guiding principle. Indeed, it is not difficult to conceive a GATT-consistent Free Trade Agreement (FTA) that by circumventing GATT coverage (for example, through creating new protectionist devices), could be discriminatory or even blatantly harmful to third countries. This view that openness means going beyond the GATT is not uncommon in the western Pacific. As Noordin Sopiee, chairman of the Pacific Economic Cooperation Council, has said, "GATT represents the lowest common denominator. We should hold our region to a higher standard."[2] That standard is becoming enshrined in the Asia Pacific as open regionalism.

It challenges the view that FTAs that have not been judged to be GATT inconsistent are necessarily "not detrimental to third parties." For such a claim to be true, trade creation effects must outweigh trade diversion effects.[3] Clearly, if the tariffs and other trade barriers of each FTA partner to the rest of the world are lowered along with internal barriers, trade distortions are minimized. This is true, for example, in the Australia–New Zealand Closer Economic Relations Trade Agreement (ANZCERTA), where both parties are unilaterally reducing barriers to third countries in addition to the removal of internal barriers. Trade creation effects would increase in proportion to the extent of the liberalization.

Quantification of trade creation and diversion effect is possible using econometric models and other methods. However, such quantification is usually not necessary, because the general openness of an FTA can be assessed more simply, for example, by inspecting the rules of origin. As a rule of thumb, FTAs are unlikely to be particularly open but are likely to be more open if they are accompanied by unilateral liberalization. Conversely, a trade bloc is defined, for the purposes of this paper, as a trade agreement (even one that has not been judged to be GATT inconsistent) in which preferential treatment and trade diversion are manifest. In a trade bloc, the greater the difference between internal and external barriers, the more marked are its characteristics as a bloc.

With these definitions, it is useful to briefly compare and contrast some existing examples of regionalism, in terms of their openness and the relative involvement of the private and public sectors.

REGIONALISM IN EUROPE

Although the formation of the European Community (EC) was clearly motivated by close private sector economic integration stemming from geographic proximity together with shared democratic values and policy objectives concerned with the future stability of Western Europe, there appears to be a greater degree of institutional economic momentum underlying the formation of the single European market. In the 20 years from 1970 to 1990, the proportion of intra-EC trade in total EC trade rose only marginally (from 50 percent to 51 percent for imports and from 53 percent to 56 percent for exports).[4] In contrast, West Europe's intraregional trade increased by more (62 percent to 69 percent for imports, 67 percent to 72 percent for exports).

Looking first at the benefits to third countries from the EC, we expect supposedly higher economic growth prospects, with associated growing import demand and capital supply. It is difficult, however, to compare actual EC growth and import demand with what "would otherwise have been the case" if the EC did not exist. There is also the argument that in developing common external tariffs, higher tariffs would be moved in line with lower ones, supporting overall trade liberalization. However, in reality, although protection has fallen somewhat in some sectors, nontariff barriers (NTBs), for example, in agriculture, have increased in general. On a more positive note, some evidence certainly exists to indicate that benefits have been derived for foreign firms operating in Europe from economies of scale (the springboard effect), from the harmonization of standards, regulations, and infrastructure in Europe, and from the introduction of facilitative mechanisms such as the Business Cooperation Network (an investment matchmaking service).

The costs of European integration to non-Europeans include the trade diversion effects. The Dillon, Kennedy, and Tokyo Rounds of the GATT were largely responsible for the EC having developed in as open a fashion as it has, at least in manufactures trade (to date, that is). As such, it has not raised trade barriers to third countries explicitly, but there is no commitment by its members to reduce such barriers. Moreover, policies like the Common Agricultural Policy, which has major depressing effects on world prices for many products (including coal, grains, meat, and dairy products), have considerably expanded in scope since their creation. This policy penalizes efficient third country agricultural producers — in terms of prices, lost exports to Europe, and loss of third country market share to subsidized EC exports. In Australia's case, the costs are around A$1 billion annually, and it is most unlikely that this loss is outweighed by trade creation effects (total Australian exports to Europe are over $6 billion annually).

Furthermore, integration in Europe has been characterized by a preoccupation with European affairs, to the exclusion of multilateral priorities. The European Economic Area will now extend the Single Market to include the European Free Trade Association,[5] except Switzerland, moving toward free intraregional movement of factors of production (labor and capital) as well as free movement of goods and services accounting for 56 percent of world trade. Association agreements with Malta, Poland, Hungary, the Czech Republic, the Slovak Republic, Romania, Bulgaria, Turkey, and Cyprus are being strengthened and represent longer-term candidates for accession to the EC. Eurocentrism and the spread of the Common Agricultural Policy and other EC trade distortions grow more serious as the EC grows, so, extension is another possible cause for concern.

REGIONALISM IN THE AMERICAS

Across the Atlantic, the Canada-U.S. Trade Agreement was firmly based on the logical extension of private sector cross-border economic activity, together with close sociopolitical relations. There is similar but less compelling motivation for links between the United States and Mexico, and the inclusion of Canada in NAFTA is based largely on political motivation and strong center-periphery links, rather than on genuine economic regionalism. Canada-Mexico trade and investment is small, and intraregional trade has, in fact, fallen over 1970–90 (from 38 percent to 27 percent for imports, although exports have risen slightly from 33 percent to 34 percent).

The Canada-U.S. Trade Agreement is an agreement that, in practice, covers mainly trade that was free before the agreement came into effect, so new trade diversion is not great. NAFTA is argued by North Americans to complement and reinforce the multilateral trading system and not divert trade away from third countries. However, there is to be some degree of reluctance to accept this claim on the part of western Pacific nations in particular, who perceive potential trade diversion effects in a number of sectors, including textiles, automotive, agriculture, and financial services. Investment diversion to Mexico may be an even greater concern, particularly of Southeast Asian nations, in part because of the tight rules of origin for some sectors in NAFTA. The bottom line is that NAFTA, like the EC, was devised with no provision for liberalization of imports from nonmember parties.

Furthermore, it would seem likely that plans to extend NAFTA, although still some way down the track, perhaps first to Chile or other Latin American nations, would not be on a most favored nation basis. Former President Bush spoke about establishing a framework of linkages between NAFTA and other countries in the Asia Pacific and

Europe. President Clinton, who has much more enthusiastically embraced Asia Pacific Economic Cooperation (APEC) as his regional economic policy focus, has so far avoided articulating a similarly comprehensive agenda of extending NAFTA on a hub and spoke basis;[6] he has, however, not ruled out such action completely and has, in fact, made guarded references to possibly extending NAFTA to some South American nations. The greater the emphasis the United States places on bilateral and subregional agreements and unilateral actions to achieve its trade objectives, the less committed it is likely to be to trans-Pacific and multilateral priorities.

In sum, North American regionalism would, at first glance, appear to be inconsistent with the kind of open regionalism defined above, although it may have benefits for the development of the Latin American economies.

WESTERN PACIFIC REGIONALISM

Crossing the Pacific, we encounter ample evidence of regionalism in the western Pacific, where intraregional trade has increased markedly over 1970–90 (from 34 percent to 47 percent for imports and from 35 percent to 43 percent for exports). However, few formal FTAs are found in the western Pacific,[7] and at this stage, integration is almost wholly private sector driven. The forms of regionalism that governments are pursuing generally involve the facilitation and promotion of trade rather than preferential agreements. The Singapore-Riau-Jahore growth triangle and the Pearl River Delta are cases in point, arguably the purest examples of open regionalism in evidence in Asia.

The spectacular economic success of the Pearl River Delta has been spurred largely by government initiative to take advantage of economic complementarities. The Chinese government has set up, since 1979, three special economic zones (SEZs) in Guangdong Province (Shenzhen, Shatou, and Zhuhai) as conduits for foreign investment and trade, which have successfully integrated the province with Hong Kong, Macao, and the broader overseas Chinese community. Guangdong now acts as Hong Kong's workshop and Hong Kong as Guangdong's shop window. From the perspective of openness, Hong Kong's uniquely liberal external policies provide a gateway for third country access to the very rapidly growing market of southern China. National treatment is widely observed (even in the case of Taiwanese trade with the mainland via Hong Kong and directly to Fujian Province, although this is not officially recognized). The SEZs are clearly GATT consistent, with government initiative spurring even greater private sector integration and with trade creation effects achieved with seemingly no trade diversion.

Encouraged by the success of the Chinese SEZs, Singapore has promoted since late 1989 a similar growth triangle concept based on providing information about the benefits of pooling the comparative advantages of Singapore (skills, services, capital), Malaysia, and Indonesia (labor, land, energy, water) to attract foreign investment. There are no special incentives or tariff breaks for businesses of the three countries relative to others, but the national treatment principle is strictly honored. The three governments facilitate the growing integration by coordinating economic regulations (for example, dealing with the movement of capital and people), providing infrastructure and encouraging investment. The concept has been enthusiastically embraced by the Indonesian government, which has invested heavily in developing infrastructure on Batam Island and invested jointly with Singapore in developing the Batam Industrial Park in Riau province. Malaysia regards more even development on the Malaysian peninsula as a priority and is interested in a possible northern triangle linking Sumatra, Malaysia, and southern Thailand. The triangle/SEZ concept provides a useful model for building greater liberalization — for example, the Philippines is interested in stimulating subregional links between Mindanao, Indonesia, Malaysia, and Brunei.

For a number of years, trade and investment between China and the Republic of Korea have also been growing very rapidly. This may have implications for trade between the Republic of Korea and Taiwan and, in the long term, for rapprochement between North and South Korea. At present, however, this rapid crossborder integration simply represents the removal of previous distortions as the relationship has normalized, rather than any preferentialism. A similar conclusion could be reached regarding the integration of the Indochinese nations into the broader East Asian economy.

By contrast, government efforts to build economic cooperation within the Association of Southeast Asian Nations (ASEAN)[8] have been somewhat spasmodic, and intra-ASEAN trade remains low, although ASEAN has been more successful in achieving common economic goals and positions, in particular in its relations with the broader region. At the ASEAN Summit in January 1992, heads of government agreed to begin working toward an ASEAN Free Trade Agreement (AFTA), which is being implemented over a 15-year period (which started on January 1, 1993) through tariff reductions on intra-ASEAN trade to a Common Effective Preferential Tariff of 0–5 percent. Provision is made for accelerated tariff reductions in up to 15 sectors that are still subject to final agreement. Agricultural products and services have been excluded from AFTA at this stage, and the limited coverage is not wholly in the GATT spirit. The investment diversion possibility exists for future adoption of further liberalization measures (for example, in agriculture), which could create more significant trade and investment diversion. Provisions in AFTA allow for member countries liberalizing their trade regimes on a most favored nation basis.

ANZCERTA has facilitated close economic integration of the Australian and New Zealand markets, including free trade in goods and most services, virtually unhindered investment flows, removal of bilateral antidumping provisions, and harmonization in areas such as business law, customs, quarantine, and technical barriers to trade. In addition, both countries have embarked on ongoing reform and liberalization of their economies, which has reduced barriers to third countries to close to zero and improved the trade and investment climate through internal microeconomic reforms. The creation of a level playing field in Australasia is, like the growth triangle and China's SEZs, the type of regionalism that can truly be called open and outward looking.

ASIA PACIFIC INTEGRATION

To summarize, western Pacific regionalism is open, predominantly private sector driven, and with government functioning as a facilitator and liberator. North American regionalism has been a reflection of market-driven forces but is becoming more dominated by detailed preferential governmental agreements and with distinct dangers of new forms of protectionism emerging.

There is little doubt that the economic linkages across the Pacific are as strong as the intraregional links on each side and are growing rapidly.[9] From 1970 to 1990, Asia Pacific intraregional exports increased from 54 percent to 65 percent and imports from 59 percent to 65 percent, higher in both cases than EC intraregional trade and growing more rapidly than West European links. Increasing interdependence is also manifest in steadily rising intraindustry trade. Private sector investment ties are also growing rapidly, in particular, Japanese, Hong Kong, Singaporean, and Taiwanese investment in North America, Southeast Asia, and South China as well as well-established North American investment in East Asia and Australasia. Much of this investment is associated with the globalization processes mentioned earlier, accompanied by intrafirm linkages arising from horizontal and vertical integration. There are also rapidly developing intraregional private sector people links, in terms of tourism, business migration, educational services, and cultural appreciation.

It is not the purpose of this chapter, however, to dwell on the evidence for growing private sector economic integration in the Asia Pacific but to address the role for governments in this process to facilitate more open regionalism.

A ROLE FOR GOVERNMENTS

Economic theory suggests a role for government to correct perceived adverse externalities, to provide public goods, and to coordinate economic activity. In regional terms, correcting externalities translates into a need to reduce uncertainties in the regional economic environment by providing information in a myriad of areas, as well as international technical cooperation, and generally smoothing the paths of regional economic transactions.

Providing public goods can be equated with removing physical bottlenecks to economic activity by improving infrastructure (ports, airports, telecommunications links, and the like) as well as, to some extent, providing development cooperation. A key role for governments, however, derives from the coordination of economic activity — in particular, standardizing and harmonizing regional regulations, removing impediments to trade and investment (improving access), and improving the consistency of policy making through better understanding of developments in regional neighbors' policies. Dialogue and exchanges are important means for achieving the latter. Governments should be responsible for ensuring the development of legal and institutional mechanisms for achieving these objectives. In this respect, the Asia Pacific region has, until recently, suffered from an underdeveloped sense of regional coordination and integration. The economic changes in the Asia Pacific have, by and large, occurred in advance of the development of coordination arrangements by which regional trade relations can be dealt with cooperatively. This is one reason why we see today a great contrast between the interdependence in the actual trade pattern and the acrimony in the trans-Pacific trade rhetoric.

ASIA PACIFIC ECONOMIC COOPERATION

However, this is changing. The most important economic cooperation and dialogue mechanism to have emerged in the region is undoubtedly the APEC process. APEC was launched at a ministerial conference in Canberra in November 1989 and is the first high-level intergovernmental forum with broad Asia Pacific membership and an economic focus. APEC's objectives, as outlined in its 1991 Seoul Declaration, are to sustain regional growth and development, to enhance the positive gains from increasing economic interdependence, to develop and strengthen the multilateral trading system, and to reduce barriers to trade in goods and services among participants in a manner consistent with GATT principles and without detriment to other economies.[10]

At the 1992 APEC Ministerial Meeting in Bangkok, it was agreed to establish a small permanent secretariat for APEC, based in Singapore, with a central fund (around $2 million) to support and coordinate APEC activities. The secretariat opened its doors on January 11, 1993, and, when fully staffed, should comprise an executive director, deputy executive director, eight to nine professional staff, and over a dozen support staff (locally recruited).[11] The institutionalization of APEC marks the conclusion of APEC's formative stage and the transition to a new phase of cooperation on policy questions. A gratifying boost in the region's enthusiasm for APEC occurred in 1993, and, with little doubt, the momentum of regional coordination will now increase.

The transition is evident in the work of the ten sectoral groups that cover trade and investment data, trade promotion, investment and technology transfer, human resource development, energy, marine resource conservation, telecommunications, fisheries, transport, and tourism. Momentum has developed in many of these groups to a point where they are beginning to deliver real benefits to the business communities of APEC participants. The Trade Promotion Group has set up an electronic information network, APECNet, which provides a commercial opportunity-matching facility as well as general market information. The Telecommunications Group has published a guidebook outlining regional telecommunications infrastructure and the regional regulatory environment and has other significant initiatives in the pipeline — for example, paperless trading, where a pilot demonstration project in trans-Tasman electronic data interchange in the steel trade has been implemented successfully. The Energy Group has distributed a number of technical documents dealing with energy conservation and efficiency measures and is working on an energy supply and demand database. The Human Resources Group, in following up proposals agreed by APEC education ministers who met in Washington, D.C., in August 1992, is establishing a substantial program of exchanges of people and information at all levels of education and training and addressing fundamental policy issues such as world standards of education, regional recognition of qualifications, and enhanced university mobility in the Asia Pacific. At the 1992 Bangkok APEC Ministerial Meeting, it was decided that there should be a review of the work groups to assess the scope for energizing the few groups where progress is less rapid (with a view to possible rationalization) as well as identifying the scope for greater private sector involvement in prioritizing and developing work projects. This review will sustain and accelerate the momentum of the work groups.

REGIONAL TRADE LIBERALIZATION AND EMINENT PERSONS GROUP

Although the emphasis in APEC's initial years has been on developing common building blocks for specific policy strategies through the work groups, more recent attention has focused on trade policy issues and, in particular, on Regional Trade Liberalization (RTL). These issues form the focus of APEC activities in 1993, building on the agenda agreed by APEC ministers in Bangkok. A two-pronged strategy has been agreed upon, involving the establishment of an Eminent Persons Group (EPG) to help establish vision and agenda for action in the region in the medium term as well as a program of practical trade facilitation measures to be implemented more immediately.

In the latter category, four short-term RTL measures are being implemented.

The first is a measure to assess the viability of establishing a regional electronic tariff database for APEC members to facilitate regional trade through better information flows on tariff arrangements in member economies and to interface with other APEC electronic databases and networks; in addition, an APEC Tariff Manual detailing the tariff policy approaches of all APEC members will be published in 1994.

The second is a measure to consider viable steps for APEC to take to streamline customs procedures within the region. These steps include the preparation of an APEC Customs Guide, the holding of an APEC Customs Trade Symposium, closer cooperation in international bodies devoted to harmonizing customs procedures and tariff classification, the use of electronic data interchange to speed up trade transactions while reducing costs, and enhanced cooperation in the areas of training and enforcement.

The third measure, dealing with the administrative aspects of market access, is quite far-reaching. It involves establishing an indicative list of nontariff barriers to trade to be addressed, including phytosanitary regulations, labeling and packaging requirements, technical standards, rules of origin, customs formalities (including licensing and customs valuation), antidumping, and other measures affecting trade. In 1993, APEC members decided on modalities to decrease or eliminate the trade-distorting effects of priority barriers, a process that will continue in future years for other barriers.

The fourth measure is to publish a comprehensive guidebook on foreign investment procedures and regulations within APEC members, to provide transparency and facilitate greater investment flows. As well, a survey of business sector attitudes to investment in the region is underway.

In addition to these measures, APEC members agreed in June 1993 to commence working toward closer cooperation on standards and conformance issues. A survey of regional practice is underway, which will provide the basis for further work in this area.

More generally, APEC members are considering new arrangements for the consideration of RTL issues to replace the current ad hoc arrangements. Discussions are focused on the development of an appropriate framework for handling trade and investment issues in APEC, including the establishment of a high level Trade and Investment Committee with a substantial and forward-looking work program. It is envisaged that the work program for 1994 will include further development of the short-term measures listed above, as well as other trade facilitation initiatives, including suggestions from the report of the EPG.

The EPG comprises 11 Asia Pacific statesmen, senior business figures, and leading intellectuals, nominated by APEC member governments but taking a regional perspective rather than representing national interests. The EPG, which met first in March 1993 in Singapore, is considering the likely shape of trade and investment relationships in the Asia Pacific to the year 2000, identifying constraints to the growth of trade and investment and analyzing the scope for governments to address these impediments. The group presented a report, with recommendations, to APEC foreign and trade ministers at the Ministerial Meeting held in the United States in November 1993.

The mandate for the EPG is broadly to "think big thoughts" and to establish a longer-term agenda for trade and investment facilitation and liberalization in the region. There are exciting possibilities for any such agenda. New trade facilitation initiatives could build on the existing short-term agenda and on ideas already floated in APEC by Australian Prime Minister Paul Keating. Possible measures might include the development of a common set of principles governing the treatment of regional investment. Another possibility, with significant potential commercial benefits, would be to work toward mutual recognition and greater regional harmonization of technical standards and associated certification and accreditation processes. A region-wide mechanism for addressing trade conflicts, APEC statements of principles in nontariff areas (for example, import licensing) and, in the longer term, agreements in more sensitive areas such as intellectual property or competition policy are all potential options that could remove structural impediments and facilitate the flow of capital, technology, and trade as the key to the region's continuing dynamism.

At some stage, APEC will come to look at more traditional trade liberalization issues, tackling less controversial matters first and more difficult issues in the medium term. For example, products for which intraregional trade is high (for example, steel, minerals processing, or some manufactures) could be addressed initially. Liberalization could then be extended to areas like aviation where the rationale for protection is fading and where political sensitivities are less entrenched than in areas like agriculture or textiles.

In pursuing all of this, it is vital that participants do not lose sight of what is at stake and what is there to be achieved. All this is worth doing because we can, with every passing month, now speak confidently of a growing Asia Pacific economic community, built on a principle of open regionalism and made up of 2 billion people producing (already) half the world's output (with a promise of more) and bound together by the integrated economic rules that would flow from the agenda of action sketched out above. Participants in APEC should be able to do all these things and more because they will benefit all the countries of the Asia Pacific region. Whatever else, APEC must be built on the principle of open regionalism. APEC must forge a truly open regional economic community, one that has a will to address its own particular economic priorities but that does not seek to harm those outside.

ASIA PACIFIC ECONOMIC COOPERATION'S OPEN REGIONALISM

The time is ripe in APEC to build on the progress soon, hopefully, to be achieved in the Uruguay Round and to begin working toward a substantial package of facilitation and liberalization. The commitment of APEC, as agreed in Singapore (1990) and reiterated in Seoul (1991) and Bangkok (1992), is that any liberalization should not be detrimental to third countries. To quote former Singapore Prime Minister Lee Kuan Yew:

> All countries present today have grown faster because of the GATT-IMF multilateral free trade regime. It is in all our interests to keep open the system of free and fair trade. Indeed APEC countries should set themselves up as examples of good GATT-abiding citizens of the world and oppose the formation of trading blocs. In that way we will contribute to world economic growth.[12]

Also, at Seoul, APEC ministers reaffirmed that "Any trade policy actions involving APEC participants should be designed to maximize trade creation, should not lead to new barriers to trade or investment, and should be consistent with APEC's overriding objective of an open and free multilateral trading system."[13]

APEC has adopted a consensus approach to its work, with no mandatory obligations, for example, to participate in a work project if a member does not wish to do so. This approach to RTL has merits, where participants join a broadening consensus at their own pace without penalty. For this reason, first steps in RTL have been in areas where nonparticipation is unlikely to substantially impede the progress of the initiative while being unlikely to provide a "free ride" for any nonparticipating economy, for example, in areas where intraregional trade is greatest (although, to date, no member has requested to be excluded). Australia has advocated an incremental approach to RTL due to a positive experience in the ANZCERTA negotiations — no end point was discussed initially, but, rather, each step was taken when the last was completed, and the final product is very successful integration.

APEC RTL can also play another, more immediate and increasingly important defensive role in monitoring subregional trade arrangements within the region and encouraging them to reinforce multilateral liberalization, as well as in preventing the development of inward-looking or self-defeating trade policies, not least between the United States and Japan. The relationship between the United States and northeast Asia, in particular, Japan, is likely to be one of the most critical influences on trans-Pacific and even global trade performance in the next decade. A real risk exists that frictions over bilateral trade imbalances, structural impediments, unilateral trade policy actions, and other tensions could snowball into antagonistic measures that would damage the interests of the emerging regional economic community. The positive dialogue and opportunity for third country representations presented in the APEC RTL trade policy dialogue is a key mechanism for resolving difficulties in the U.S.–East Asia relationship and for building constructive solutions to problems that, in the absence of APEC and in a worst case scenario of a deterioration in world trading relationships, could cause a fracture in trans-Pacific trade relations. As indicated earlier, Asia Pacific economic integration being what it is, North America and the western Pacific are infinitely better off if they work together than if they drift apart.

In sum, APEC offers a new form of economic cooperation for the Asia Pacific across traditional boundaries and draws together key economies of great diversity at a high policy level. APEC would be greatly enhanced by periodic meetings at head of government level, which are prevalent among other common interest groupings. Such meetings, as suggested by Prime Minister Keating to be held under the APEC umbrella, would fill an important structural gap and add political impetus to the APEC process, in particular to its economic cooperation and trade liberalization work. President Clinton's invitation to host an informal leaders' meeting in Seattle in November 1993, following the APEC ministerial meeting, was an important first step in realizing such a goal. Future U.S. involvement would also help to consolidate APEC's potential for a powerful role in addressing new global issues and in contributing to the evolution of a positive new world economic order.

CONCLUSION

East Asia, with private sector drive, open economic integration, has experienced dynamic economic transformation with high growth benefits. Western Pacific openness is stronger than GATT consistency — it is genuine trade-creating liberalization on a nonpreferential basis. The western Pacific is watching other forms of regionalism in the Americas and Europe as they emerge or evolve and, in particular, remains very alert to the directions that U.S. trade policy, so critical for trans-Pacific harmony, could take. Both the passage of NAFTA and ratification of the Uruguay Round represent litmus tests in the transition to a new world economic order. To ensure that the emerging environment, where regionalism will be more predominant than ever before, is open in the true sense of the word, Asia Pacific cooperation must be maintained and strengthened. The APEC process is the primary vehicle for achieving this objective. APEC is committed to open regionalism, to developing Asia Pacific regionalism and cooperation in a way that maximizes trade creation, minimizes trade diversion, and preserves the prosperous income growth of the region and the world.

NOTES

1. A. Stoeckel, D. Pearce, and G. Banks, "Western Trade Blocs: Game, Set or Match for Asia Pacific and the World Economy?" Centre for International Economics report commissioned by the Confederation of Asia Pacific Chambers of Commerce and Industry, 1990, compare the rise in nontariff barriers in Europe and North America in the 1980s with the falls in NTBs and tariffs in the western Pacific. In the United States, the rise in NTBs is associated also with a broadening of import coverage and a doubling in the induced decrease in imports.

2. USIS, Wireless File EPF505, September 9, 1992, was quoted at PECC IX (see note 3).

3. Trade diversion arises when a lower cost third country supply is replaced by duty-free imports from an FTA partner, leading to welfare losses in aggregate and, in particular, for the third country. Trade creation arises as a result of a switch from domestic production to lower cost imports from an FTA partner, leading to welfare gains within the FTA. Moreover, the income generated can create dynamic benefits for third parties as demand increases for the general basket of imports of the FTA partners from the world.

4. The source for these intraregional statistics, quoted throughout the chapter, is the Australian National University, International Economic Databank, compiled from United Nations, International Monetary Fund, and national statistics and presented in P. Drysdale and R. Garnaut, "The Pacific: An Application of a General Theory of Economic Integration," paper prepared for the 20th Pacific Trade and Development Conference, Institute of International Economics, Washington, September 10–12, 1992.

5. In relation to the earlier claim that there are no GATT-inconsistent FTAs, the European Free Trade Association covers only manufacturing, hardly "substantially all the trade in products," yet, it has not been challenged in GATT.

6. Under a hub and spokes arrangement, the spokes may have more limited agreements than those with the hub or, indeed, no agreements among themselves. The hub would tend to get the best arrangements, but negotiations between the spokes would tend to lack coverage and be complex, nonhomogeneous and costly in terms of negotiating time as well as maintenance costs.

7. South Asia is excluded from this analysis, although the recent agreement by the South Asian Association for Regional Cooperation countries to establish common preferential tariffs by 1995 as a first step toward greater economic cooperation is notable. This association comprises Bangladesh, Bhutan, India, the Maldives, Nepal, Pakistan, and Sri Lanka. There are also AFTA and ANZCERTA.

8. ASEAN comprises Singapore, Indonesia, Malaysia, Thailand, the Philippines, and Brunei.

9. The linkages between the western Pacific and Latin America are not as strong, although these may grow in the future. For this chapter, the Asia Pacific is defined as the 15 APEC members — Australia, Brunei, Canada, China, Hong Kong, Indonesia, the Republic of Korea, Japan, Malaysia, New Zealand, the Philippines, Singapore, Taiwan (Chinese Taipei), Thailand, and the United States.

10. Asia Pacific Economic Cooperation, "Record of the Third APEC Ministerial Meeting 1991," Seoul, 1991, p. 25.

11. For the first three years, the executive director is nominated by the current APEC chair, the deputy executive director by the incoming APEC chair, and the professional staff by member governments. There is an option for staff to be openly recruited rather than nominated after the first three years.

12. Asia Pacific Economic Cooperation, "Record of the Asia Pacific Economic Cooperation Ministerial Meeting 1990," Singapore, 1990, Document 3, p. 1.

13. Asia Pacific Economic Cooperation, "Record of the Third APEC Ministerial Meeting 1991," Seoul, 1991, p. 17.

10

Regional Groupings in the Pacific Rim: An East Asian Perspective

Mahathir bin Mohamad

Alliances between countries were common throughout the history of nations, but at no time have such alliances been so popular as in the post–World War II period. Beginning with the European Economic Community, regional cooperation organizations sprouted in the Caribbean, the Arab world, the African continent, South Asia, and Southeast Asia.

DEVELOPMENT OF THE ASSOCIATION OF SOUTHEAST ASIAN NATIONS AND ITS ROLE IN THE PACIFIC RIM

One of the most enduring of such regional groupings is the Association of Southeast Asian Nations (ASEAN). This organization was born of political necessity, though many seem to think of it as an economic grouping patterned after the European Economic Community. The frequent confrontation between the newly independent nations of Southeast Asia led to several attempts to set up a mechanism to facilitate consultations and dialogue over the many disputes among them. After several false starts, ASEAN was proposed and accepted by the five independent Southeast Asian nations. Brunei joined later, when it achieved independence.

Clearly, it was political expedience that brought the Southeast Asian nations together. The political disputes among them were not completely resolved, but the existence of a mechanism for solving problems between neighbors tended to minimize open confrontation. Tensions were reduced, and the members were able to concentrate on economic development and the welfare of their people.

A common market for ASEAN seems to be the next logical step, but the ASEAN countries, largely agricultural, are competing economies. They produce very much the same products, namely, tin, rubber, and palm oil. They compete in the same foreign markets as well as for foreign investments in identical industries. They are trade rivals, and economic cooperation does not come easily. However, the association is not entirely without economic benefits.

It must be remembered that at the time of the formation of ASEAN, socialism was very much in vogue. The tendency of newly independent nations was to nationalize and work against the freemarket system. Even Singapore and Malaysia, staunch anti-Communists, flirted with state enterprises as vehicles for economic growth and social justice.

However, from very early on, the members of ASEAN noticed that those among them who practiced the free market system prospered. These countries encouraged both domestic and foreign investments with incentives and special tax-free industrial estates. Thus, from very early on, the ASEAN countries discarded socialist theories that were still the guiding principles in much of the then-Third World. As a result, the members of the association prospered more or less uniformly.

As a regional organization, ASEAN compares very well with the most successful of the regional associations in the world. One of its members, Singapore, is now classified as a newly industrialized economy. The others achieve growth rates that are significantly higher than growth rates in most developing countries. The manufacturing industry has overtaken, or at least become, a major contributor to their gross domestic product.

What is clear is that the association has brought about considerable economic benefits despite its largely political character. Its members have benefited from one another's economic experiences and the desire not to be outdone by their neighbors. To the ASEAN countries, regional cooperation represents a good way to achieve political stability and economic advancement. They are, therefore, very receptive to ideas that can enlarge the association or enhance ASEAN's role in a much wider region.

When the Asia Pacific Economic Cooperation (APEC) forum was proposed by Australia, all the ASEAN countries, with the exception of Malaysia, welcomed it. Malaysia's fear was that the inclusion of economic giants like the United States, Canada, and Japan would result in the domination of the grouping by these countries. In addition, the initial exclusion of China, the Indochina states, and the Central and South American Pacific Basin countries would be difficult to justify if the Pacific is to be the geographical basis for membership in the grouping.

Fear prevails that ASEAN will disappear as a group within the very much enlarged and more powerful APEC grouping. There may be conflicts between the ASEAN interest and the broader Pacific interest.

APEC is likely to dominate ASEAN and hinder its progress toward greater intra-ASEAN cooperation.

Malaysia, however, was reassured that APEC would remain an informal consultative group dedicated to helping the less developed members upgrade their overall performance. Training of personnel and economic upliftment programs would be the main activity of the APEC grouping in order to achieve this objective. Indeed, in the initial period, this objective was realized. Several programs that benefited some ASEAN and even South Pacific countries were started, including trade promotion, human resources development, and a survey to overcome transportation bottlenecks.

China, Chinese Taipei, Hong Kong and Mexico have now been admitted as members of APEC. Other Latin American countries are likely to follow. With their inclusion, APEC would become less of a misnomer. Nevertheless, the Indochina states have not been considered eligible as members, despite their geographical qualification. If APEC is not a political grouping, then ideological considerations should not influence eligibility for membership.

Despite assurances that the APEC organization would not be formalized, already a secretariat has been established and proposals for permanent offices and meetings of heads of government have been made. The implication is obvious. A U.S.-dominated Asia Pacific organization is being created in order that East Asian economies, with their powerful growth, will not be left to their own devices. U.S. interests will always be safeguarded through the APEC mechanism.

In the meantime, two major members of APEC have formed a regional organization that will inevitably further strengthen their grip on APEC. The North American Free Trade Agreement (NAFTA), comprising initially the United States, Mexico, and Canada, is obviously a trade bloc that will affect access to the huge markets of these three countries. A very substantial number of the exports of East Asia are directed to these countries. Obviously, NAFTA would become a competing group that could negate the ASEAN grouping within APEC. The NAFTA would then negatively influence the course of Asian economic development.

The recent history of U.S. trade relations is not reassuring in this regard. Every instrument, tariff and nontariff, has been used to protect the U.S. economy. Countervailing duties, intellectual property, even environmental imperatives and human rights, have been used by the United States in order to achieve economic advantage.

A free-trade grouping implies less than free trade between the grouping and the rest of the world. NAFTA is, without doubt, the richest market in the world. The European Community (EC) is a market with limited growth potential. An expanded NAFTA will represent a potentially richer market than any other trade grouping in the global economy. Further, the United States has already indicated that it will consider expanding beyond the three North American nations. The Enterprise of the Americas envisions the inclusion of the nations of Central and South America to form one huge pan-American common market. Such a market will have unlimited potential. Indeed, with massive land, labor, and natural resources, the market of the Americas will not need to depend on the rest of the world for anything. If a pan-American market can be content with certain disadvantages in technology and pricing, it can be a truly exclusive bloc, a world unto itself.

EAST ASIA ECONOMIC GROUP

Fair and free trade were advocated initially by the free market nations of Western Europe and North America. The closed economies of the Communist states were soundly condemned for their managed trade. This occurred when the countries of Europe and North America were practically the sole exporters of manufactured goods, made largely from cheap raw materials found in and imported from the poor countries that were their colonies. It was a great arrangement while it lasted, but colonialism was terminated, and the colonies became independent states responsible for their own destiny.

Then, Japan began to produce quality products that were cheaper than those produced elsewhere. Within a very short time, the Japanese goods were gaining market share over Western-produced goods. The situation was still tolerable, however, and the West still believed in its superior capacity to compete. However, when products from Korea and Taiwan entered these same markets, alarm bells sounded all over Europe and North America. The West felt that these new competitors must be stopped; if free trade had to be curtailed, then so be it.

In the meantime the Uruguay Round of trade negotiation had bogged down because the United States and Europe could not agree on a number of issues. A failure of the round would affect most of the emerging industrial economies of East Asia. Very early on, it became clear to the East Asian nations that, individually, they had little say in determining the course of world trade. The idea of an East Asian Economic Grouping was mooted in order to give them a powerful and coherent voice in trade negotiations (the East Asian Economic Grouping was later renamed the East Asia Economic Caucus [EAEC]).

The EAEC is not an East Asian replica of the EC or NAFTA. The grouping is meant to be only a forum for discussing common trading problems, particularly those related to the discriminatory trade practices of the West. If a common stand can be formulated by East Asian countries during trade negotiations in the General Agreement on Tariffs and Trade rounds or elsewhere, the chances of being heard and of being taken seriously would be better, but the caucus should not be anything more than a discussion forum. It should certainly not be a trade bloc, imposing common restrictions and tariffs against those outside the group. Such restrictions would deprive the members of the caucus of their freedom to take advantage of the small and relatively undeveloped countries of the region. They do not want to be the exclusive market of the developed members of the group, particularly Japan.

Additionally, the EAEC can help the process of developing the less developed countries the same way that ASEAN had done. Not only can policies and methods for successful economic development be copied, but also the more advanced and prosperous members of the EAEC can invest in the less developed members. Although the West has helped the developing countries of Southeast Asia by investing in numerous industries, the main source of investments has been the successful economies of East Asia. Now the former recipients of investment funds in Southeast Asia are investing in other East Asian countries. Coordinated and stimulated by the EAEC, investments in the less developed East Asian countries could be accelerated. The EAEC will, thus, contribute toward a more prosperous East Asia, and a prosperous East Asia will be more committed toward peace in the region, for cross-investments can take place only in a climate of peace.

If the United States can accept the EC, if the United States can become a member of NAFTA, why is the United States opposing the EAEC, a grouping that conforms to the concept of open regionalism and is dedicated to upholding free trade? I believe that the United States is using unfair pressure on Japan and some of the ASEAN countries to abort the proposed EAEC. At the same time, the United States is promoting the consolidation and formalization of APEC, in which the United States plays a prominent role. It would seem that the United States is against an East Asia that is free of U.S. dominance.

Much has been said and written about the Pacific Century and the Pacific Rim. The twenty-first century is slated to be the century of the Pacific as much as the twentieth century is supposed to be the century of the Atlantic. In actual fact, there is no such thing as an Atlantic or a Pacific community. These bodies of water are too big to bring the countries on their rims together. Instead, they tend to divide. For example, the countries on the Atlantic coast of Africa have never been regarded as Atlantic Rim nations. Similarly, the countries of Central and South America and Oceania seem to be excluded from some definitions of the Pacific Rim.

If there are people on the rim of the North Atlantic who are united, they are united not because of geographical location but by ethnic and cultural origins. On the other hand, the Pacific separates peoples of different cultures. On the eastern rim are the Americans of largely European origin; they have an affinity for the Central and South Americans, the New Zealanders, and the Australians. On the western rim of the Pacific are the Asians, who are culturally roughly similar but have hardly anything in common with people of European stock.

The people of the east and the west Pacific Rim cannot form a single homogeneous community. The abrasiveness of those of European origin is incompatible with Asians.

For a Pacific Rim community to emerge, a common cultural background is necessary. Pure economic imperatives alone are not enough. Even in Europe, Turkey is rejected. No doubt Albania, Macedonia, and what remains of Bosnia will also be excluded from membership in the EC because their Muslim culture is unacceptable. It is painful to say this, but it is true. A Pacific Rim community will not materialize because culturally there are two different groups. Unless the Asians are bludgeoned into becoming members of a Pacific community, there will be no such grouping, in my opinion. Already, on the question of human rights, the Asians and the Europeans are in conflict. It may not lead to war, but it would certainly prevent the close kind of cooperation needed for a regional grouping.

11

New Directions for the Future

Hector Cardenas

The twenty-first century and the new millennium appear to have commenced at the turn of the 1990s, lending a new dimension to the solution of political, economic, and social issues. In the 1990s, we are witnessing the globalization of the economy and a boom in world telecommunications and, perhaps, as a consequence, the gradual disappearance of socialist regimes and closed societies, which have for many years constituted one of the main political concerns of the West and an obstacle for economic development. In this new age, the Pacific Basin has acquired the importance for which it was destined in a long process initiated many centuries ago.

The geopolitical importance of the Pacific Basin emerged only in the twentieth century, when it became the theater of hostilities during World War II in the Far East. In the postwar period, the Pacific region became a vital space for the implementation of U.S. containment policy against communism in the Far East. The economic dynamism associated with this region today was recognized at the beginning of the 1980s when the United States, the major export market for several anti-Communist Asian nations, Japan among them, recorded a greater volume of trade with the Asia Pacific than with its traditional Atlantic partners. However, in spite of the importance that Mexico currently places on its role in the Pacific region, we must remember that the concept of a "Pacific community," as coined by Masayoshi Ohira in 1978, is a relatively novel one, and Mexico has adopted it as a main goal of its foreign policy only within the more recent context of its economic openness and the diversification of its commercial ties.

FROM A "LOST DECADE" TO ECONOMIC OPENNESS (1980–90)

Until the 1980s the Mexican economy underwent an industrialization process based upon an import-substitution model that maintained economic growth with price stability for 40 years and accumulated pronounced structural imbalances as a result of a decade of fiscal deficit and protectionism. The external sector registered serious limitations, such as a lack of export-oriented policies, a strong dependence on oil revenues, and excessive foreign debt service payments. Such was the economic climate of Mexico when President Miguel de la Madrid took office in December 1992 and decided to give priority to the solution of the problems created by lack of liquidity and excessive debt to stabilize the economy and to return confidence to the private sector.

In order to achieve these goals, the immediate program for economic restructuring included the creation of the necessary financial and budgetary conditions to recover growth. Most prominent among these measures was the devaluation of the exchange rate by 90 percent and the realignment of the prices of public services with production costs and international prices. The quantitative objective in budgetary terms was to gradually reduce the financial deficit to 3.5 percent of gross domestic product (GDP) by 1985.

During 1985–86, the Mexican economy suffered national disasters such as the Mexico City earthquake, which caused material damages in the order of 2 percent of GDP. At the beginning of 1986, oil prices plummeted by 50 percent, reducing the income from oil exports from $14.8 billion in 1985 to only $6.3 billion in 1986, a loss of 25.4 percent in export goods. By 1989, when Mexico was paying 6 percent of its GDP to service the debt, the difficulty of recovering economic growth with price stability became evident.

In the face of this scenario, the government acted on two fronts: internally, an agreement was reached among the principal economic actors, namely, by the Economic Solidarity Pact, signed in December 1987, and, externally, by restructuring debt until 1990. By means of this debt restructuring agreement, which involved a $48 billion public sector foreign debt, an instant savings of $3.8 billion in interest was achieved for the period 1990–94. The Solidarity Pact, on the other hand, has proved to be an efficient means of reestablishing economic growth and controlling inflation. In 1989, inflation fell to 19.7 percent from 1,005 percent at the end of 1982. It rose again to 29.8 percent and fell to 18.8 percent in 1991. The GDP has grown 3.3 percent, 4.4 percent, and 3.6 percent, respectively, in these three years.

THE NEW MEXICAN ECONOMIC PROJECT

The Mexican "lost decade" left behind several scenarios; perhaps the only positive one is the awareness of the structural limitations of the import-substitution model and, consequently, the need for a new economic project. Mexico had to implement such a program in connection with the modernization of the country consistent with main international market trends such as the emergence of new economic poles in North America, the Pacific Basin, and Europe, and, finally, the globalization and deregulation of international capital markets. This new economic project would assume the following characteristics: commercial openness, divestiture of public enterprises, and modernization of the financial system.

Commercial Openness

In 1982 the Mexican economy was highly protectionist, and imports were strictly regulated by a system of import licenses and average tariffs of 27 percent, with some reaching 100 percent.

In 1983 a gradual process of openness started that has witnessed a reduction in tariffs from 16 percent in 1982 to 5 percent in 1989, while the total value of imports requiring import licenses has shifted from 100 percent in 1983 to 14 percent in 1991. A further step in this direction was taken in 1986 when Mexico formally joined the General Agreement on Tariffs and Trade. Similarly, measures were adopted to stimulate and diversify exports, particularly those with higher value added. Thus, although nonoil exports represented only 26 percent of total exports in 1982, this figure rose to 85 percent in 1991.

In April 1991, Mexico signed an agreement with the European Community to increase investment and trade flows and reinforce technical assistance between both parties. In September, an Agreement of Economic Complementation was signed with Chile, the first bilateral free-trade agreement between two Latin American countries seeking to eliminate nontariff restrictions for imports in 1992 and tariff barriers within a period of four years thereafter.

In February 1993, the Tuxtla Gutiérrez Accord signed by Mexico, Costa Rica, El Salvador, Guatemala, Honduras, and Nicaragua aimed to eliminate tariffs and nontariff barriers among those countries. Finally, in August 1992, the negotiations of the North American Free Trade Agreement concluded, projecting a date for implementation of January 1, 1994.

Divestiture of Public Enterprises

The program of divestiture of state-owned companies launched by the government became a fundamental element of private and public sector structural reform. Here, the main goals were strengthening public finances, focusing upon priority areas, and eliminating unjustified expenses and subsidies in social and economic terms. Thus, of the 1,155 companies that the public sector held in December 1982, 916 enterprises had been sold, merged, or transferred by December 1991. By July 1992, the sale of commercial banks had been concluded. From December 1988 until June 1992, the income generated by 192 sales operations rose to $8.6 billion, not counting the sale of commercial banks.

Modernization of the Financial System

Structural reform served the strategic purpose of developing and increasing domestic savings and became an efficient channel to finance the productive sector. The logic behind this reform was the creation of economies of scale designed to reduce costs and increase competitiveness, ensure a greater degree of specialization, and provide greater security to the consumer.

The financial liberalization initiated toward the end of 1988 sought to deregulate banking, stimulate savings, and improve financial operations. In the aftermath of these measures, Mexican banks presently face more profitable investment options for channeling their resources. Obligatory investment regimes (that is, selected credit pockets) and legal requirements were suppressed. In short, the privatization process of the commercial banks sought to encourage competitiveness of financial intermediaries in the new international environment.

THE PACIFIC BASIN: AN ECONOMIC SPACE IN THE TWENTY-FIRST CENTURY

Some of the most prosperous economies of the world are now located in the Pacific Basin, particularly in the Asia Pacific, where high rates of economic development over the past few decades have prevailed despite recession and slow growth in the world economy. In addition to Japan, the second largest economy in the world, high levels of economic growth have been registered by the newly industrialized economies, namely, Hong Kong, Taiwan, Singapore, and Korea, a trend also seen among the economies of Southeast Asia. Evidence of the growing importance of the Pacific Basin is the increasing volume of intraregional commercial transactions. In the past 20 years, trade among the countries of the zone has increased sixfold. The Pacific economies represent 40 percent of world trade, and future trends point toward a progressive increase of this share.

The Pacific region plays a relevant role as an international financial center. Japan is currently the world's largest capital exporter, with direct investments reaching a total of $310.8 billion in 1990, of which

$210 billion, or 68 percent, was distributed across the region. Also, since 1989, Japan has become the world's major donor of economic assistance.

It should be noted that Japanese investment is geared toward selected higher value-added production sectors in the region, with a multiplying effect on the production processes of the area. Thus, a new regional division of labor has been created in the Pacific Basin based on reciprocal complimentarity that translates into multilateral and mutually beneficial cooperation. As such, the concept of cooperation in the Pacific Basin can be seen as an eminently economic community sustained by free and open ties of interdependence among the nations of the region — in other words, as a community of industrialized and developing nations with market economies coordinating their interests in favor of joint prosperity.

MULTILATERAL PACIFIC FORA: MEXICO'S INVOLVEMENT IN THE PACIFIC RIM

One fundamental goal of Mexican foreign policy is to expand and diversify Mexico's relations with most nations of the world and to promote international cooperation in all areas. Mexico is not interested in belonging to a closed trade bloc. The North American Free Trade Agreement does not inhibit Mexico from widening its economic ties with the rest of the world. A case in point is the recent signing of a framework agreement with the European Community and the efforts underway to encourage trade liberalization among Mexico's Latin American neighbors.

In this context, Mexico has taken firm and sustained steps to reassert its presence in the dynamic Pacific region through a two-way strategy: by broadening its diplomatic representation in the Asia Pacific region and by increasing its participation in the multilateral fora of the Pacific Basin. Until recently, Mexico's economic ties in the region were concentrated almost exclusively on Japan. However, in the past few years, serious efforts have been made to diversify exchanges with other nations of Asia and the South Pacific, which have prompted those nations to reciprocate in trade and investment with Mexico.

Aware of the risks presented by closed trade blocs in the region, fora like the Pacific Economic Cooperation Council have sought to stress the importance of integrating complementary regional economies, a vision that has been crystallized in its so-called doctrine of open regionalism. The Asia Pacific Economic Cooperation (APEC), a governmental forum, also promotes a more pragmatic economic cooperation. In fact, Mexico's participation in APEC is a significant step forward in the composition of this high-level organization, which incorporates in its forum the vision of Mexico, its first Latin American member country, and the third member of the North American Free Trade Agreement.

Mexico places considerable importance on the future role of organizations such as APEC in coordinating and deepening strategies for regional economic cooperation in an area that it increasingly considers to be the focal point of the world economy. This vision becomes all the more relevant as the world witnesses the emergence of new economic players in the Pacific region. These include the recovered economies of Mexico, Chile, and Argentina in the American Pacific, nations that seek to reinforce economic ties among themselves as manifest by the aforementioned Free Trade Agreement between Chile and Mexico.

On the other side of the Pacific, China's unique model of economic development has already had an impact on the region, the effect of which is likely to be reinforced when China fully recovers Hong Kong in 1997. Not only has China had an important impact on the economies of Taiwan and Hong Kong and vice versa, but also a substantial trade network has developed between the People's Republic of China and many of the Chinese ethnic communities in Southeast Asia. More recently, Chinese direct foreign investment has increased in the Pacific economies, particularly in Mexico and the United States.

Complementary triangles of economic development have also started to emerge in the North Pacific, incorporating previously closed economic areas like Mongolia and Pacific Russia, and are playing a crucial role in defusing the political tensions of the zone. The nations of the Association of Southeast Asian Nations are also in the process of consolidating regional economic integration, giving due attention to new regional players, like Vietnam, and encouraging greater participation from other Indochinese nations.

From Mexico's standpoint, new directions for the future rest upon several decisions and definitions of policy that involve not only the countries of the American Pacific but also every nation of the Pacific Basin. From our perspective, the future points toward a greater awareness of the strategic necessity to integrate the Latin American economies within the framework of a vast continental cooperation mechanism. Within this dynamic, Mexico seeks to consolidate its sovereignty by raising the standards of living of its population and reducing its economic vulnerability. In this sense, Mexican policy toward the region is drafted along long-term lines that aim to exploit the advantages that the nation's 8,000 kilometers of Pacific coastline afford for the westward expansion of its economy and thereby revalidate its historical legacy in the area. The excellent bilateral ties that Mexico maintains with Pacific Basin countries will undoubtedly go a long way toward fostering these new economic alliances.

However, these policy objectives imply overcoming both an objective and subjective set of barriers that hinder Mexico's ambitions in the Pacific region. The obstacles refer to the physical impediments represented by the geographical distance of Mexico from the countries of the Asia Pacific and an inadequate commercial shipping fleet. Internal obstacles point to the need to arouse Mexican entrepreneurial interest in the vast potential markets of the zone, breaking away from a traditional inertia resulting from dealing almost exclusively with North America.

REFERENCE

Kerber, Victor. *The Pacific Basin: A Field of Power Competition in the Global System, Japan's Strategy*, Master's thesis, Sophia University, Tokyo. Kerber refers to Masayoshi Ohira and the ter "Pacific commuity."

12

Asia Pacific Economic Cooperation Potential and the U.S. Interest: "Going Multilateral"

Allen C. Choate

The Asia Pacific Economic Cooperation (APEC) has rapidly emerged in the past several years as the only Pacific Rim formal intergovernmental organization seeking to improve regional economic cooperation. The establishment and speedy development of APEC can be attributed to two basic factors. First, and most obvious, is the continuing dramatic private sector driven economic growth of the region, characterized by increasing intraregional trade. This growth and its consequent economic interdependence have led to an increasing recognition by the governments of the region — the United States included — of the need to find new means and mechanisms for managing this transnational interdependence. In fact, what is surprising is not APEC's relatively rapid development but the long passage of time before action was taken in establishing APEC in the first place.

Second, in the period immediately prior to the end of the Cold War, the Asian "middle powers" (Korea, Australia, the Association of Southeast Asian Nations [ASEAN]) have stepped into the partial power vacuum created by the collapse of Soviet power projection, and the perceived ebbing presence of the United States, by showing leadership through a new kind of diplomacy. This diplomacy is not built on power and structure factors but on coalition-building skills, intellectual and technical ability, and entrepreneurship. This new entrepreneurial diplomacy seeks to multilateralize the management of transnational issues, and one of its most noteworthy successes to date has been APEC — largely the result of ASEAN, Australian, and Korean initiatives.

The views expressed in this chapter are those of the author and do not necessarily represent the opinions of either The Asia Foundation or the Harvard University Center for International Affairs.

How has the United States regarded the development of APEC? What positions has the United States taken with regard to the APEC agenda? Most importantly, what U.S. interests may be served (or disserved) through the further development of this regional body? What does the United States stand to gain or lose? It will be argued below that U.S. international economic policy goals can best be achieved through more assertive and engaged leadership participation in APEC. To play such a role in APEC, U.S. diplomacy must employ the same entrepreneurial techniques utilized successfully by the Asian middle powers to date. The United States must also be prepared to accept shared decision making in a multilateral organizational context. First, however, it is necessary to review what the founding members of APEC have in mind for that organization's aims.

THE ASIA PACIFIC ECONOMIC COOPERATION: ITS PURPOSE AND FUNCTIONS

APEC has advanced in a relatively short period from an idea to an information-sharing and partially consultative body. APEC's character reflects the economic realities of the region. It is market oriented and encourages private sector participation in its work program. To this end, the Pacific Economic Cooperation Council has observer status at APEC meetings. Clearly, APEC must retain enough flexibility to keep a range of private sector organizations involved in its work. APEC's establishment of an Eminent Persons Group in March 1993 was a recognition of this need. That group, composed of distinguished private economists and business people, was mandated to produce a future vision for APEC focused on trade liberalization for the Seattle APEC ministerial meeting in November 1993.

APEC has identified three basic priorities for itself: exchange of information, development of strategies to reduce regional trade and investment barriers, and activities to promote regional trade and economic growth. The United States, which hosted the APEC ministerial meeting for the first time in Seattle, already has signaled its primary interest in APEC as lying in that organization's ability to liberalize regional trade. Indeed, regional trade liberalization was the key theme of the November 1993 Seattle Ministerial.

Currently, the APEC work program is a busy one but is focused very heavily on the gathering and distribution of information and data, with a view in some cases to providing the basis for future policy coordination. That work program consists of the following projects:

trade and investment data collection;
trade promotion activities (for example, missions, fairs);
investment and technology transfer information network;

information exchange and education/training linkages in human resource development;

regional energy database development;

information exchange on marine resource conservation;

telecommunications — data development, studies on regional networks, human resource development training;

transportation — data collection and analyses;

tourism — data exchange; and

fisheries — surveys.

Although all of this data development is necessary and needed, it is not sufficient in and of itself to move APEC to the next plateau of organizational development. That next step must be to move from information sharing to consultations in forming consistent policies. The final and most important organizational development step will be to move to policy coordination. The results of such policy coordination would be made manifest in the adoption of regional agreements and consistent policy application. As recommendations begin to emerge from the data acquisition and research now underway, it will be critical for APEC to demonstrate that it can be more than just another "talk shop." The operationalization of APEC in terms of regional agreements and policy coordination on specific issues and needs will be APEC's true test. APEC's primary motivation has been to see the Uruguay Round of the General Agreement on Tariffs and Trade (GATT) talks successfully completed. However, if it has a larger vision, it is to go beyond GATT in blazing new trails for regional economic cooperation while remaining faithful to GATT principles. Indeed, an appropriate vision for APEC is not simply to be GATT consistent but to be GATT sustaining. That phrase connotes a mission for APEC that generates continued momentum on trade liberalization in the post-Uruguay Round period. Now that the round is concluded, the framework and discipline that has restrained protectionist sentiments no longer exists. APEC's larger role, then, will be to continue to provide that framework and momentum for the Asia Pacific region.

ASIA PACIFIC ECONOMIC COOPERATION AND THE U.S. INTEREST

The United States has called for a more results-oriented agenda for APEC, with particular regard to regional trade liberalization. This agenda, the United States suggests, would consist of a number of practical agreements including, among others, a regional charter on investment, establishment of a trade dispute settlement mechanism, a regional agreement on customs harmonization, and intellectual property rights, an aviation agreement (open skies), and common rules of origin. To achieve any one of these will require that APEC evolve rapidly to the next generation of intergovernment organization status, where such pacts are negotiated. If APEC does not, it is not likely to be taken seriously in the future. Admittedly, some regional agreements, such as open skies, are more difficult and sensitive than others. The U.S. challenge to APEC should be to identify those multilateral actions that appear feasible — a regional investment treaty, for example. "Achieving the doable" is a suitable slogan for APEC, which characterizes itself as a practical body.

The U.S. challenge to APEC should be regarded by the other APEC members as a healthy sign of a renewed U.S. interest in and commitment to the region. Increasingly, the United States is aware of how critical that region is to U.S. future economic health. That growing recognition is producing a two-track trade diplomacy. On the one hand, the United States is deploying or proposing to deploy trade power diplomatic weapons such as a renewal of the so-called Super 301 status (assigned by the U.S. trade representative to some U.S. trading partners) and other responsive measures. On the other hand, it is indicating its desire to see APEC become a policy coordinating body, using new entrepreneurial diplomacy techniques. The two are not contradictory. Both U.S. and other APEC officials should consider the former approach as a prod and an incentive to advance APEC's ability to multilateralize the resolution of regional trade issues. To the extent that the United States must resort to power diplomacy moves, it will be — or should be — because APEC has been unable to operationalize itself to meet the goals of at least a portion of the agenda suggested by the United States.

The United States, then, should give first priority to making APEC work, holding its "doctrine of comparable action" in reserve. That doctrine as it has been articulated to date does not seem to be a program of protectionist retaliation. U.S. Trade representative Mickey Kantor has described that doctrine as based on mutuality and comparability. Those would appear to be appropriate values to bring to the APEC table.

Most U.S. experts would agree that the twin goals of U.S. trade policy should be to greatly reduce and eliminate the U.S. current account trade deficit and to contribute to eliminating barriers to market access, wherever they exist. The latter is also an objective of APEC, while the former is more of a national aim. On the surface, these two aims would appear contradictory, because realizing the second goal (through removal of subsidies to U.S. agriculture, for example) may weaken U.S. ability to achieve the first. However, the two aims can be viewed as consistent with one another *if* the strategies employed to achieve them are agreed upon and synchronized. It is suggested here that the United States stands the best chance of realizing its trade policy goals through the encouragement of APEC's development and through APEC's adoption of a common regional strategy.

Although there are a number of components to a U.S. trade strategy that are nation specific (for example, export promotion and incentives, increasing export credit, retooling industry to make it internationally competitive), other aspects of the strategy will require making fuller use of APEC and urging its further development as a mature intergovernment organization. First, at the macro level, there must be regional consensus on an economic growth strategy, especially for the less developed countries (LDCs). This is important to the United States if it is going to see foreign markets grow and is a key to the economic vitality of the region's LDCs. APEC appears tailor-made to advance this strategy, being composed not just of wealthy advanced economies but also including newly industrialized economies and LDCs. What was originally regarded as a problem for APEC (that is, the North-South nature of its membership) and the consequent diversity of interests may in fact be one of its distinctive strong points in activating this strategy. To this end, coordination of foreign economic aid should logically be included in the APEC agenda as a means of realizing this economic growth goal.

Trade deficits and market access barriers also can most efficiently be reduced by arriving at regional agreements recognizing common rules. The United States already has proposed a number of initiatives to arrive at such common rules, as outlined earlier. It needs to sustain that initial display of leadership and not be too quick to resort to retaliatory measures. Producing a condition of common rules on a region-wide basis will be a lengthy and complex task, requiring the utilization of technical and entrepreneurial skills in a multilateral setting. The United States is not used to this kind of diplomacy, but economic realities necessitate their development. APEC is a natural vehicle for developing regional common rules. U.S. participation in APEC, however, will need to be based on a shared decision-making and partnership basis.

A U.S. trade strategy for the Asia Pacific region should include the establishment and development of regional trade dispute settlement mechanisms. The United States undoubtedly would find a regional/multilateral dispute settlement mechanism both more effective and, certainly, more efficient than its current pattern of strained and repetitive series of bilateral negotiations. However, to be effective, such a multilateral mechanism must have its findings honored by the contesting parties, the United States included, even when the judgments are not considered favorable by the United States. Currently, APEC does not have this objective in its work program. The United States has proposed it, however, and can reclaim its higher standing in the Asia Pacific region by continuing to promote its establishment. It would be one of the clearer signals by the United States to its Asian partners of its commitment to the region and economic cooperation.

Multilateral trade negotiations should be results oriented, with the results measured by benchmarks and standards commonly agreed upon. These measurements may include market shares, percentages, and the like but need not be confined to just those factors usually defined as comprising managed trade. Instead of the managed trade concept, which is usually considered in a bilateral context, the notion of measurable results can be part of a multilateral undertaking. Here, too, APEC, with its extensive research and survey work program, could prove a useful vehicle. The main issue within APEC concerning measurable results would appear to be the political will among the members to reach agreement on the type and content of measurements. Without such multilateral agreement and consistency, the boundaries of measurable results will undergo continual resetting, producing tensions and misunderstanding.

A final item on the APEC agenda concerns Asia Pacific region exchange rate regulation for competitive pricing. Thus far, financial regulation has not made its way onto the APEC agenda, and it is probably asking too much at this time for it to be on the agenda, given the opposition of various APEC financial authorities.

Participation in any meaningful intergovernmental organization means that each participating nation must yield some small segment of what it regards as its own sovereign rights in order for all to benefit. No less is true for a meaningful APEC. The key for the United States is to regard APEC and whatever regional agreements it can reach as a vehicle furthering U.S. trade interests. If the United States can retain this perspective, it will regain its respected standing in the Asia Pacific region while moving closer toward achieving its own trade policy objectives.

ASIA PACIFIC ECONOMIC COOPERATION AND SUBREGIONAL TRADE AGREEMENTS

At least as perceived by various APEC members, the greatest present threat to APEC's further usefulness and relevance is the emergence of subregional trade arrangements. These would include North American Free Trade Agreement (NAFTA), ASEAN Free Trade Agreements, and the proposed East Asian Economic Caucus. These are seen by some as potentially undermining APEC because of possible exclusionary trade diversion possibilities.

In the case of NAFTA, the United States has told its APEC partners repeatedly that it views NAFTA as trade creating, not trade diverting. NAFTA also includes "docking" provisions that allow other APEC members to join *if* (and it is a big if) they agree to the liberal trade NAFTA conditions. Despite these assurances, other APEC members are concerned that NAFTA is evidence of a declining U.S. interest in East and Southeast Asia and is a precursor of future bilateral trade agreements with other Latin American countries. Although the United States consistently has denied these views, words alone will not suffice in this instance. Even though the United States has pointed out the inclusion of an accession provision in NAFTA, it already is evident that Asian nations, even those desiring to join, will not be able to easily gain such access. If, indeed, APEC is so critical to the successful achievement of U.S. trade policy goals, and given the paramount importance of the region's economic growth to U.S. economic recovery, then any agreement that the United States enters into should fall under the APEC umbrella. The United States should indicate its willingness for this to happen and work with its APEC partners to define the parameters of that inclusion. At a minimum, it would mean that all subregional trade agreements entered into by APEC members will be consistent with the principles and goals of APEC as outlined in its Seoul Statement.

This same concept also should hold true for ASEAN Free Trade Agreements, which the ASEAN countries have touted as a "foreign investment platform." It should also apply to the proposed East Asian Economic Caucus — which, on the face of it, would be a yen-dominated and at least partially diversionary enterprise. APEC's charter allows for and even encourages subregional trade agreements, but only when they are APEC consistent and GATT consistent. Here, too, the key to successful implementation is accurate and agreed-upon measurement standards. If such arrangements are found to be trade diverting according to these measurements, then those arrangements would need to be modified.

A PACIFIC FREE TRADE AGREEMENT?

Given the foregoing considerations, logic would seem to lead to the following question: Why not a Pacific Free Trade Agreement instead of a number of subregional agreements falling under the APEC umbrella? The advantages are obvious. Asian concerns about NAFTA and U.S. worries about market access in the region would be dissipated. APEC, with a functioning secretariat in Singapore, would provide a solid multinational organizational base for developing, managing, and monitoring a regional free trade agreement. The impetus for sustained long-term comprehensive trade liberalization would be ensured. To be sure, this would be a difficult and lengthy undertaking, covering one to two decades. What would be needed now is an effort at dialogue to determine if APEC members and potential members might agree on accepting this long-term objective. The problems, however, cannot be minimized. Countries such as Malaysia and China already are leery about APEC overwhelming or obstructing their national economic interests. The Asian APEC members, recognizing the diversity of the region, have successfully insisted on a gradualist approach to economic cooperation. A Pacific Free Trade Agreement represents a major leap in regional cooperation with which a number of APEC members may be uncomfortable. Recognizing this obstacle, it would be necessary to design an incremental strategy to achieve such an ambitious goal, with several parallel steps being taken.

These initiatives would include early inter-APEC consultations to examine the pros and cons of adopting a Pacific Free Trade Agreement as an ultimate goal of APEC; a wide-ranging series of seminars and research projects exploring the concept and proposing implementation approaches to be conducted by the Pacific Economic Cooperation Council, the Pacific Basin Economic Council, the Pacific Free Trade and Development Conference, and other independent research centers in the region; continued pursuit by APEC of proposed practical next steps in functional cooperation, such as customs harmonization, which would lay the foundation for a regional free trade agreement; and policy dialogue to achieve consensus with regard to subregional free-trade agreements as steppingstones to a regional agreement. A Pacific Free Trade Agreement is an ambitious and complex proposal. Consequently, it is significant that the United States has put the concept into play at the Seattle summit. It now needs to carry out a range of activities required of a new entrepreneurial diplomacy.

CONCLUSION

It may sound trite to say APEC is at a crossroads, but it is true. To succeed, it must both evolve in the scope of its mandate and begin to produce coordinated results. It has been argued here that the U.S. stake in APEC is very high — probably higher than generally considered. By now it is clear that the current Uruguay Round has not resolved the continuing Japan-United States trade problem. The options for the United States are to continue its difficult bilateral negotiations with Japan or to be more forceful in bringing these bilateral problems onto the APEC multilateral table.

China, although not yet a GATT member, is an APEC participant. Its exploding economic growth and consequent difficulties and opportunities for the United States on trade matters thus far also have been difficult to resolve in a bilateral context. As a rough and ready new international trade, China is creating problems of competition for its neighbors as well. A set of APEC-managed regional trading rules agreements may offer the best prospect for resolving these problems. At the same time, only a multilateral organization like APEC can provide a comprehensive forum for dealing with the new economic territories crossing national boundaries in the Asia Pacific region (for example, China/Taiwan/Hong Kong and Singapore/Malaysia/Indonesia) and the structural adjustments that have to take place to accommodate this new regional reality. APEC has the promise, and the United States has much to gain, if it is prepared to "go multilateral."

IV

SECURITY: NEW AND EMERGING ISSUES

13

A Framework for Regional Security Cooperation in Asia

Robert A. Scalapino

The Asia Pacific region is both a part of, and apart from, the rest of the world. It shares in the first global revolution in human history, a revolution reaching every corner of the earth. Indeed, its more dynamic portions are front-runners in that revolution, taking advantage of the latest phases of scientific-technological progress, pushing development at unprecedented speed, with rapid social transformation and political restructuring the inevitable consequences. At the same time, by virtue of its size and diversity, Asia has its special characteristics and problems. Thus, any attempt to impose upon it a simple, monolithic formula, whether the issue at hand be economic, political, or strategic, is doomed to failure.

Our first task is to define "security" in both its global and its Asian contexts, keeping in mind the elements of commonality and difference. In simple terms, security for a nation-state is achieved when the defenses against external threats are sufficient to reduce the risk of attack to a minimum and when the internal structures of society and state underwrite a dynamic combination of order and development, thereby affording maximum protection against decay, strife, or collapse. In Asia, where differences in developmental stage, historic traditions, geopolitical circumstances, and cultural-political values are extensive, security also involves the complex task of reaching a harmonious

This chapter was originally prepared for the Japan Institute of International Relations (JIIA) symposium "The Prospects of Security Cooperation in Asia," held in Tokyo, June 19–20, 1992, and first published in *The Korean Journal of Defense Analysis*, 5 (2) (Winter 1993).

relationship with neighbors, a task frequently arduous given the obstacles to be overcome.

Beyond this, Asia, in common with other states, faces global problems that are mounting rapidly as the twentieth century comes to a close and that affect the security of mankind as a whole — the proliferation of weapons of mass destruction, environmental degradation, overpopulation, drugs, and such new hazards as AIDS. These are issues that must be handled in a variety of ways but with as wide a range of active participants as possible.

The challenges come at a unique period for the nation-state. As in certain other regions, in many parts of Asia, the nation-building process is still underway, but at the same time, national sovereignty is under unprecedented challenge from both above and below. Simultaneously, an effort, driven largely by economic necessity, is being made to create decision-making mechanisms and institutions above the nation, and a process of reallocating power to regions and localities below the national level is taking place, again, heavily influenced by economic considerations.

There are further domestic challenges. The diversity and generational cleavages that are inevitable products of rapid development combine with the difficult effort to mesh borrowed institutions — economic and political — with indigenous cultures that are often significantly different in their main thrust. In one sense or another, all Asian societies are "follower" societies in various stages of catching up with a Western industrial revolution that is now several centuries old. Only Japan, starting at a relatively early point and employing remarkably successful techniques, has achieved that goal thus far, but a number of other Asian societies are not far behind.

Asia must also deal with historic issues projected forward. Many of these issues were postponed because of the lengthy colonial rule to which much of the region was subjected. Now, they are reemerging with vigor, augmented by the new issues thrown up as a result of World War II and its immediate aftermath. Ethnic and religious cleavages, territorial disputes, divided states, and economic controversies, thus, demand attention. It is in this context that a new framework for security cooperation in Asia should be explored.

Today, the collapse of the Soviet Union and, more broadly, the profound political shift away from Leninism (except in a few enclaves) together with the triumph of the market economies have brought us into an entirely new age. Suddenly, the Eurasian heartland has become weak, its peripheries strong. Virtually overnight, the type of global balance to which we had become accustomed has vanished, as yet not replaced by any new international order. Patron-client relations are disappearing, but partnership is still a phrase, not a reality. The old alliances are undergoing alterations, shedding their tightness and exclusiveness. Understandably, the swiftness of the change has left all nations groping.

However, as events in Eastern Europe and certain other regions indicate, the failure of Leninism was not uniquely a Russian phenomenon. On a much larger stage, the Stalinist economic strategy proved incapable of meeting developmental requirements after its initial big spurt. This, together with the basic conservatism — and inner corruption — of the Leninist political system, created conditions making dramatic change inevitable.

It is true, of course, that in Asia, Leninism survives in four states. Even here, however, economic reform is underway in varying degrees, and it is primarily in the political realm that the old order — or a modified version thereof — prevails. The current economic goals are to turn outward, making greater contact with the market economies in order to secure technology, capital, and export opportunities. The impact of these policies upon the political system cannot be avoided; the only issues are those of the timing and nature of the change.

SECURITY CONCERNS IN THE ASIA PACIFIC

Under the conditions outlined above, where is the threat? To a considerable extent, it lies within, not outside the state. Note the extensive pressures upon the remaining socialist states of Asia. China faces three far-reaching challenges in the political realm, quite apart from the hazards of trying to combine a largely closed politics and an increasingly open economy. A change in leadership lies directly ahead, involving not merely new individuals but also a new generation. In a few years, the octogenarians who still occupy the political heights will have passed from the scene. As pioneers, they can be defined as generalists, having a reach into party, government, and the military. The third and fourth generation leaders who follow will be "specialists," having a far more limited reach. Hence, the premium will be upon collective leadership, but China has always found such a course difficult to pursue; throughout this century, it has had either a supreme leader or a sizeable degree of instability.

The second major issue relates to the allocation of authority among center, region, and locality. The process of decentralization, born out of the requirements of economic reform, has now advanced to a point where it is irreversible in any fundamental sense. Nor is this manifest merely in developments within China. Natural economic territories (NETs) whereby portions of China are joined with external sources have been formed or are in the offing: Guangdong-Hong Kong-Taiwan, Fujian-Taiwan, Shandong-South Korea, and Southwest China-Southeast Asia. These NETs together with the uneven development of China's diverse domestic regions raise profound issues of jurisdiction and authority. What power to the center? What power to other levels?

China's security, indeed, its existence as an entity, hinges upon resolving these challenges effectively and in the midst of the enormously difficult task of modernizing over 1 billion people.

A third political challenge relates to the future role of the military, a crucial element in China throughout the Communist era. Will the military remain united and under party control? Can its regional power be curbed, especially in border areas where security considerations are more compelling?

It is not surprising that Chinese leaders play upon two contradictory themes: China as a part of the poor, underdeveloped world, and China as a major power with both global and regional interests that must be served. How the issues surrounding both of these images are handled, first by China, then by others, and, most particularly, by other Asian states, will be a major determinant of security throughout the region.

In the other Asian Leninist states, a similar quest is presently underway to move away from an autarkic, command economy while maintaining political Leninism in the name of stability. The thrust in this direction is pronounced in Vietnam, moderate in Laos, and only beginning in North Korea. Mongolia and Cambodia now represent ex-Leninist states. In Ulaanbaatar, Mongolia, very young political leaders wrestle with complex economic problems that have caused public dissatisfaction to rise, but they remain committed to both a market economy and political pluralism. The outcome in Cambodia naturally hinges upon whether the civil conflict can now be ended. The most recent signs are hopeful but by no means conclusive.

The success or failure of the developmental process in the Leninist states will not only affect their internal stability and prospects for peaceful change but will also impact upon the entire region in diverse ways. A chaotic China, for example, would create serious problems for all of China's neighbors, as it did in the earlier decades of this century. A bitter internal struggle in North Korea might result in one or more factions turning out to obtain support, with uncertain consequences. The region has already witnessed the problems engendered by the outflow of Indochina refugees.

Clearly, the future desired for these societies by Asia Pacific neighbors is that neither chaos nor a high-posture militarist authoritarianism prevails. As noted earlier, the primary responsibility for the path taken lies with those holding power within these states. Prodigious mistakes in both economic and political policies have been made in the past and, in some arenas, continue. Systemic change is never easy and rarely takes place without pauses and retreats. There may well be serious internal struggles in the period immediately ahead.

At this time, however, these are societies ripe for further change in every field. The major task of others is to support constructive change by various forms of economic and cultural interaction and by drawing the Leninists into a wide-ranging dialogue on the principal issues relating to development and security. In the course of this exercise, they should be made a part of such multilateral institutions and processes as are relevant. Isolation feeds the cause of extremism just as backwardness supports hard authoritarianism.

The movement toward greater political openness in the remaining Leninist societies will be forwarded as a growing network of ties are constructed with the market economies and the economic and political-security mechanisms available at regional and global levels. This should become easier to accomplish because in the not too distant future, the political continuum within Asia will narrow, with the remaining traditional societies and the classic Leninist states at the extremities of this continuum being either modified or fundamentally changed.

The non-Leninist states of Asia also have multiple problems relating to internal cohesion and growth. On balance, to be sure, such states represent a success story, with rapid economic development in recent decades and changes in political institutions without chaos. Moreover, the broad trend has been toward greater political openness. Nevertheless, there have been and continue to be hazards. Three factors with deep political significance accompany rapid development: diversity, inclusiveness, and porousness. Within both classes and regions, the complexities of growth manifest themselves quickly in myriad differences, making a highly centralized, command structure increasingly less feasible and gradually challenging all forms of bureaucratic dominance. As urbanism and education advance, moreover, the demand for meaningful inclusion in the political process rises and must be met. Finally, the society is brought into much greater contact with the external world, with culture and ideas as well as technology introduced from the outside.

In varying degree, these by-products of modernization are conducive to an increase in instability. Whether the political system is that of parliamentary democracy or some form of authoritarian-pluralism, the issue of governability emerges. Special interests in the private sector, many of them very powerful and often in competition with each other, seek to influence or control those who hold political power. The media becomes a critical force, vying with government in shaping public opinion and, hence, in a very real sense, in determining attitudes and policies. Confronted with sharply conflicting views and subject to a great deal of negativism regarding politics, the citizen can easily become cynical or indifferent, a pronounced trend in current democratic states. In southern Asia, moreover, deeply rooted ethnic, religious, and regional cleavages remain relatively intact, promoting periodic violence and constant division.

Thus, the challenges confronting the open, rapidly modernizing society are scarcely less than those confronting the Leninist states. The central issue in both cases is how to combine stability and development. In the first instance, it is crucial to promote continued economic advances, and here again, the burdens fall upon both internal and external sources. Most Asian market economies are evolving from a state-dominated capitalism resting upon mercantilist policies, with domestic access limited to outsiders and a heavy concentration upon exports as the engine of growth. Whether they can move rapidly toward a more open economy compatible with such economies as that of the United States is of vital importance if greater international harmony is to be achieved.

At the same time, it is incumbent upon the major global economies — the United States, Japan, and Germany — to sustain the level of growth that will preserve their role as sources of capital, technology, and markets for late developers. Thus, this is a time when a nation's domestic economic policies are of vital consequence to all others. We stand at a crossroad. The threat of greater protectionism in various forms — national and regional — is real, and it will take truly enlightened leadership to advance an open, equitable international trading and investment system.

It should be clear that these are issues quite as crucial to the strengthening or weakening of regional and global security as matters involving arms or territory. Hence, the logic of bringing together a consortium of nations in an effort to assist the Russian Republic economically is as solid today as was the logic of building an alliance structure against Soviet expansionism 40 years ago. Similarly, keeping the economies of the advanced industrial nations strong will be crucial to states like India and China, as each in its own way seeks greater transparency and economic interaction with the international market system.

SUBREGIONAL CONFLICTS

Let us look next at the subregional conflicts or tensions that remain in the Asia Pacific, examining whether cooperation on a broader scale can be helpful in resolving or containing them. In East Asia, the principal sources of friction are the remaining cases of divided states, namely, the two Koreas and China-Taiwan, the Russia-Japan controversy over the Northern Territories, the unresolved territorial disputes in the South China Sea relating to the Spratley and Paracel islands, and the continuing uncertainties that surround Cambodia.

It is doubtful whether a large, undifferentiated multilateral approach to any of these issues would be constructive. Rather, experience to date has shown that the most promising approach is a situation-specific set of concentric arcs, building outward and bringing to bear a variety of incentives and influences. The term "arcs" is used in place of "circles" because there must be easy access between involved parties upward and downward in the course of developments.

In the case of Cambodia, the first arc was composed of the four Khmer factions. Their effective interaction, or at least the willingness of a majority of them to interact positively, has always been critical to the outcome. As is well-known, that has remained an extremely difficult effort, and, hence, the long-term outcome of the Cambodian conflict remains uncertain. Nevertheless, the forces within Cambodia constitute the first, indispensable element in any ultimate resolution.

A second arc has also been extremely important, namely, China and Vietnam. As the two neighboring states having had the deepest involvement, their willingness to compromise was critical to reducing the external components in the struggle. This second arc, moreover, although strongly influenced by the domestic concerns of these two countries, especially in the case of Vietnam, was also provided with incentives by the third and fourth arcs, in the first instance, the Association of Southeast Asian Nations (ASEAN) members and, subsequently, Japan and the permanent members of the Security Council apart from China. At a later phase, various international organizations, most especially the United Nations, have been brought in to play crucial roles.

At this point, it is far from certain that a lasting peace in Cambodia can be achieved, notwithstanding multiple efforts. Whatever the outcome, however, this case provides a model of importance. With respect to the problems of the Korean peninsula, a similar approach has evolved. The first arc is clearly composed of North and South Korea, with their relations — still subject to innumerable advances and retreats — obviously critical to progress. A second vitally important arc is composed of the four large states long involved with the Korean peninsula — the United States, China, Japan, and Russia. The crisis over North Korean nuclear activities clearly illustrates the significance of this arc, with close consultations taking place despite certain differences of position, notably on the part of China. Indeed, if the tensions are to be alleviated and advances made, the big four must continue constructive involvement, each playing a special role. Beyond this, moreover, lies the possibility once again of the engagement of international bodies, old and new. Indeed, the United Nations Development Program has already played some role in connection with the exploration of the Tumen River project, and there are many other possibilities if North-South relations improve and the North pursues a program of economic reform.

In the case of China-Taiwan, significant progress has been made within the first arc — the two parties immediately involved. Economic and cultural ties are thickening, and two liaison bodies for the handling of disputes are in place. On the People's Republic of China (PRC) side, the Association for Relations across the Taiwan Straits and, on the

Taiwan side, the Straits Exchange Foundation are now in operation, with meetings held in the spring of 1993 and certain agreements reached pertaining to documents and mail. Although these contacts are billed as "unofficial," they involve individuals with intimate connections to government and can be accurately described as the closest approach to official contacts yet developed.

At the same time, the political gap between the PRC and Taiwan has widened with the advent of democracy in the latter society. Further, Beijing authorities are not likely to alter their position that Taiwan is a province of China while advocating the one country–two systems approach. Consequently, PRC-Taiwan unification is a remote prospect in the foreseeable future, and China broods over the fact that time is not necessarily on its side, especially given the possibility that the Democratic Progressive Party, which officially advocates independence, may grow in strength.

With the status of future PRC-Taiwan political relations uncertain and with China unwilling to abandon the possible use of force, a second arc remains of great significance. That arc, composed of the United States and Japan, operates as a passive deterrent against the outbreak of conflict. The combined military and economic influence of these two nations is felt by both primary parties. The United States-Japan duo also poses obstacles to any declaration of formal independence by Taiwan, an action that might trigger a PRC militant response. Neither country would recognize such a move. This second arc cannot necessarily prevent violence under certain circumstances, but it can act as a restraining influence.

Further, the involvement of both China and Taiwan in a growing number of regional and international bodies introduces a third arc of importance, providing an international framework that strengthens their bilateral cooperation and renders a resort to force less likely.

One can note that with respect to the Northern Territories issue, the primary arc — that of Russia and Japan — is still the only locus of such activity. However, the United States and the Group of Seven have influenced developments through their own economic and security policies and by urging Japan to increase its contributions to the program of economic assistance to Russia. Meanwhile, within Russia, an emerging issue is almost certain to be the degree of autonomy to be given to the Russian Far East and the extent to which it will be pulled into the North Pacific economic orbit, becoming part of another NET.

The South China Sea territorial issues have also received attention, first from the Asian members themselves, meeting in 1990 and 1991, and subsequently, in ASEAN–Post-Ministerial Conference (PMC) discussions involving China. Indeed, above the bilateral level, the ASEAN-PMC constitutes a logical second arc.

In South Asia, meanwhile, with the Afghanistan tragedy possibly winding down (although many observers foresee continuing civil war), one can reflect on the important role of Russia and the United States at a late stage in this situation and the continuing importance of such neighboring states as Pakistan, Iran, and, possibly, the Central Asian Republics.

Kashmir remains a festering wound with no solution in sight and a continuing risk of major conflict. The alternatives would seem to be few. Outsiders may adopt a hands-off policy, hoping that domestic circumstances in India and Pakistan will serve to restrain both parties even if no resolution is at hand. Yet, as long as tension is high and violence is recurrent, not only will arms from external sources be sought and obtained but also nuclear weapons programs are likely to proceed.

Another option is some effort to build arcs beyond India-Pakistan. In this case, however, none of the outside major states has great leverage or, indeed, vital interests involved. Thus, incentives and pressure would probably have to flow from such sources as the United Nations via the Security Council or its permanent members. Almost certainly, one or both of the principal parties to the dispute would resist such a course at this point, but India's need to concentrate upon a new developmental program involving the support of market-oriented states and Pakistan's weak international position at present may offer some hope of a willingness to consider such a course and certain creative new steps.

REGIONAL SECURITY ISSUES AND COLLECTIVE DECISION-MAKING MECHANISMS FOR THE FUTURE

My emphasis thus far has been on adopting a situation-specific approach to certain identifiable conflicts or tensions that jeopardize Asian security. However, this cannot be the only approach to security. As noted earlier, there are a wide range of issues impossible to handle in such a fashion. Thus, there is a strong case to be made for subregional consortiums focusing on basic security issues within the compass of their immediate area. For example, it is appropriate that the ASEAN members have looked toward a more meaningful dialogue among themselves on such matters and have encouraged the ASEAN-PMC to include security concerns on its agenda.

Naturally, a counterpart development in the North Pacific is more difficult at this point, given the unresolved problems that remain here. Yet, there are certain issues upon which the states of this region need to focus: greater transparency and confidence building in military matters; the development of NETs cutting across political lines, such as the Sea of Japan rim and the Tumen River Basin; and nuclear issues, centering on the production of enriched uranium or plutonium, strengthening the International Atomic Energy Agency with respect to verification procedures, and not excluding the possibility of a nuclear-free zone that would encompass portions of Russia and China as well as the Korean peninsula and Japan. A step in the direction of a North Pacific dialogue to be commended was the earlier effort initiated by the Canadians to hold conferences that involve both unofficial and official representatives. Currently, several new "second track" efforts are underway, promoted by various institutes in Asia and the United States.

FUTURE RISKS AND OPPORTUNITIES

Whatever the format, there is also an urgent need for multilateral cooperation in controlling weapons of mass destruction, limiting strategic weapons transfers, and reducing military budgets. In much of Asia, military expenditures continue to rise, even in states that desperately need additional funds for developmental purposes. Certain proposals, including that of former Prime Minister Kaifu, have been made to consider military budgets, the production of weapons of mass destruction, and strategic weapons sales when determining economic assistance, but it is unclear whether such proposals are scheduled to be implemented. The time has come to pen these issues to multilateral discussion at various levels.

The risks of a major power conflict, either in Asia or elsewhere, are at their lowest level in the twentieth century. Russia, the strongest military power next to the United States, is completely preoccupied with its internal problems. The United States will continue to have an important presence in Asia. Physically, it is a part of the western Pacific, inextricably joined to Asia, and the western United States is increasingly involved in one of the many NETs that are emerging. Thus, Asia is of vital economic and political significance. However, no one can doubt that the age of pax Americana is over and that the United States is in the process of reevaluating its international role. Almost certainly, it will move from being *the* leader to being *a* leader, from unilateralism toward an acceptance of collective decision making in return for risk and cost sharing.

Consequently, the responsibilities of the small and medium Asian states are rising. Moreover, although the window of opportunity is open now, if advantage is not taken of the unique circumstances currently existing, the twenty-first century may pose new threats. Already, a number of Asian states worry about the possibility of an economically successful and militarily strong China eager to play a more powerful regional role and dissatisfied with its status or boundaries. Others evidence concern about a Japan that has continued to expand its power, increased its independence from the United States, and defined its interests in ways detrimental to others.

Some expect India, having achieved hegemony over the subcontinent, to seek greater influence in Southeast Asia. Also, who can say that Russia, possessed of great human talent and abundant natural resources, will not get its economic and political act together over time and reemerge as a major player, in Asia as well as in Europe?

Thus, the 1990s represent a great opportunity to build a network of institutions and ties that will serve as restraints on the future proclivity of any state to pursue its own interests without regard to those of others. Whatever the precise structure, the world now needs permanent discussion and decision-making bodies at subregional, regional, and global levels dealing with the full range of issues that should be subsumed under the label "security." Naturally, this includes environmental and health issues as well as the conventional economic, political, and security concerns. The Tokyo Declaration on Financing Global Environment and Development, issued in April 1992, and the June Earth Summit meeting in Rio are small steps forward.

In this age, we are condemned to live with complexity. Bilateral relations will continue to be highly important, especially between such states as the United States and Japan. Regionalism is upon us in many ways, and we must work to prevent it from succumbing to exclusivist tendencies. The pioneer global institutions from the United Nations to the General Agreement on Tariffs and Trade are still fragile and in the process of evolving but are of crucial importance. Naturally, there are contradictions among these levels, and one task is to reduce those contradictions to the fullest possible extent, but it is not possible to abandon any level of suprastate interaction at this time.

Further, we shall be deeply involved in the process of sharing authority despite the efforts of certain states to hold doggedly to the nineteenth century Western concept of absolute state sovereignty. To be sure, the strong internationalist tides have evoked a sharp nationalist response, not only in the so-called developing states but also in advanced industrial nations. Indeed, the competition among localism, nationalism, regionalism, and globalism will be the epic drama of the coming decades.

Nevertheless, the tides of internationalization will continue to roll forward, not only in economics but also in political matters. What a nation does to its own people, for example, now receives global attention, given the communications information revolution, and, correspondingly, influences the attitudes and policies of others. It is not surprising that both authoritarian and democratic states presently feel obliged to defend their human rights record before the world. Gradually, we should proceed to broaden the international standards pertaining to such matters and strengthen the role of the international court to hear appeals.

Similarly, we should move toward a North Pacific regime on arms reduction and the peaceful resolution of disputes. Such a regime should ultimately include the United States, Japan, Russia, the PRC, the Republic of Korea, the Democratic People's Republic of Korea, Mongolia, and Taiwan. It may be necessary to proceed bilaterally and with smaller groups at first, but in reality, a regional framework should strengthen, not weaken, the prospects for lower level agreements. In any case, this region is as vital as any in the world in holding the key to future global stability and prosperity.

In sum, there is no single approach to regional cooperation, and economic, political, and security issues are becoming increasingly intertwined, as are domestic and foreign policies. Over time, it may be possible to consolidate certain institutions, joining their functions. At this point, however, the premium should be upon making certain that all key issues are encompassed in various regularized dialogue and policymaking structures, with lower level organs feeding into more comprehensive bodies. A growing number of national leaders recognize the necessity of such a course. Further, it is important to preserve flexibility and avoid rigid structures and to encourage multiplicity of approaches, even at the risk of some duplication. In a transitional and uncertain era, we should not assume that we can present final programs or construct permanent institutions. Nonetheless, this is a time for experimentation with fresh ideas and new dialogue and decision-making mechanisms.

14

Asia Pacific Security in a Time of Change

Bih-jaw Lin

Recent changes in the international system and the subordinate system of Asia and the Pacific inspire us to think about new arrangements for maintaining peace and stability in the region. This chapter will examine structural changes at global and regional levels and then go on to analyze some important security issues and the mechanisms required to deal with them. In this way we may shed some light on current discussions about regional collective security.

GLOBAL CHANGES

For the past 40 years or so, Asia and the Pacific have been characterized by steady growth and political stability. These trends are the result of the consistent application of a carefully designed development model within a bipolar international system. Both the Asian development model and the international system have now changed significantly, however. Several aspects of this change are familiar: political democratization, social changes, the collapse of the former Soviet Union, the disintegration of Eastern Europe, and Japan's rise to economic primacy. Domestically, the Asia Pacific countries have become more open, liberalized, and plural than before, while the international system has transformed itself from bipolarity to multipolarity. The traditional state system embedded in the Westphalian model can no longer cope with these changes, making some form of adaptation inevitable.

In the past the maintenance of stability and order depended very much on a balance of power between the United States and the former Soviet Union. At the time when the two superpowers were involved in military confrontation, the international system was simple and rigid.

Because of the self-destructive nature of nuclear war, the world was actually stabilized by a balance of terror. The threat of massive retaliation worked only when the United States had military superiority and the former Soviet Union accepted this reality. Even the strategy of flexible response was effective only for the two superpowers because they realized that any nuclear war would inflict unbearable damage on humankind. The line between friend and foe was clear; no country would risk a nuclear war by crossing it.

From time to time, Moscow and Washington experienced tension in their mutual relations or used proxies to advance their interests, but they managed crises with reasonable success. In short, one can describe the structure of the international system as confrontational and competitive. Although the situation was sometimes quite tense, the two major actors in international politics were able to prevent crises from escalating into all-out war. During this period, each side put a great deal of effort into upgrading its military capability. A bitter arms race, unprecedented in the history of international politics, dominated the world scene for more than three decades. It was halted only after repeated rounds of difficult negotiation. The greatest irony occurred when the two major arms producers decided to dismantle or scrap their weaponry after spending so much money on military development.

Gorbachev's "new thinking" and reform policy played a critical role in producing the momentum for change. This chapter is not the place to evaluate the results of his policy or to judge Soviet policy makers according to standards set by outsiders. However, it is fair to say that the pressure for change was so strong that Gorbachev and his supporters had no choice but to loosen their hold on Eastern Europe and withdraw from that part of the world, thus, making the disintegration of the former Soviet empire inevitable. One man's decision certainly could not change everything. There was consensus that the Soviet political system and economy had failed to meet the expectations and demands of society. The country had probably gained the upper hand in the arms race but had fallen seriously behind in other nonmilitary areas. Its national power was overstretched to such an extent — as exemplified in Angola, Somalia, Afghanistan, Vietnam, and Cuba — that it could no longer serve its own people. The leadership in Moscow had to face reality and adopt a more reasonable policy toward the rest of the world.

Successive events, such as German unification, the changes in Eastern Europe, and European economic integration, also contributed to the transformation of the international system. Other factors had an impact as well, namely, the influence of information technology, growing interdependence among nations, and common concerns about global issues. At the time of writing, no one can be sure of the type of international system in which we are living. Is it a unipolar or multipolar system? Are order and stability maintained once again by the "concert of Europe"? These questions are still debated among policy makes and policy analysts, and we simply do not have an answer.

REGIONAL STRUCTURE

What about the changes at the subordinate level of the Asia Pacific region? In general, the regional structure has been influenced by East-West relations and the respective policies of the two superpowers. Asia Pacific regional politics have long been shaped by power politics and will remain this way for a very long time. Thus, at a time when the world was divided along ideological lines, member countries of the two blocs found it very difficult to maintain normal relations. With the emergence of détente, initial contacts were made and relations normalized. The People's Republic of China (PRC), the former Soviet Union, Vietnam, and, to a certain extent, North Korea followed this path. The United States, Japan, and South Korea also established relations with countries of the former Communist bloc. Even the Republic of China (ROC) on Taiwan has adopted a new policy toward Russia, Vietnam, and North Korea. Together they have created a trend toward further relaxation of tension, peaceful coexistence, and mutual respect among nations.

For the purpose of discussion, we can divide the regional structure into two parts, Northeast and Southeast Asia. The structure of the Northeast Asian system still reflects traditional power politics, deeply imbued with concern for security. In Southeast Asia, the subsystem is more institutionalized, predictable, and practical, with a clear emphasis on economic cooperation. Southeast Asian ruling elites exhibit consistent support for the U.S. military presence in the region and the spirit of the Zone of Peace, Freedom, and Neutrality (ZOPFAN). They are concerned about foreign threats but are reluctant to form a military alliance and clearly exhibit a high degree of confidence in the Association of Southeast Asian Nations (ASEAN) as an institution to improve regional relations. The ASEAN summit, the annual ASEAN ministerial meeting, and the post-ministerial conference are the three main tiers of that institution.

The success of ASEAN will continue to depend on the ability of its member states to cooperate and the support of the major powers in the region, particularly Japan and the United States. The PRC will play an increasingly important role as the territorial dispute in the South China Sea builds up. For the moment, the ASEAN countries prefer to concentrate on economic cooperation and to only gradually extend their dialogue to security issues. It is unlikely that ASEAN will transform itself from a regional forum into a defense and security organization, despite the fact that member states are paying increasing attention to security, including such issues as the protection of sea lanes, maritime surveillance, and the arms build-up in the region. On the whole, economic issues occupy first place on the agenda, and some ASEAN countries have performed rather well, though infrastructural problems, such as labor, technology, income disparity, capital, and communications, remain to be solved. Nevertheless, the ASEAN countries are joining the ranks of the newly industrialized economies, and their prospects look quite promising.

Two sets of regional structures, therefore, are working to forge a stable environment in which Asia Pacific countries can interact. A geopolitical structure exists in Northeast Asia, and a geoeconomic structure, by contrast, supports ASEAN and the Asia Pacific Economic Cooperation (APEC) forum. The former entails traditional power politics in which an established relationship is carefully maintained among nations sensitive to military balance, strategy, deterrence, and crisis management. The area remains the last outpost of the Cold War, but it is inconceivable that another war will break out there. The PRC, Japan, and the United States will form a new triad replacing the old strategic triangle of Beijing, Moscow, and Washington. Russia will continue to play an important role in the area, but it has become more inward looking and less eager to influence regional events. The geopolitical structure here is now directly related to the Beijing-Tokyo-Washington triangle.

The geoeconomic structure of Southeast Asia denotes a regional setting in which states have developed a new awareness of and sensitivity toward economic competitiveness, access to world markets, investment, and other aspects of international political economy. ASEAN is an essential part of a movement toward greater regional cooperation. Dialogue and discussion among regional leaders, together with a genuine desire to practice a market economy, help to facilitate this. Three proposals have been made to promote economic cooperation: the Common Effective Preferential Tariff, the ASEAN Economic Treaty, and the ASEAN Free Trade Area. A consensus needs to be built among member states before these proposals can be realized. A deep feeling prevails among the ASEAN countries that further institutionalization of their cooperation must be pursued with care and patience. They welcome proposals for regional cooperation and enter into dialogue with frankness, but they shy away from rash action and quick solutions. The question is whether APEC can serve as a broad framework to accommodate both ASEAN and the geopolitical structure of Northeast Asia. The countries concerned are certainly making efforts to encourage that movement, particularly Australia, Japan, and the United States. Again, the process, in my view, is bound to be slow and subtle.

SECURITY ISSUES

Security issues that stem from the regional structures noted above reflect both change and continuity. For more than 30 years, the former

Soviet Union was the major threat. Today, there is growing concern about the PRC's military expansion. Analysts point to the fact that Beijing's military spending increased by about 6–8 percent annually between 1984 and 1992.[1] This year's budget called for a 12.5 percent increase. According to a Radio Moscow report, mainland China ordered 26 Sukhoi-27s and six Ilyushin-76 military transport planes in May 1990 and has taken delivery of most of these aircraft. During Boris Yeltsin's visit to Peking in December 1992, Russia agreed to sell 72 Sukhoi-27s, 4 Backfire-26 bombers, 100 surface-to-air missiles, 72 T-72 tanks, and three submarines. The two sides are still negotiating the sale of advanced MiG-29 and MiG-31 jets and even aircraft carriers.[2] The frequent exchanges of visits between the top brass of the two countries and the staging of a display of Russian military hardware in Beijing indicate that their security cooperation is very close indeed. No wonder the ASEAN countries, Japan, and Taiwan look at these developments with anxiety and apprehension.

Given this background, one can fully understand the security concerns raised by the Asia Pacific countries when they discuss the territorial dispute in the South China Sea.[3] It is well-known that the PRC attaches a great deal of importance to the Paracels and the Spratlys. Surely the Beijing leadership's determination to modernize its navy and air force is a clear sign that the PRC's territorial claims will soon be backed up by military muscle. Beijing has repeatedly stressed its intention to develop the South China Sea in cooperation with the ASEAN countries and shelve its territorial claims for the time being, but the prospects for cooperation look uncertain because of the lack of trust among the countries involved. The ASEAN countries know that the PRC has built an air base in the Paracels that will be capable of supporting Su-27 operations. If the country eventually acquires an aircraft carrier, the fragile military balance in that area will be seriously affected.

Related to this is the third issue area, namely, North Korea. Pyongyang's refusal to allow international inspection of its nuclear facilities has prompted growing regional concern that North Korea may soon develop the capability to produce a nuclear bomb. The rationales behind the North Korean nuclear program are difficult to list with certainty. One can only speculate that the regime may see it as a bargaining chip to win concessions from South Korea, Japan, and the United States. We should also not forget that the North Koreans have wanted to develop nuclear weapons for a long time.[4] It is only logical to presume that the regime is willing to pay a high price to fulfill its ambition. For the past 20 years or so, the economic balance of power has moved decisively in South Korea's favor, and North Korea is now in a very desperate situation. The leadership in Pyongyang may view nuclear weaponry as a last hope to reverse that trend. The potential dangers are so serious that all countries concerned must take concrete steps to cope with this issue effectively and safely.

It would be wrong to suggest that all Asian security problems have their origins in the Leninist states. Some ASEAN countries worry about Japan's militarization and the role of the United States in Asia Pacific affairs. Will the only remaining superpower withdraw from Asia and the Pacific? If that is the long-term trend, can or will Japan replace the United States as a guarantor of regional security? Enjoying as it does a competitive edge in computers, microelectronics, and information technology, Japan could easily convert its civilian technology to military use. Those who still remember the bitter legacy of Japan's militarism during World War II harbor anxiety at the prospect of a remilitarized Japan. In all likelihood, however, Japan will continue its normal role in world affairs and the U.S. commitment to constructive involvement in the Asia Pacific will remain largely intact. There is a greater need for the two major industrial democracies to conduct regular consultations on their policy toward Russia, the PRC, and, indeed, the rest of the Asia Pacific region.

Looking south, we see a great deal of continuity in Taiwan's foreign policy. Like other newly industrialized economies, the ROC has moved steadily toward democratization and pluralization. Its national unification policy reflects a genuine desire for a further reduction of tension in the area and the development of a peaceful relationship with the mainland. Although Taiwan's economic relations with the other side of the Taiwan Strait have grown closer, the government is still cautious in its dealings with the authorities on the mainland. Representatives from both sides have concluded talks in Singapore, although the meeting served only to settle some practical issues involving postal services and document verification. The ground has been broken, however, and there will be more negotiations in the future, but some fundamental problems await solutions. Viewed in this context, one gets a strong impression that the movement toward Chinese unification will be incremental and evolutionary. An economic triangle comprising Hong Kong, Taiwan, and southern mainland China is gradually appearing on the horizon. For such a triangle to take shape, the participants will need to adopt a pragmatic attitude and agree to respect each other's positions in the international community. The spirit of peaceful coexistence has imbued relations across the Taiwan Strait for some time; there are good reasons for policy makers on the two sides of the strait, and, above all, for Hong Kong, to preserve it.

ADAPTIVE MECHANISM

How can Asia Pacific countries devise an effective mechanism to deal with all these problems? A continued U.S. military presence in the region, based on treaty ties, arms transfers to friendly nations such as the ROC and Singapore, and the stationing of troops in Japan and South Korea, is obviously crucial to the preservation of stability in our region. In addition to keeping this "hub and spokes" approach, is it feasible and instrumental to argue for collective security or, more precisely, multilateral arrangements for security cooperation? Europe has shown remarkable achievements in this area, and support for this approach is being echoed in Asia. Opponents of collective security quickly point out that Europe and Asia differ greatly in political background, foreign policy, and their economic situation. Indeed, history shows that a collective security system has worked only on special occasions; in most cases, bilateral alliances have been more effective and reliable. The Conference on Security and Cooperation in Europe (CSCE) became possible only after the Western countries accepted the European status quo and decided to coexist with the former Soviet Union. The formation of the CSCE was such a lengthy process that the Asia Pacific countries will find it very difficult to copy. The Asia Pacific lacks a clearly defined alliance structure, a sphere of influence dominated by a hostile power, and a common willingness to accept existing boundaries. The South China Sea, the PRC's border with the former Soviet states, Japan's Northern Territories, and the Pinnacle Islands in the East China Sea are all still in dispute. It will be very difficult, almost impossible, to organize an Asian security conference under these circumstances. In addition, opposition will be quite strong when issues such as human rights are raised.

Supporters of Asian collective security, however, ask this question: "Is the European experience truly inapplicable to the Asia Pacific region?" We have to understand that the CSCE represented an effort to stabilize Europe after a period of tension between the two superpowers. Backed up by the peace movement in Europe, it realized a series of arms control agreements aimed at preventing the outbreak of nuclear war. More important, it served to create an atmosphere for lowering tension and promoting transnational cooperation. The members of NATO and their counterparts in the Warsaw Pact were encouraged to pursue self-restraint and moderation, thus, laying the foundation for current reforms in Russia and Eastern Europe. Through this process, a common European identity gradually emerged that linked Western and Eastern European interests. Without the CSCE, it would never have been possible for smaller states to participate in the process of shaping a European order. Even the countries of southern Europe were involved in the process, making the setting of a European security agenda a common aspiration. This aspiration was rendered more credible by the signing of agreements on economic cooperation, human rights, and relations between the opposing power blocs. These agreements became effective regimes that, according to Robert Keohane, provided "rules, norms, principles and procedures" that made it easier for European countries to realize their interests collectively.

A close examination of the Asia Pacific reveals that a common concern for regional affairs does exist. Korean and Chinese national unification, territorial disputes in the South China Sea, Cambodia, and other problems certainly have no easy solutions. However, these issues are viewed more and more in a regional context. Japan's relations with the ASEAN countries have become very close. South Korea, Taiwan, and mainland China are all very active economically in Southeast Asia. Indeed, Japan, the newly industrialized countries, ASEAN, Australia, and New Zealand are bound by a new awareness of common interests and a steady growth of trade, investment, technology transfer, and academic exchanges. As the process of Asianization grows, the Asia Pacific countries will need a framework to deal with their common problems. Policy makers, entrepreneurs, and public opinion leaders have given more support for regionalism than before. It is, therefore, not surprising to see that the Eminent Persons Group to APEC ministers has argued strongly for the creation of an Asia Pacific Economic Community. The APEC together with the Pacific Economic Cooperation Conference, the Pacific Basin Economic Council, and the Pacific Trade and Development Conference have gradually developed a useful process of consultations among their members. On the basis of these experiences, one can hope for some spillover effects in the area of security cooperation as a nongovernmental organization known as the Council for Security Cooperation in the Asia Pacific was set up in June 1993 and the ASEAN regional forum was formed in July 1994. It will be grossly misleading to view these as replications of the European experience, but similar patterns of regional development are hard to ignore. When we look at the increasing links among Asia Pacific countries and a growing interlocking of institutions, what appears is an interdependent transnational linkage that helps to benefit regional cooperation and reduce tension as the European experience demonstrated in the past.

LOOKING AHEAD

For practical reasons, bilateralism will continue to serve the security needs of the Asia Pacific in the foreseeable future. Common security concerns will be discussed more openly in regional forums, and conditions for multilateralism will become more favorable. Undoubtedly, the Asia Pacific countries will continue to search for an acceptable regime in which multilateral arrangements can be made. Some countries would like to see further internationalization of their security problems. Taiwan and South Korea are good examples. For others, there is a need for burden-sharing and collective measures to enhance national security. Foreign policy elites in Japan, Canada, Australia, and Taiwan have engaged in a process of consensus building to increase trust and confidence in the security area. As President Lee Teng-hui of the ROC has indicated, Asia Pacific collective security has no target enemy. It is to be expected that the common purpose of maintaining stability will help to create a sense of trust and lead to the harmonization of policies. Here, the spillover effects of economic cooperation will hopefully pave the way for a regional security forum. All of these require patience and hard work. Before this goal can be achieved, APEC and the ASEAN-Post-Ministerial Conference will continue to serve the Asia Pacific countries well.

NOTES

1. James Harris et al., "International Trends in Chinese Military Spending," in *China's Economic Dilemmas in the 1990s: The Problems of Reforms, Modernization and Interdependence*, Vol. II (Washington, D.C.: U.S. Government Printing Office, 1991), pp. 676–84.

2. *China Times* (Taipei), April 20, 1993; Desmond Ball, "China's Disturbing Arms Buildup," *The Independent Monthly*, February 23–24, 1993; "China's New Muscle," *Time*, April 12, 1993.

3. Leszek Buszynski, "ASEAN Security Dilemmas," *Survival* 34 (Winter 1992–93): 90–107; John W. Garver, "China's Push through the South China Sea: The Interaction of Bureaucratic and National Interests," *The China Quarterly*, December 1992, pp. 999–1028.

4. Nicholas Eberstadt, "Can the Two Koreas be One?" *Foreign Affairs* 72 (Winter 1992–93): 150–66; James Cotton, "North Korea's Nuclear Ambitions," in *Adelphi Paper*, No. 275 (London: International Institute for Strategic Studies, 1993), pp. 94–106.

5. Paul M. Evans, "Emerging Patterns in Asia-Pacific Security: The Search for a Regional Framework," in *Towards a New Pacific Order*, ed. Jawhar Hassan and Rohana Mahmood (Kuala Lumpur: Malaysian Institute of Strategic and International Studies, 1991), pp. 51–67; Amitav Acharya, "A New Regional Order in South-East Asia: ASEAN in the Post-Cold War Era," in *Adelphi Paper*, No. 279 (London: International Institute for Strategic Studies, 1993).

15

Prospects for Cooperative Security Arrangements

Harry Harding

Asia today is more prosperous and stable than at any other time in its history. The end of the Soviet-U.S. confrontation, the nearly simultaneous resolution of the Sino-Soviet dispute, and the growth of economic ties between former enemies have significantly reduced international tensions across the region. Nonetheless, security concerns have not disappeared from the agenda of the Asia Pacific region. Domestic political and economic problems, ethnic disputes that span international boundaries, controversies over borders on land and on sea, subregional disputes left over from the Cold War, increases in military procurements and deployments, and such transnational issues as emigration, drug trafficking, and environmental pollution — all of these could readily lead to an increase in tension and even the use of armed force. Moreover, the growing national power of some regional actors (such as Japan, China, and India), coupled with the retrenchment of the two superpowers (Russia and the United States), produces a fluid, and potentially imbalanced, international strategic environment.

In addressing this long agenda of security concerns, the governments of the Asia Pacific region view cooperative security mechanisms with both considerable skepticism and growing interest. There is increasing awareness that many unconventional threats to national security can be effectively addressed only through cooperative measures. There is also a growing realization that more conventional security

---

This chapter was originally prepared for the Workshop of the Cooperative Security Consortium, Snowmass, Colorado, August 3–7, 1992. An expanded version will appear in Janne E. Nolan, ed., *Global Engagement: Cooperation and Security in the 21st Century* (Washington, D.C.: The Brookings Institution, 1994).

problems can be dealt with more economically through cooperation than through unilateralism. Nonetheless, many governments remain suspicious that cooperative security could be detrimental to their national interests: that the process could be dominated by a few powerful states, that the proposals presented for consideration could be imbalanced, that the principles of transparency and verification associated with cooperative security could prove intrusive, and that the creation of new cooperative security mechanisms might weaken existing military capabilities and strategic alliances.

Yet, echoes of cooperative security can be seen in a surprising number of subregional disputes, ranging from the Korean peninsula to the Russo-Chinese border to the South China Sea. To be sure, in all these cases the current approaches to the management of conflict reflect both substantially more and considerably less than the standard definitions of cooperative security. They constitute less than full-fledged cooperative security regimes because few of them involve formal agreements to regulate the numbers and deployments of military forces. At the same time, they represent more than cooperative security in that they generally involve extensive economic interaction as well as military dialogue. Nonetheless, the core concept behind cooperative security — the idea that potential adversaries can cooperate to reduce tensions and prevent conflict — lies at the heart of the recent developments in several subregional disputes.

In addition, there is growing interest in the creation of some kind of regionwide dialogue on security matters. The former Soviet Union, Australia, Canada, and the Association of Southeast Asian Nations (ASEAN) have all presented proposals along these lines, and the Canadian and ASEAN initiatives have already resulted in preliminary discussions. Although other major powers, notably Japan, the United States, and China, were initially cautious about the idea, the political context has forced them to participate in the process so as to avoid exclusion. Moreover, both Tokyo and Washington have begun to display greater enthusiasm for multilateral security dialogue than was true in the past.

The most promising approach to cooperative security in the Asia Pacific region involves considerable diversity. The more collaborative attempts to manage or resolve subregional issues should be intensified. Unofficial dialogue among knowledgeable scholars and analysts should be launched on both a regional and a subregional basis. On the official level, it may be possible to start government-to-government exchanges on military strategies and force postures, as well as on the economic dimensions of regional security.

THE SECURITY ENVIRONMENT IN CONTEMPORARY ASIA

The improvement of relations among the major powers, and the moderation of several important subregional disputes, can be traced to the end of Asia's two cold wars: the confrontation between the former Soviet Union and the United States dating from the late 1940s and the conflict between Moscow and Peking that began in the late 1950s. This has permitted the improvement of a number of bilateral relationships that had been enmeshed in these superpower rivalries, notably those between India and China, China and Vietnam, Vietnam and ASEAN, and Mongolia and the United States. In addition, virtually every government in the region, with the possible exceptions of Burma and North Korea, has now established economic development as its central national priority. This encourages, in turn, a reduction of international tensions, so that each country can gain the greatest possible access to markets, capital, information, and technology from abroad. This economic imperative has been particularly evident in the recent improvements in the relations between China and South Korea, China and Mongolia, Taiwan and mainland China, and Taiwan and Vietnam, to name but a few.

However, the end of these two cold wars in Asia has not removed all the security challenges facing the region. Instead, the threats to regional stability and security, although in many ways less pressing than in the past, remain complex and daunting.

A number of Asian countries still face serious internal problems of political instability, economic stagnation, social inequality, and demographic explosion. In the past, these problems gave rise to political insurgencies, which, in turn, often attracted external support either to the government or to the opposition. Today, the prospects for sustained insurgencies are substantially reduced, except perhaps for the Philippines and Cambodia, and the chances for the internationalization of domestic unrest are even more remote.

Instead, domestic problems are presently arousing a different set of concerns. One is that internal collapse or decay could encourage emigration abroad, on a scale that could be destabilizing. The flow of Chinese to Hong Kong in the 1960s and 1970s, the flood of Vietnamese to China and Hong Kong in the 1970s and 1980s, and the extensive refugee camps along the Thai-Cambodian border are examples of this kind of problem. Many Asians fear that turmoil or collapse in China or North Korea could send waves of refugees flooding into Hong Kong, Taiwan, South Korea, and Japan for the remainder of the 1990s and into the next century.[1]

A second problem is the effect of internal disorder on a nation's military capabilities. The collapse of the Soviet Union illustrates several aspects of this problem, including the control over the nation's nuclear forces, the fate of its conventional forces, and the prospects of substantial arms exports by a successor government as a way of reducing the scale of the military and acquiring foreign exchange. All these problems would be raised by severe instability in China, and the collapse of North Korea would raise questions about the disposition of its conventional forces and the fate of its nuclear weapons program.

Asia is home to a number of ethnic disputes, many of which span international borders. In an era of growing nationalism, ethnic unrest could be an increasingly serious regional security problem. Examples include the presence of large numbers of overseas Chinese in Southeast Asia, the continued Vietnamese settlements in Cambodia, the links between Islamic minorities in western China and the newly independent Moslem states in central Asia, the presence of a sizable Tibetan exile community in India, the existence of substantial Mongol populations in China and Siberia, and the large Korean population in Japan. Tensions between any of these ethnic communities and their governments could readily take on international overtones if they produced substantial emigration or if they produced tensions between the two governments concerned.

East Asia is also plagued by a large number of territorial disputes, both on land and at sea. Vietnam, China, Taiwan, and most of the ASEAN countries have conflicting claims to the Paracel and Spratly islands in the South China Sea. There are similar disputes between China and Japan over the Diaoyutai or Senkaku islands and between Japan and Russia over the Northern Territories. On land, China's borders with Russia, the central Asian republics, India, and Vietnam are all either disputed or incompletely demarcated.

A variety of unconventional security issues are beginning to assume a place on the Asian agenda. Drug trafficking, particularly from Burma through southern China to markets abroad, is a growing concern. Piracy is again a growing problem in the shipping lanes of Southeast Asia, as is smuggling in the Taiwan Strait and in the waters around Hong Kong. Atmospheric pollution, particularly the acid rain produced by Chinese industry, is a growing issue in northeast Asia.[2] The depletion of fishing and the stocks of marine mammals in the northern Pacific is of concern to governments and environmental groups. More than ever before, the governments of the Asia Pacific region are adopting the concept first articulated by Japanese analysts in the 1970s that "comprehensive security" involves not just military threats but also threats to economic viability, to social order, and to environmental safety.[3]

Despite some promising developments in recent years, all of which will be discussed below, none of the three principal subregional crises that were the principal flashpoints of Asia's two cold wars — Korea, the Taiwan Strait, and Indochina — has been completely resolved. There remains a significant possibility of armed conflict between North and

South Korea and a residual chance of military confrontation between China and Taiwan. Although a collapse of the Cambodian peace accords is not likely under present circumstances to directly involve any outside powers, it could certainly give rise to renewed civil war inside Cambodia itself.

Finally, there are disturbing signs of an arms race in the Asia Pacific region. In large part, this arms race is being fueled by strategic uncertainties. The decline in the military deployments of both Russia and the United States and the closing of Russian bases in Vietnam and U.S. bases in the Philippines are creating a perceived strategic vacuum that other governments are tempted to fill. Many of those regional actors, in turn, are suspicious of each other's long-term intentions, with the growing military power of China, Japan, and India and the strategic potential of a reunified Korea the most frequently cited grounds for concern.

In addition, the arms race in the region is being triggered by other factors, including the growing financial resources available to most governments, the prominence of the military in many political systems, the obsolescence of the military equipment acquired in the 1960s and 1970s, especially in the light of the technological advances made since then, and the bribes and commissions paid to military procurement agents by arms exporters overseas.[4]

So far, the arms race in East Asia has remained conventional in nature. If, however, North Korea were deemed to have developed a nuclear weapons capability, it would be difficult to prevent the spread of nuclear weapons at least to South Korea and Japan and possibly to other parts of the region as well.

To a large degree, the nations of the Asia Pacific region are dealing with this new security agenda in the same way as they have in the past: through unilateral action and through alliances. China, Japan, India, Taiwan, and most of the ASEAN countries are, as already noted, modernizing their armed forces, in some cases through the acquisition of the capability to project force by air, at sea, and by missile. Alliances with the United States remain the cornerstone of the national security policies of Japan, South Korea, and Australia, and residual U.S. security guarantees play a large part in Taiwan's defense posture as well.

At the same time, many governments and policy analysts in the Asia Pacific region are showing increased interest in the development of cooperative security measures to address these issues. There is a growing awareness that most of the unconventional threats to national security (such as piracy, smuggling, emigration, drug trafficking, and pollution) can be dealt with effectively only through international cooperation. In addition, there is also an emerging realization that cooperative security mechanisms can provide less costly solutions to conventional security concerns (such as territorial and ethnic disputes, subregional conflicts, and regional arms races) than can either unilateralism or alliances. Calls for multilateral security dialogue, on both regional and subregional issues, are now regularly heard from virtually every capital in the Asia Pacific region.

Still, there remains considerable skepticism about the merit of cooperative security. Although the reservations vary from one country to another, they tend to fall into several broad categories.[5] First, and most basic, is the concern that the strategic situation in Asia is so complex and the level of interaction among various Asia Pacific nations is so low that cooperative security mechanisms similar to the Conference on Security and Cooperation in Europe (CSCE) would simply prove unfeasible. The Asian security environment has always been multipolar, rather than bipolar, greatly complicating the negotiation of arms control or other confidence-building measures. Several pairs of actors (Taiwan and mainland China, North and South Korea, Japan and North Korea, the United States and North Korea, and the United States and Vietnam) do not have diplomatic relations with one another, making sustained official dialogue difficult. There is virtually no experience with regionwide discussions of security issues, and official multilateral dialogue on economic issues has a history of but a few years.

Second, there have been apprehensions that a single major power might control the agenda of a cooperative security dialogue and, thus, achieve unfair advantage in any agreement that was produced. This was one reason why Soviet proposals for naval arms control and nuclear-free zones were dismissed out of hand by Japan and the United States in the mid-1980s. It also explains why, even today, any proposal for cooperative security issued by Japan, the United States, or China would encounter extreme skepticism from other nations and why the most successful initiatives have, thus far, come from such smaller powers or groupings as Australia, Canada, and ASEAN.

Third, there is an awareness that the implementation of cooperative security mechanisms inherently entails limitations on secrecy and sovereignty. Transparency is an accepted concept in pluralistic, democratic societies, but it is an unfamiliar and profoundly troubling idea for authoritarian systems. The level of trust among many Asian states, some of which have been engaged in open conflict or in intense military confrontation with each other in the past several decades, is so low that open discussion of security policies would be regarded as a significant threat to their own defense.[6] Moreover, the limitations on sovereignty that would be involved in addressing either conventional or unconventional security issues would be staunchly resisted by many states in the region, especially the remaining Leninist systems, which cling to nineteenth-century notions of absolute national authority and autonomy.

Fourth, effective cooperative security arrangements presuppose that the various participants are essentially status quo powers, which are, therefore, willing to renounce the development or use of offensive military power. In Asia, as noted above, at least two nations have irredentist claims — North Korea over South Korea and China over Taiwan, the South China Sea, and potentially Mongolia — that lead them to the deployment of projective force and, therefore, complicate the negotiation of any agreements on maintaining purely defensive armed forces.

Finally, several Asia Pacific governments, most notably the United States and Japan, have been persuaded that regional security problems can be addressed best through existing alliance mechanisms or through collective security arrangements such as the United Nations. At best, cooperative security proposals are irrelevant diversions, regarded by some skeptics as "solutions in search of a problem." At worst, those same proposals are viewed as dangerous distractions in that, if adopted, they might lead to the erosion of more proven mechanisms in favor of devices whose effectiveness has never been tested. Attitudes in the United States are gradually beginning to change, however, as the concept of cooperative security gains more proponents in the region and as U.S. policy makers seek ways of compensating for projected reductions in U.S. forces in the region.

Given these conflicting calculations, cooperative security in the Asia Pacific region has a checkered present and an uncertain future. Thus far, there has been some progress in applying concepts of cooperative security to subregional disputes and to territorial issues, but the development of regionwide cooperative security mechanisms has made only preliminary headway.[7]

APPLYING COOPERATIVE SECURITY TO SUBREGIONAL DISPUTES

Since 1990 the countries of the Asia Pacific region have made considerable progress in managing some of their longest-standing subregional issues and territorial disputes. In no case has a full-fledged cooperative security system been created, in the sense of formal agreements on levels and types of military deployments, nor has any of the controversies in question been fully and finally resolved. However, in each instance, the parties to the dispute have made some progress in reducing the chances of armed conflict through a combination of military redeployments, diplomatic negotiation, and economic cooperation. In short, in these subregional disputes, cooperative security arrangements have represented one piece of a partial solution.

Cambodia

For nearly a decade, the most recent confrontation in Indochina — the one caused by Vietnam's intervention in Cambodia in 1978 — was conducted according to the classic principles of the balance of power. In opposition to the Vietnamese action there formed a multinational coalition, centering on China and the ASEAN states, that sought to force Hanoi to withdraw. China applied military force directly and, along with the members of ASEAN, tried to isolate Vietnam diplomatically and economically and provided material and military assistance to the anti-Vietnamese Cambodian resistance.

Over time, these diplomatic and military pressures laid the groundwork for a negotiated settlement.[8] Successive concessions by Moscow, Hanoi, and Peking made it possible for the five permanent members of the UN Security Council to reach an agreement on Cambodia, which was embodied in the Paris Accords of October 1991. That agreement called for a cease-fire, the creation of a provisional government under UN supervision, and then elections for a new national assembly. Unfortunately, the Khmer Rouge refused to cooperate with the military demobilization or participate in the elections. This raises the possibility that they may also try to obstruct the process of forming an effective national government.

Even if the Paris Accords should collapse, however, the likelihood that the outside powers would reenter in the Cambodian conflict is reasonably small. Vietnam is preoccupied with its domestic economic and political problems and seems reluctant to reactivate a confrontation with China, ASEAN, or the United States. For its part, China seems willing to remain aloof from the Cambodian problem as long as Vietnam stays disengaged. In this sense, the Cambodian settlement represents the operation of a subregional concert of powers, whose members have decided to end their own competition over Cambodia and to broker a political settlement. Even if that concert of powers proves unable fully to resolve the Cambodian dispute, it may well be able to prevent any renewed further internationalization of the issue.

Korea

A similar process is at work on the Korean peninsula, albeit with far more uncertain results. As in Cambodia, the turning point was the emergence of an informal concert of regional powers, united in their desire to avoid the resumption of military hostilities in Korea. Moreover, each participant in the concert of powers began to expand its network of diplomatic and, in some cases, economic contacts on the Korean peninsula. The former Soviet Union and China have established diplomatic relations with Seoul, and the United States and Japan have cautiously expanded their diplomatic dialogue with Pyongyang.

With the emergence of a concert of powers interested in preventing the renewal of armed conflict, the two Korean governments began to expand their bilateral relations. In 1990, North and South Korea inaugurated a series of talks at the prime ministerial level, which led to limited cultural, economic, and humanitarian exchanges. In 1991, both

Koreas agreed to enter the UN as separate and equal political entities. At the end of the same year, North and South Korea signed an agreement to avoid conflict and to expand bilateral relations. In 1992, North Korea finally accepted international safeguards of its nuclear program once the United States had announced the withdrawal of its tactical nuclear weapons from South Korea.

Then, in 1993, the emergence of a cooperative security regime on the Korean peninsula came close to collapse. Concerned that its production of plutonium was about to be discovered, North Korea refused further inspections of its nuclear facilities and announced its withdrawal from the Nonproliferation Treaty. As of this writing, it remains uncertain whether the other regional powers can persuade North Korea to resume active participation in the nuclear nonproliferation regime and whether Pyongyang's nuclear weapons program can be placed under credible international safeguards. If not, South Korea and the United States will seek international economic sanctions against North Korea through the UN. In such a case, a cooperative security process incorporating Pyongyang will have been replaced by a collective security arrangement against it.

If the nuclear issue can be resolved, however, the most promising directions for cooperative security arrangements on the Korean peninsula are reasonably clear. The next step would be to construct a fuller network of diplomatic, cultural, and economic ties between Pyongyang and the West, possibly including the creation of the proposed Tumen River development zone spanning portions of North Korea, China, and Russia. Then, the two Koreas could implement traditional confidence-building measures along the armistice line, including the true demilitarization of the demilitarized zone, advance notification of troop rotations and exercises, and constraints on provocative deployments and maneuvers. Finally, the two sides could seek to negotiate a reduction in the level of their conventional forces and the redesign of their military establishments along purely defensive lines. These bilateral arrangements should be supplemented by restraints on the external supply of advanced conventional weapons to both North and South Korea.[9] Unfortunately, none of these agreements can be readily reached or implemented without significant economic reform in North Korea and some preliminary liberalization of its political system.

The Sino-Russian Border

Perhaps the most promising, although still incomplete, set of cooperative security arrangements in the Asia Pacific region are those being put in place along the Sino-Russian frontier. The normalization of relations between Moscow and Peking also has enabled their bilateral border negotiations, conducted fitfully and inconclusively since the 1960s, finally to achieve some success. Alongside the negotiations concerning the demarcation of the border, Chinese and Russian officials have been conducting discussions, apparently as yet inconclusive, of military confidence-building measures between their two countries. The negotiations are apparently aimed at reducing force levels in Siberia and northern China, demilitarizing the frontier, and allowing for greater transparency in military deployments and exercises.

These are all promising initiatives that need to be continued and elaborated. The construction of a fuller cooperative security regime would involve resolving the remaining differences between China and Russia on their eastern border, conducting successful negotiations between China and the Central Asian republics over the western section of the former Sino-Soviet frontier, and concluding the military confidence-building measures outlined above. Economic cooperation between China and the Central Asian republics, Mongolia, and Siberia should be expanded, in part by improving the transportation and communications facilities crossing the relevant frontiers. In addition, some kind of security guarantees will have to be constructed for Mongolia, which fears Chinese irredentism but can no longer rely upon Russian protection.

The Taiwan Strait

Along with the Korean peninsula, the Taiwan Strait is one of the other subregional disputes that contemporary Asia has inherited from the original Cold War between the United States and the former Soviet bloc. Here, the breakthrough came from the parties directly involved. Beginning in the late 1970s, mainland China opened its door to trade and investment with the outside world and made it clear that it welcomed economic relations with Taiwan. Then, starting in the mid-1980s, Taiwan began to relax its ban on commercial and cultural contacts with the mainland. As a result, travel across the Taiwan Strait has soared, trade has boomed, and Taiwanese investment in the mainland has increased dramatically. Tensions between Taiwan and the mainland are arguably at their lowest point since the Communist seizure of power in 1949.

Nonetheless, several knotty problems require further attention. The Taiwan government still prohibits direct communication or transportation links with the mainland. Many members of Taiwan's opposition party advocate formal independence from the mainland. As a result, Peking is refusing to renounce the use of force against Taiwan and is developing the capability to apply military pressure against the island. The threat of mainland attack, in turn, is leading Taiwan to purchase advanced aircraft and naval vessels from abroad. Accordingly, a military confrontation between Taiwan and the mainland still cannot be ruled out.

Several steps would help consolidate and extend the improvements in the relations between Taiwan and the mainland. Because neither reunification nor independence is feasible in the foreseeable future, the best approach for the middle run is to negotiate a modus vivendi between the two sides, involving concessions by both Peking and Taipei. The mainland should renounce the use of force against Taiwan, except in response to a unilateral declaration of independence by the Taiwanese government. It should also welcome Taiwan's membership in a broader range of international organizations. Although Peking presently does not accept dual membership in the United Nations, or dual recognition by foreign governments, the experiences of Korea and Germany show that such policies are not incompatible with ultimate reunification. To reciprocate, Taipei should also renounce any unilateral declaration of independence, except perhaps in response to a military assault by the mainland. It should relax its restrictions on commercial, cultural, and political relations with the People's Republic, opening direct communications and transportation links across the Taiwan Strait and welcoming visitors and investment from the mainland.

Given the mainland's insistence on maintaining the military capabilities to deter a unilateral declaration of independence, it will be extremely difficult for the two sides to develop the customary military confidence-building measures. However, it might be feasible to construct a multilateral regime reducing the flow of arms to the two sides, particularly those that would give the People's Republic an extensive projection capability. A first step would be to discourage further sales of Russian attack aircraft to Peking, in exchange for restraints on the sale of advanced Western fighters to Taiwan. Given the widespread nervousness across the region about China's growing military capability, such a regime would have beneficial consequences extending far beyond the Taiwan Strait.

The South China Sea

Finally, a fifth subregional dispute to which the principles of cooperative security might be applied is the controversy over the two principal island groups of the South China Sea: the Paracels, which are claimed by both China and Vietnam and the Spratlys, all of which are claimed by China (including Taiwan) and Vietnam and parts of which are claimed by the Philippines, Malaysia, and Brunei. Although small and barren in themselves, the islands are important because they sit along important sea lanes of communication and rest atop undeveloped petroleum and gas reserves. China and Vietnam engaged in two military clashes over the islands in 1974 and 1988.

Since 1990, there have been annual multilateral workshops on the South China Sea. These informal meetings have recommended that the interested governments pursue their claims through negotiation rather than force and that they adopt cooperative programs on such problems as piracy, environmental protection, and navigational safety. They have also explored the idea that, pending the resolution of the competing claims to sovereignty, there be joint exploration and development of the area's seabed resources.

The concept of joint development is a valuable one that should be vigorously pursued. At a minimum, it could involve cooperative, government-to-government attempts to exploit the seabed resources in the South China Sea. However, more ambitious formulas have also been put forward that might supplement joint development with demilitarization or provide for joint development through the creation of a multilateral authority rather than through state-to-state agreements.[10]

The concept of joint development might also be applied to two other cases in the Asia Pacific region in which sovereignty over islands is in dispute. One is the Senkaku, or Diaoyutai, islands, off the northeast corner of Taiwan, which are claimed by both China (including Taiwan) and Japan. These islands have already been the subject of several incidents in which Chinese naval vessels fired warning shots at Japanese cargo ships passing by.[11] The other is the four islands off Hokkaido, known as the Northern Territories, which are occupied by Russia but claimed by both Moscow and Tokyo. The creation of a democratic system and the rise of nationalism in Russia make it more difficult to envision the compromise suggested in the past, in which Russia would gain sovereignty over two of the islands and Japan would take over the rest. Instead, joint development might be a more feasible approach to the issue in the short and middle term.

APPLYING COOPERATIVE SECURITY TO THE REGION AS A WHOLE

In addition to these efforts to manage or resolve subregional security challenges, there has also been increasing interest in applying concepts of cooperative security to the Asia Pacific region as a whole. At first, this resulted from concern about the danger of a Soviet-U.S. conventional and nuclear arms race in the last Cold War era. More recently, it has reflected apprehensions about an even wider arms buildup, affecting larger numbers of regional and subregional actors. In addition, the growing interest in cooperative security is also the consequence of the emergence of nonconventional threats to peace and stability, including migration, drug trafficking, and environmental pollution.

As noted above, the application of cooperative security principles to subregional disputes has been an incomplete and often halting process. This has been even more true in the regional arena. Early proposals, involving formal arms control negotiations or official regionwide discussions of security issues, failed to attract much support. More recent proposals, however, have suggested more informal confidence-building measures and have envisioned several arenas of dialogue with different sets of participants, rather than a single regional forum incorporating everyone. This second round of proposals is, therefore, proving more productive.

The first official proposals for cooperative security arrangements in the Asia Pacific region were presented in the late 1980s, first by the Soviet Union and then by Australia. The Soviet proposals, articulated by Mikhail Gorbachev between 1986 and 1989 in speeches in Vladivostok, at the United Nations, and in Peking, involved a potpourri of formal arms control and confidence-building measures, including a freeze of naval forces in the western Pacific, limitations on air and naval forces around the Korean peninsula, nuclear-free zones for Korea and for the Indian Ocean, agreements to prevent incidents at sea and in the air, and various forms of security dialogue among major powers in the Asia Pacific region.[12]

The last element in the Soviet package was also endorsed, albeit implicitly, by Australia. In 1986, Gorbachev proposed a regionwide meeting on security matters, likening it to the Helsinki process in Europe. A few years later, in 1990, the Australian foreign minister called for a similar kind of official multilateral negotiation, also comparing it to the CSCE. The use of such similes led this specific concept to be described as a Conference on Security and Cooperation in Asia.

These early Soviet and Australian proposals were viewed with considerable disfavor by many Asia Pacific governments, particularly Japan and the United States. The proposals for naval arms control were dismissed out of hand. The idea of a Conference on Security and Cooperation in Asia was derided as a naive attempt to apply ideas from Europe, where their validity had not yet been demonstrated, to a totally different strategic environment. It was argued that the Asia Pacific region was bigger, more diverse, and more complex than Europe and that its member nations were much less experienced in multilateral negotiations on security questions. As a result, it was predicted that cooperative security measures would be difficult to negotiate successfully. A regionwide dialogue aimed at formulating such measures would, therefore, be doomed to failure.

Discussions of cooperative security are, therefore, increasingly focusing on a second round of proposals, put forward in 1990–91 by Canada and ASEAN, that significantly modified the notion of a Helsinki-style dialogue on Asia. The Canadian government advocated a process that would be smaller in scale and more informal in approach. Ottawa launched a North Pacific Cooperative Security Dialogue (NPCSD), focusing not on the region as a whole but on the problems of the north Pacific. The formal participants in the dialogue were limited to Canada, the United States, Japan, the two Koreas, China, Russia, and, later, Mongolia. Moreover, the NPCSD emphasized unofficial discussions among scholars and policy analysts, with government officials playing subordinate roles. By 1993, however, waning support from the Canadian government had forced the end of the NPCSD as a multilateral dialogue.

In 1991, ASEAN presented the most promising proposal yet for an official regional security dialogue. It proposed that its annual post-ministerial conference, which had previously been restricted to economic issues, be enlarged to include security questions. It suggested that this security dialogue begin with ASEAN and its seven dialogue partners (the United States, Canada, Japan, Australia, New Zealand, South Korea, and the European Community) but that it also be broadened to include Russia, China, Vietnam, and North Korea. The following year, Indonesia also proposed that military personnel be included in this post-ministerial security dialogue.[13]

Although both Japan and the United States had reservations about the ASEAN proposal, its sponsorship made it difficult to reject out of hand. Both Tokyo and Washington agreed to send official representatives to the preliminary workshops designed to discuss and elaborate on the concept. They also assented to the extension of the post-ministerial conferences to include security matters. After two preliminary meetings in 1990, the parties agreed to form an ASEAN Regional Forum on security, with an initial session in 1994.

The fate of a regionwide multilateral security dialogue will depend on the attitude of the major powers. Russia, as already noted, has always been enthusiastic, and the United States is considerably more sympathetic to the concept of cooperative security under the Clinton administration than it was in the past. Previously, U.S. officials portrayed the U.S. bilateral alliances as the central element in the region's security architecture and likened them to the spokes of an Oriental fan centering on Washington. Toward the end of the Bush administration, however, they were willing to envision some kind of multilateral security arrangement, which they portrayed as the fabric that stretches across the ribs of the fan, as a way of permitting the United States to withdraw military forces from the Asia Pacific without destabilizing the region.[14] Then, during his confirmation hearings as President Clinton's nominee as Assistant Secretary of State for East Asian and Pacific Affairs, Winston Lord stated that the new U.S. administration would not only participate enthusiastically in the security dialogue organized by ASEAN but also was interested in creating a parallel dialogue on security issues in Northeast Asia.

Tokyo has also taken a more supportive approach toward multilateral security dialogue. It has been willing to enlarge the agenda of the ASEAN post-ministerial conferences to cover security issues, as long as the process remains as informal and flexible as possible. It also endorses the creation of additional forums to discuss subregional problems or specific functional issues.

Of the four major powers, therefore, China is the most reserved about the concept of cooperative security. To be sure, Chinese policy analysts are willing to participate in unofficial conferences on security matters, and Peking has played an active part in official discussions of such subregional issues as Cambodia, Korea, the Sino-Russian border, and the South China Sea. On regionwide issues, however, China appears more comfortable with a series of bilateral conversations than with a multilateral dialogue, because it fears that it would become the principal target of demands for transparency on military doctrines and deployments.

Thus, although there is more interest in regionwide cooperative security arrangements than before, progress remains slow. Few official forums have been established, and those that have been inaugurated have produced few concrete results. On balance, the application of cooperative security to subregional issues has been more successful than its application to the Asia Pacific region as a whole.

PROSPECTS AND RECOMMENDATIONS

At this point, the application of cooperative security principles to the Asia Pacific region will necessarily entail a considerable degree of diversity, creating what several policy analysts have variously called a "multilayered" or a "multifaceted" approach. Such an approach would, in fact, closely parallel the region's experience in developing multilateral economic organizations. That process, which began in the late 1960s, involved several different tracks: the creation of subregional organizations, such as ASEAN and the South Pacific Forum; the formation of unofficial dialogues of academics and businesspeople through the Pacific Trade and Development Conference and the Pacific Basin Economic Council; the subsequent development of organizations such as the Pacific Economic Cooperation Council (PECC) in which officials could participate in their private capacities; and, finally, the creation of the Asia Pacific Economic Cooperation (APEC) conference as an official multilateral forum.

In the case of security issues, the most feasible multifaceted approach would comprise three elements:

First, the nations of the region should continue to address subregional issues, along the lines suggested above. This involves the full implementation of the Paris Accords on Cambodia, the implementation of confidence-building measures in Korea, full resolution of the disputes involving the Sino-Soviet border and the reduction and redeployment of forces along it, the negotiation of a formal modus vivendi in the Taiwan Strait, and the adoption of the principle of joint development of disputed island territories in the western Pacific. The Asian experience suggests that such issues can be managed most effectively when there are economic incentives for the parties directly involved to cooperate with each other. The key to addressing these subregional disputes, in short, is to provide mechanisms for economic development as well as for cooperative security.

Second, the time has come to organize a more formal, but still unofficial, dialogue on regionwide security issues. A number of such forums have been created over the past several years, but none has yet gained the status that Pacific Basin Economic Council, Pacific Trade and Development Conference, or the PECC have gained in the economic sphere. One that seems to be gaining such recognition is the Council for Security Cooperation in the Asia Pacific (CSCAP), created in Kuala Lumpur in June 1993. Like PECC, CSCAP will be composed of national committees across the region, including not only scholars and policy analysts but also government officials participating in their private capacities. This permits a franker and more tentative discussion of sensitive issues than is possible in an official setting.

CSCAP can discuss the full range of security problems confronting the Asia Pacific region. It can help identify the most feasible ways of continuing the progress toward managing subregional disputes. It can discuss nonconventional security threats and recommend the most appropriate forums for addressing them. It can begin to formulate the norms that could prevent arms races by regulating national military deployments. It can also consider some of the most central — but also the most sensitive — issues in Asia Pacific security, including ways of helping Japan come to terms with its past. Harmonizing Chinese ambitions with those of its neighbors, and coping with the implications of the eventual unification of Korea.

Finally, it should also be possible to build a security dialogue on an official level in settings such as the ASEAN Regional Forum, but the topic for such a dialogue must be chosen with care. One often-mentioned candidate, naval arms control, is highly sensitive for a number of countries in the region, and it should not be the opening item on the agenda. Other potential issues, such as the development of rules to prevent conventional weapons proliferation and environmental pollution, must be dealt with primarily on a global level.

Instead, regionwide security dialogue should focus on the emerging arms race in the region. The process could start with efforts to increase transparency, by exchanging information on national security strategies, defense budgets, and military deployments, in the hope that each nation can reassure its neighbors of its capabilities and intentions. This could then lead to a consideration of multilateral norms to govern those deployments, building on the prior work done at the unofficial level. The ultimate purpose of the dialogue should be to construct what Geoffrey Wiseman has called a "defensive intent regime," in which each country's military forces are clearly configured and deployed for defensive purposes and in which each nation's military budget can, therefore, be limited.[15]

In addition to the most promising topic, it is also necessary to consider the most useful format for such a dialogue. The best approach at this point is to work simultaneously in three venues, each of which has its own advantages and shortcomings:

The ASEAN Regional Forum will have particular credibility in addressing security problems in Southeast Asia but will be less effective in considering other parts of the region. It should be expanded to include India, whose military deployments have a direct impact on the balance of power in Southeast Asia.

A comparable forum should be created to discuss security issues in Northeast Asia, as has recently been proposed by both U.S. and South Korean officials. A principal focus of these discussions should be the international dimension of security on the Korean peninsula. Other topics could include the Russo-Japanese dispute over the Northern Territories and the security of Mongolia. The four major regional powers — Russia, China, Japan, and the United States — should participate in these discussions, as should the two Koreas. Mongolia and Canada should also be considered for membership.

Finally, APEC could usefully devote secondary attention to security issues, even as it continues to focus primarily on economic matters. APEC has the advantage of being the only official regional forum to include both Taiwan and mainland China, although it simultaneously suffers from the absence of Russia, Mongolia, and Vietnam. APEC would be a particularly appropriate venue for considering the intersection of economic and security questions, including the use of economic sanctions to enforce multilateral nonproliferation regimes and the solution of the unconventional security problems most closely linked to economics, such as smuggling, piracy, migration, and environmental pollution.

Eventually, it may be feasible to create a single regionwide security organization, analogous to the CSCE in Europe. For the foreseeable future, however, it is more practical to build a reasonable number of overlapping and reinforcing forums, each allowing a different set of actors to address a distinctive set of issues.

NOTES

1. One of the first attempts at an objective assessment of this problem can be found in Takashi Sugimoto, "Mass Migration Pressures in China," Working Paper No. 5, Toronto, North Pacific Cooperative Security Dialogue, York University, 1992.

2. Vaclav Smil, "Potential Environmental Conflicts Involving Countries of the North Pacific," Working Paper No. 4, Toronto, North Pacific Cooperative Security Dialogue, York University, 1992.

3. On comprehensive security, see Robert W. Barnett, *Beyond War: Japan's Concept of Comprehensive National Security* (Washington, D.C.: Pergamon-Brassey, 1984).

4. The growing arms imports by many Asian nations are described and analyzed in Gerald Segal, "Managing New Arms Races in the Asia/Pacific," *Washington Quarterly* 15 (Summer 1992): 83–101; Andrew Mack, "Arms Proliferation in the Asia-Pacific: Causes and Prospects for Control," paper presented to the Workshop on Conventional Arms Proliferation in the 1990s, sponsored by the World Peace Foundation, Washington, D.C., July 1992. The role of corruption in Thai military procurements is described in the *Far Eastern Economic Review*, July 2, 1992, p. 13.

5. Many of the reservations are summarized in Richard Fisher, "Why Asia Is Not Ready for Arms Control," Asian Studies Center Backgrounder No. 113 (Washington, D.C.: The Heritage Foundation, 1991).

6. As Andrew Mack has pointed out, "Transparency — military openness — is not the norm in the region. No Southeast Asian state, for example, publishes defense 'White Papers'; none publish the sort of lengthy analyses of various aspects of defense policy which are commonplace in European states, in the US and in Australia." Mack, "Arms Proliferation in the Asia-Pacific," p. 14.

7. For a useful overview of the confidence- and security-building measures that have been adopted or proposed in the Asia Pacific region, see Douglas M. Johnston, "Anticipating Instability in the Asia-Pacific Region," *Washington Quarterly* 15 (Summer 1992): 103–12.

8. This discussion of the Cambodian peace process is based on Robert S. Ross, "China and the Cambodian Peace Process: The Value of Coercive Diplomacy," *Asian Survey* 31 (December 1991): 1170–85; Michael Leifer, "Power-Sharing and Peacemaking in Cambodia?" *SAIS Review* 12 (Winter-Spring 1992): 139–53.

9. See Tong Whan Park, "Issues of Arms Control between the Two Koreas," *Asian Survey* 32 (April 1992): 350–65; Dong-Won Lim, "An Urgent Need for Arms Control on the Korean Peninsula: A Framework for Implementation," *Korean Journal of Defense Analysis* 3 (Summer 1991): 49–66.

10. These alternative formulas are explored in Huyng-Yu Chen, "The Prospects for Joint Development in the South China Sea," *Issues and Studies* (Taipei) 27 (December 1991): 112–25. Chen pessimistically concludes, however, that "the case of the South China Sea is just too complicated for any program of joint development to be realized in the near future."

11. See Reuter News Service, July 23, 1992.

12. Some of the best reviews of cooperative security proposals for the Asia Pacific region have been prepared by officials in the Canadian government. See, for example, Stewart Henderson, "Canada and Asia Pacific Security: The North Pacific Cooperative Security Dialogue, Recent Trends," Working Paper No. 1, (Toronto, North Pacific Cooperative Security Dialogue, York University, January 1992); Peggy Mason, "Asia Pacific Security Forums: Rationale and Options: Canadian Views," paper presented to the Sixth Asia Pacific Roundtable, Kuala Lumpur, June 1992.

13. For the ASEAN proposal, see Henderson, "Canada and Asia Pacific Security," pp. 11–14; for the Indonesian elaboration, see *Far Eastern Economic Review*, May 14, 1992, p. 20.

14. This connection between cooperative security and U.S. force reductions was made explicit in James R. Winnefeld, Jonathan D. Pollack, Kevin N. Lewis, Lynn D. Pullen, John Y. Schrader, and Michael D. Swaine, *A New Strategy and Fewer Forces: The Pacific Dimension* (Santa Monica, Calif.: Rand Corporation, 1992).

15. Geoffrey Wiseman, "Common Security in the Asia-Pacific Region," *The Pacific Review* 5 (1992): 42–59.

16

From Confrontation to Cooperation in Southeast Asia: Lessons and Prospects

Donald K. Emmerson

Indonesian President Sukarno enjoyed mixing words from different languages. In 1964 he combined Indonesian with Italian to name that year *Tahun Vivere Pericoloso*, "The Year of Living Dangerously."

He had a point. In 1964, inside Indonesia, inflation soared by 900 percent above one official exchange rate while living standards in parts of rural Java and Bali fell to starvation levels. Abroad, Sukarno campaigned to "crush Malaysia" — the independent country whose creation in 1963 out of formerly British Malaya, Singapore, Sabah, and Sarawak he deemed an imperialist intrigue against Indonesia. Incursions by Jakarta's forces into Sabah and Sarawak were augmented in 1964 with coastal landings and parachute drops of several hundred Indonesian guerrillas into peninsular Malaya. Bombs set by Indonesian saboteurs exploded in Singapore and the Malayan city of Malacca.[1]

Malaysia retaliated against Sukarno's embargo on Indonesian trade with Malaysia by banning all sea and air traffic from Malaysia to Indonesia. Increased outlays for defense against Sukarno's government in Jakarta obliged Malaysian authorities in Kuala Lumpur to scale down their five-year development plan; U.S. aid to Indonesia effectively ceased while Soviet aid rose; and Sukarno responded to Malaysia's election to a seat on the Security Council by threatening to withdraw from the United Nations. (In 1965 Indonesia would become the first UN member ever to take this step.)

In 1964 an Association of Southeast Asia (ASA) did exist, but it grouped only three of the ten territorial units — seven countries, two

Whatever errors or infelicities may mar this chapter, they are no fault of Chandran Jeshurun or Michael Malley, for whose helpful comments on an earlier draft I am most grateful.

de facto states, and one colony in the region at that time.[2] Powerless to mediate the conflict between Jakarta and Kuala Lumpur, ASA would soon atrophy out of existence. Nor was the also doomed Southeast Asia Treaty Organization (SEATO), whose eight full participants included only two in Southeast Asia (the Philippines and Thailand), about to restore security.[3] SEATO members, above all the United States, were too busy losing the war against nationalistic communism then raging in South Vietnam, where in 1964 the Viet Cong substantially enlarged their "liberated zones" while Saigon lurched from coup to coup in the wake of the assassination of President Ngo Dinh Diem.

In 1964 the United States was being drawn deeper into the Indochina quagmire. The Gulf of Tonkin incident escalated into the first direct U.S. attack on North Vietnam. U.S. aircraft also bombed and strafed Communist positions in Laos. Over the course of the year the size of the U.S. military presence in South Vietnam grew by a fifth. Elsewhere in the region, mobs attacked U.S. diplomatic offices in Cambodia and Indonesia, while in the Philippines, demonstrators furious over the killing of two of their countrymen by guards at local U.S. military bases torched the U.S. ambassador in effigy.

In other news from Southeast Asia in 1964, despite an agreement between Kuala Lumpur and Manila to open consulates in each other's countries, Philippine authorities refused to extend full diplomatic recognition to Malaysia pending settlement of the Philippine claim to Sabah. Racist rioting in Singapore took more than 30 lives. In Indonesia, which in 1964 had the largest nonruling Communist Party in the world, Sukarno for the first time appointed a Communist to his cabinet. Meanwhile, the militant Maoist wing of the Vietnamese Communist Party was reported to be gaining influence in Hanoi. (Two years later, the Great Proletarian Cultural Revolution would convulse China, threatening repercussions in parts of Southeast Asia and presaging Pol Pot's brutally antibourgeois purges in Cambodia in 1975–78.)

In 1993 a time traveler arriving in Southeast Asia on stop from 1964 would have been in for quite a shock. Perhaps most startling would have been the economic contrast. While global per capita gross national product (GNP) rose a modest average 1.5 percent annually in 1965–90, four of the ten countries in Southeast Asia did considerably better: Malaysia grew 4.0 percent; Thailand, 4.4 percent; Indonesia, 4.5 percent; and Singapore, 6.5 percent. The Philippines, at 1.3 percent, lagged the world average. Comparable figures are unavailable for the countries that were set on a "socialist" path in 1964 — Burma, Cambodia, Laos, and North (later plus South) Vietnam, but all four clearly fared worse than most, if not all, of their capitalist counterparts in the region.[4]

Wishfully thinking observers on the left, who in the 1960s extrapolated the revolutionary tide in Southeast Asia into a general collapse of capitalism and a vindication of the power of socialism to raise production and reduce poverty, turned out to be mistaken on both counts. In 1990, even on a Human Development Index that combines adjusted real gross domestic product (GDP) with life expectancy and educational achievement to yield a more welfare-focused standard of comparison — social development, not just economic growth — all four "socialist" countries underperformed all six "capitalist" ones.[5]

Alongside this evidence of rising regional prosperity, a time traveler direct from 1964 would have been amazed, too, by the reduction of regional conflict and the rise of regional cooperation. In all likelihood the year 1993 in Southeast Asia would have seemed to him or her a *Tahun Vivere Securo*, or "Year of Living Safely," compared with conditions three decades before.

Interstate tensions in 1993 did not begin to approach the intensity of the Indonesian-Malaysian quarrel, let alone the North-South Vietnamese war. Both confrontations had long since disappeared, as had the meddling by Indonesia in Bruneian affairs. Electoral and constitutional politics had, at least temporarily, replaced civil war in Cambodia, partly due to the willingness of Vietnam to cooperate with its non-Communist neighbors. Hanoi's leaders had even signed a treaty of amity and cooperation with their old Cold War antagonists in Southeast Asia, including the erstwhile "front-line state" against once-feared Vietnamese expansion, Thailand.

In 1993 this combination of national development and regional stability was unique in the so-called former Third World. Nowhere else, not in Northeast or South Asia, not in Africa or Latin America, and certainly not in the Middle East or the Balkans, were economic growth and interstate security — welfare and peace — as evident as they had become in most of Southeast Asia.

To be sure, in 1993 the Southeast Asian region was still split between an upper tier of five relatively wealthy or dynamic economies — Brunei, Indonesia, Malaysia, Singapore, and Thailand — and a laggard set of five comparatively poor and straitened ones — Burma, Cambodia, Laos, the Philippines, and Vietnam. What prosperity there was had not been evenly distributed.

For the future of Southeast Asia, however, at least as important as this bifurcation was the trend toward the economic opening of Indochina to its more dynamic neighbors. Even if the Philippine economy were to stay in the doldrums — in 1992 it registered zero growth[6] — and Burma were to retain its lowly status as a least developed country, there was in 1993 a good chance that Vietnam, for one, could joint the queue behind Malaysia, Thailand, and Indonesia to become a newly industrialized economy after the example of South Korea, Taiwan, Hong Kong, and, locally, Singapore. If that were to happen, the economies of Cambodia and Laos, thanks to their location between booming Thailand and recovering Vietnam, might be expected to expand as well.

Frustrated by their failure to win the Vietnam war, U.S. policy makers occasionally rationalized their stand against communism in Indochina as having created a protective shield behind which the capitalist states of Southeast Asia could fashion their prosperity and security. Had Hanoi's troops quickly reunified Vietnam without facing U.S.-backed resistance, greater pressure might well have been exerted on the rest of the region to propitiate and imitate socialist revolution as the wave of the future. Even so, if China's reverse course away from Maoism in the mid-to-late-1970s had occurred on schedule, local experiments in radical agrarianism would have lost a major beacon. As for Cambodia, the slaughterhouse socialism practiced there by Pol Pot in the mid-1970s was self-injurious enough to allow one to wonder how much longer such a regime could have lasted even if Vietnam had chosen not to destroy it by invasion in 1978–79.[7]

Above all, the reversal of Southeast Asia's seemingly leftist fortunes in 1964 must be attributed not to U.S. policy but rather to internal events in Indonesia in 1965–66 over which Washington had little control. The left-wing conspirators who kidnapped and killed six generals in Jakarta on the morning of October 1, 1965, set the stage for General Suharto to blame the murders on the Indonesian Communist Party. On these grounds, he proceeded in effect to exterminate communism in Indonesia while slewing the country 180 degrees: from Sukarno's romantic leftism, indifference to economics, anti-Western rhetoric, and excoriation of Malaysia toward market-sensitive economic policies, cooperation with neighbors, and active solicitation of Western and Japanese assistance and investment on generous terms for the sake of economic growth. Some observers have tried to portray the assassinations of October 1, 1965, as a cynical machination by the CIA to murder (or permit the murder of) six of its Indonesian army friends in order to provoke an anti-Communist backlash. But the crucial initial aboutface in Jakarta was driven by internal events that Washington had neither the sophistication nor the influence to mastermind. Both the anticapitalist left and the anti-Communist right in the United States have had an interest in magnifying U.S. responsibility for reversing Indonesian history, and both are mistaken.

The Indonesian turnaround had far-reaching repercussions. Without it, Jakarta would not have reconciled with its neighbors in 1965–66 or been so willing to join with Malaysia, the Philippines, Singapore, and Thailand to form the Association of Southeast Asian Nations (ASEAN) in 1967. (By 1984, with the independence and addition of Brunei, ASEAN grouped six of the region's ten countries.) Although few realized it at the time, the new body would become the single most successful indigenous organization of developing countries for regional cooperation and stability in the world.

In its early years, ASEAN was underestimated from opposite directions. Critics from the left were inclined to dismiss it as another Western scheme to stem revolution — SEATO with a local face. However, ASEAN's organizers were neither kowtowing to nor bandwagoning the West. They were preparing for the prospect of Western military disengagement. Already in London there was talk of repatriating British forces from "east of Suez." (The decision to do so would be announced in 1968.) If the United States lost its war in Vietnam and withdrew from Indochina, neighboring dominoes would be left to their fate. (In 1969 on Guam, U.S. President Richard Nixon would make an Asia-for-Asians speech that seemed to rationalize that prospect.) ASEAN was an effort by the dominoes themselves to remain erect.

Meanwhile, ASEAN's birth was skeptically received in a different quarter for a different reason. Observers who, far from rejecting Western models, championed them, looked at the European Economic Community and found ASEAN ineffective by comparison, but the comparison was unfair. Precisely because the obstacles to regional economic, let alone political, cooperation were so much greater in Southeast Asia than in western Europe, ASEAN could not and did not expect to become a European Economic Community. The association succeeded in part because its founders did not rush into premature schemes for economic integration. When the Bangkok Declaration creating ASEAN was signed in 1967, the Treaty of Rome had existed for a decade and the Schuman Plan to pool European coal and steel was six years older still.

Geographically, demographically, religiously, racially, linguistically, politically, the members of ASEAN are stunningly diverse. Indonesia, the Philippines, and Singapore are mega-, meso-, and micro-archipelagoes, respectively. Thailand is a chunk of subcontinent trailing into an isthmus. Tiny Brunei consists of two enclaves scooped out of Malaysian Sarawak on either side of a tongue of land (Limbang) whose allocation to Malaysia Brunei still does not accept.

Malaysia comprises a western peninsula and an eastern coastal margin separated by the width of the South China Sea. That width includes the island of Natuna Besar, which is larger than Singapore, belongs to Indonesia, and is north of Kuala Lumpur. Natuna could, in theory, be used as an air and naval base to help prevent the Malaysian government from defending Sarawak and Sabah, not to mention Brunei, from Indonesian annexation and absorption into Jakarta's portion of Borneo (Kalimantan). The obvious parallel here is with Pakistan from 1956 to 1971, divided as that country's western and eastern wings then were by the breadth of India. Although there was in 1993 no prospect of Malaysian Borneo seceding from Kuala Lumpur to become a Southeast Asian Bangladesh, the popularity of Christian politicians and the strength of regionalist sentiment in Sabah in particular indicated a potential for politically centrifugal events.

In 1992, some 185 million people lived in Indonesia, making that country the fourth largest in the world. That same year, the population of Brunei numbered a mere 300,000. Indonesia and Singapore cover, respectively, 1.9 million and 600 square kilometers of land. In 1992, Thailand was 94 percent Buddhist; Indonesia, 87 percent Muslim; and the Philippines, 83 percent Catholic. Among respondents to a 1988 survey of religious affiliation in cosmopolitan Singapore, 18 percent said they had none at all, while in next-door Indonesia, atheism was and remains, in principle, illegal.[8] Meanwhile, in also-next-door Malaysia, Islam is the official religion.

Among peninsular Malaysians, 55 percent were racially Malay and 34 percent, Chinese in 1988. Just across the causeway from peninsular Malaysia, Singapore's racial make-up reversed these proportions to 15 and 77 percent, respectively. Hundreds of linguistic groups dot the ethnic maps of Indonesia and the Philippines. Although the population of Singapore, a city-state, is entirely urban, as late as 1990, only one in four Thais lived in cities.[9] In 1993, the Philippines was a U.S.-style presidential democracy, while neighboring Indonesia had virtually institutionalized military rule. Not even the three monarchies in Southeast Asia were alike: Thailand had emerged from a long history of coups d'état to become an increasingly civilianized, if still fragile, parliamentary democracy. As it had for 30 years, Brunei banned all forms of political representation including parties and elections; there, the sultan was the state. Still different was the Malaysian monarchy, whose figurehead "paramount" ruler-by-rotation enjoyed neither the prestige, power, nor permanence of his Thai or Bruneian counterpart. It cannot even be said of the ASEAN countries that they are all ex-colonies, because Thailand was never formally subjected to European rule.

The first challenge faced by ASEAN was not how to ensure cooperation across all this diversity. A necessary prior step was to help member states get to know each other well enough to be able to cooperate. When ASEAN was born in 1967, ex-British Singapore and Malaysia had been independent states for a scant two and four years, respectively, and the controversy surrounding Singapore's divorce from Malaysia in 1965 had not been forgotten. Barely a decade had passed since Indonesia had severed its economic ties to Holland by nationalizing Dutch properties.

As for Filipinos, although formally they had been free of U.S. tutelage since 1946, the United States continued to imprint their previously Hispanized culture. In novels, films, and conversations in the 1960s and 1970s, airing anxieties over one's national identity became something of a pastime for urban Filipinos. Were they Spanish, Americans, Asians, Pacific Islanders, or all of the above? "You wouldn't know who you were either," ran a standard joke, "if after 300 years locked up in a Catholic convent you had spent the next 50 watching Hollywood movies." In 1967, the members of ASEAN were, in effect, neighbors without a neighborhood.

Neighborhood making required ASEAN to help its members get to know each other without threatening them and without endangering their ties to foreign countries such as Britain or the United States. Among member countries with almost nothing in common, ASEAN taught what might be called the "Three Rs of Regional Cooperation": reach out to one another in noncontroversial ways, respect each other's sovereignty, and reassure everyone else.

Collective defense was controversial in 1967. It still was in 1993. The genius of ASEAN's founders lay in the sophistication of their naiveté. They knew full well that they were creating an association for the sake of regional security among its members, yet, they refused to create any military arrangements conducive to that goal. They did this knowing that the views of the five founding states on regional security and how to bring it about, not to mention the founders' affiliations to powerful outsiders, were disparate enough to doom any effort to establish or even to anticipate establishing ASEAN as a military alliance. Even as it turned away from the gestural Third Worldism of Sukarno, Indonesia supported nonalignment and appreciated the nationalist spirit of North Vietnam's struggle against the mighty United States. Yet, that same U.S. might was embodied in ships and planes on U.S. bases that Thailand and the Philippines, unlike Indonesia, were willing to host on their own soil. Even if ASEAN's makers had been able to agree on a military pact, the failure of SEATO either to prevent or to win the ongoing war in Vietnam augured ill for the effectiveness of another, competing alliance. Such a pact could have infuriated China, the former Soviet Union, and Vietnam without corresponding benefit to Southeast Asia.

Thus, what seemed to some at first naive — a scheme for regional security that said nothing about the military means to achieve it — was the opposite. The way to foster the long-run security of the ASEAN area in 1967 was to divert the attention of member countries to constructive domestic tasks, notably, economic development. To the extent that U.S. forces in the Philippines protected the members of the association, it was better not to mention that protection at all, or, rather, to note, as the Bangkok Declaration did, that although in the long run Southeast Asia would be free of foreign bases, those that were already there could, in some (wisely unspecified) meantime, remain.

To summarize how ASEAN practiced its Three Rs of Regional Cooperation: First, members reached out to each other in a wide variety of specialized meetings and organizations using the ASEAN name. What seemed from the outside like all talk and no action meant putting first things first. Not only diplomats but also a range of other governmental officials, businesspeople, and professionals traveled to each other's countries under ASEAN auspices. Second, ASEAN decisions had to be unanimous. What seemed from the outside like reducing progress to the pace of the slowest member meant that the association respected the sovereignty of each constituent country so that none would want to leave the group. Members also were not obliged to participate in all ASEAN activities. But most did so, either not to lose face by being absent or because they did not wish to pass up whatever opportunities ASEAN cooperation might offer them. Third, by not forming a defense pact or aligning themselves formally with any outside power, the ASEAN members reassured prospectively hostile outsiders, notably China, the Soviet Union, and Vietnam, while keeping nonaligned Indonesia inside the group.

The responsibility of ASEAN for the peace and development its members have enjoyed should not be exaggerated. Contributing to that success were Hanoi's preoccupation successively in defeating U.S. and South Vietnamese forces, digesting its new southern extension, invading and controlling Cambodia, and fending off Chinese attacks, all while trying in vain to make a command economy work. To the extent that Vietnam's Leninist leaders were absorbed in a domestic struggle to defend socialism against its enemies, the ASEAN countries could ignore Vietnam and get on with their own development. To the extent that Vietnam was in conflict with China, those ASEAN members who feared Chinese power could be glad to see it tied down in the north, and that gave China an incentive to improve its relations with ASEAN if only to outflank Vietnam.

Still more consequentially, in December 1978, Vietnam overran Cambodia. Hanoi soon installed its own Khmer clients to head a Peoples Republic of Kampuchea — the lineal ancestor of Prime Minister Hun Sen's State of Cambodia in the early 1990s. The invasion enabled ASEAN to rally world opinion against Vietnam for violating Cambodian sovereignty (never mind that one of the century's most sanguinary regimes had been routed and denied its killing fields) and to spearhead the economic isolation of Vietnam. That isolation, combined with the collapse and disintegration of Vietnam's Soviet creditor and the intransigence of Vietnamese leaders themselves, sapped the Vietnamese economy. In the early 1990s, far from being able to threaten ASEAN's members, Vietnam wanted desperately to join them and benefit from Western trade and investment the way they had.

Hanoi's invasion of Cambodia was for Vietnam what Moscow's roughly simultaneous invasion of Afghanistan was for the Soviet Union: enough of a threat to outsiders to trigger the invader's isolation, but not enough of a threat to them for the invader to expand its influence. However, if, therefore, ASEAN and the West in effect won these two cold wars, respectively, ASEAN did so at vastly less cost to itself, for it refused to engage in an arms race against Vietnam, and although no one (save perhaps Pol Pot) expected U.S. troops to oust the Viet-namese from Cambodia, the presence of U.S. forces in the Philippines and Japan made it easier for ASEAN not to become a military pact.

In the light of this record of success, how optimistic can one be about the future of regional cooperation to maintain the security of Southeast Asia?

The answer to that question will depend on the Southeast Asian policies of China, Japan, and the United States; on the ability of ASEAN leaders to mesh their member economies for mutual advantage and to rebalance external and internal security; and on how the association handles its own probable expansion.

China's real GNP boomed in 1992 and 1993 at an estimated 13 percent annual clip.[10] On top of more than a decade of rapid growth set in motion by the post-Mao reforms in Chinese agriculture in 1978, this performance was propelling the world's largest country into Asian-Pacific prominence. (If the outputs of different countries are made comparable not simply by converting them into dollar values at current rates of exchange but by taking into account the domestic purchasing power of each country's currency, China's GDP in 1992 soars from tenth to third largest in the world, behind only the United States and Japan.[11])

By the late 1980s and early 1990s, the ASEAN countries no longer feared Maoist revolution. They were more concerned by Chinese exports of a more commercial kind, not just to Southeast Asia but also to industrial country markets that the ASEAN economies themselves already served or wanted to serve. Also discomfiting to ASEAN were signs that China might be using its new wealth to become a major military power, as illustrated by Chinese arms purchases at bargain prices on the ex-Soviet market. More disquieting still was Beijing's decision in 1992 to write into Chinese law its claim to all of the Spratly Islands — a zone already contested in whole or in part by Brunei, Malaysia, the Philippines, and Vietnam — including China's right to use force as necessary to implement that claim.

On the other hand, China cooperated with the UN Transitional Authority in Cambodia to try to settle the war between the originally Vietnamese-installed State of Cambodia in Phnom Penh and the formerly Chinese-supplied Khmer Rouge in the countryside. In 1993 it remained to be seen whether the results of the successful — remarkably participatory and relatively fair — elections organized by UN Transitional Authority in Cambodia in May could become the basis for assuring the sovereignty, stability, and democracy of Cambodia — a tall order in view of that country's past. It was possible that China's line on Cambodia could change again, but in 1993, at least one could be encouraged by the constructive participation of China in containing and seeking an end to the Khmer conflict.

In the long run, the pivot of Chinese influence on ASEAN lies in Vietnam. More likely than a frontal attack on the Spratlys, which would line up all four Southeast Asian claimants against it, Beijing may try as best it can to separate Vietnam from ASEAN. Policy makers in China must be concerned lest the opening of the Vietnamese economy to Southeast Asian capital and the growing cooperation between Vietnam and ASEAN pull the "smaller dragon" southward out of the ambit of the larger one. That concern may in part explain Beijing's decision to build figurative and literal bridges to the military dictatorship in Rangoon, including upgrading the network of roads from Chinese Yunnan into the Burmese highlands. Along with its continuing interest in special relations with Thailand and possibly Singapore as well, China's *démarche* toward Burma may reflect a desire to outflank Vietnam.

For ASEAN, the risk from Japan is that Tokyo could begin using its massive economic presence in Southeast Asia as leverage to outflank the United States. In 1993, the delinking of Japanese from U.S. foreign policy was already underway. Although the Clinton administration championed "managed trade" by demanding that Tokyo meet specific numerical targets to buy U.S. goods, Japan sought and found sympathy in ASEAN, notably, in Indonesia, with the argument that someday the arrogant Americans might also try to make ASEAN firms and governments buy American as well. Malaysian Prime Minister Mahathir Mohamad's pet project, the East Asian Economic Caucus (EAEC), which would exclude the United States and position the ASEAN states as privileged partners of Japan, began to look more attractive in 1993, not as a realistic proposal — both Japan and ASEAN depended on U.S. consumers far too much to exclude them — but as threatened recourse if the North American Free Trade Agreement or the European Community turned out to discriminate too much against the Pacific Rim.

Fortuitous in this context was the Clinton administration's scheduled hosting of the annual Asia Pacific Economic Cooperation (APEC) forum in Seattle, Washington, in November 1993. Apparently buoyed by his earlier meetings with world leaders, Clinton invited the heads of the fifteen APEC member countries to gather in Seattle for a first-ever Asian Pacific summit. The transoceanic character of APEC, incorporating as it does the United States, Canada, Australia, and New Zealand — countries pointedly omitted from Mahathir's roster for the EAEC — made it a natural framework for allaying economic fears and tensions between East Asia and North America.

The success of the Seattle meetings, which Mahathir boycotted to no avail, and the promise by Indonesia to host a second APEC summit in 1994 diminished trans-Pacific tensions. In Seattle APEC was able to exert pressure on the European Community to help complete the still unfinished Uruguay Round of the General Agreement on Tariffs and Trade. Although APEC's stand for global free trade was one contributing factor in the outcome, within a month a General Agreement on Tariffs and Trade had been reached. The prospective reinvigoration of global trade symbolized by this success further reduced the temptation to seek regional protection in a tripolar world of Asian, American, and European blocs.

Crucial to this process was the confidence of ASEAN — Malaysia excepted — that far from drowning ASEAN as an entity, APEC could be energized by ASEAN to the benefit of both organizations. APEC had already agreed to hold its annual economic ministers' meetings in Southeast Asia every other year and to locate its secretariat in Singapore. By deciding to continue the precedent of an annual summit established in Seattle, Suharto had, in effect, given Mahathir a choice: come to the 1994 APEC leaders' meeting in Indonesia and stand up for trans-Pacific cooperation, or stay home again at the risk of antagonizing the most important ASEAN country.

In 1993 it seemed unlikely that the Malaysian prime minister would take the latter path, notwithstanding his passion for an Asians-only EAEC. Nor should one infer from that passion a disinterest in having good economic relations with Western countries. Malaysia was, for example, scheduled in March 1994 to host the tenth plenary session of the Pacific Economic Cooperation Council (PECC). (The United States, Canada, Australia, and New Zealand all belong to PECC.) In any event, whatever the differences between Mahathir and his ASEAN neighbors, the association itself was never in danger.

Compared with its creativity within APEC, the Clinton administration, in its first year, showed a varying but, at best, only modest inclination or ability to: make the ASEAN states more aware of the interest they shared with Americans in opening Japan's market; support the efforts of U.S. investors to do business in Southeast Asia and, thus, help pull more U.S. exports into the region; follow up the interest of some Southeast Asians in retaining a modest U.S. security profile in return for local market access; or stop blaming the trade deficit with Japan for problems of the United States' own making, notably, low private savings and spendthrift public policy, not to mention millions of choices by U.S. consumers. Incredibly, no one in the upper reaches of foreign policy making in the U.S. government in 1993 could even speak Japanese, let alone a Southeast Asian language.

In June 1993, the single most productive step that the United States could have taken, but did not take, toward regional security in Southeast Asia was to end its embargo against U.S. investment and trade with the region's second most populous economy, Vietnam. Having as a young man escaped being drafted to fight in the Vietnam War and scoring lower in the polls than any post–World War II president at a comparable time in office, Bill Clinton was understandably unwilling in June 1993 to open the door completely and risk criticism from Americans still willing to hold U.S-Vietnamese relations hostage to the hope of learning what happened to all of those missing in action (MIAs). Yet, integrating Vietnam into a peaceful, stable, and prospering Southeast Asia was surely a logical priority for U.S. foreign policy. Meanwhile, on the ground in Vietnam, Asian and European corporate competitors of the United States were taking full advantage of its absence.

In July 1993, President Clinton did quietly drop U.S. objections to French and Japanese plans to pay Vietnam's defaulted debts to the International Monetary Fund (IMF). Once those arrears were cleared, Vietnam could borrow fresh money from the IMF, the World Bank, and the Asian Development Bank. Yet, until the embargo itself was canceled, U.S. firms could not bid on the projects such loans were expected to pay for. The U.S. government, thus, found itself in the politically untenable position of funding international institutions to finance projects in Vietnam on which U.S. firms were still forbidden to bid. Meanwhile, U.S. diplomats were, for the first time, stationed in Hanoi, ostensibly to help find MIAs but clearly also to prepare the way for eventual normalization. In mid-1993, the MIA lobby notwithstanding, it was hard to believe the embargo could last much longer.[12]

As for the future of ASEAN, that will depend partly on its ability to replace its successful diplomacy of containment against Vietnam in Cambodia with other initiatives toward keeping the region economically vigorous and militarily secure.

One such initiative, the ASEAN Free Trade Area (AFTA), was announced at the association's 1992 summit in Singapore. If it is implemented on schedule, the scheme will cut intra-ASEAN tariffs on goods in agreed categories to a minimal 5 percent within a decade, give or take a few years depending on whether a given product has been placed on a "fast" or a "normal" track. The launching of AFTA was already a considerable achievement in view of the natural temptation for Indonesia to fend off imported goods while nurturing infant industries to produce those same goods for its vast domestic market, compared with tiny, free-trading Singapore's natural interest in lowering barriers to commerce with all countries, including next-door Indonesia. However, as might be expected, only the three smallest members of ASEAN — Brunei, Malaysia, and Singapore — appeared fully committed to making AFTA work. Indonesia, the Philippines, and Thailand were going along, but the economic integration of ASEAN was still by no means around the corner. Nor should it be. Only about one-fifth of ASEAN's total trade was with itself in the early 1990s, and if these economies were to prosper into the 2100s, they would need above all to expand total trade, including their access to Japan and the West.

Even if AFTA does not significantly expand intra-ASEAN trade, the fact of its existence will enable ASEAN to bring to the negotiating table a resource: access to a dynamic regional market. The more the world economy regionalizes, the more value that resource will have. One can hope that U.S. leaders will be able to look beyond the demands of domestic industries that are clamoring for protection from imports and guaranteed market shares abroad through managed trade, that is, trade by privilege and intimidation, to realize the opportunities for the U.S. economy that AFTA affords. At least 40 percent of the content of a product must have been produced in one or more ASEAN countries in order for it to qualify for tariff-cutting under AFTA. However, a glass that is two-fifths empty is also three-fifths full. U.S. exports to ASEAN could account for up to 60 percent of that same product and it would still enjoy preferred ASEAN-market access under AFTA.

In this context, linking AFTA to the North American Free Trade Agreement within APEC to form the embryo of a would-be trans-Pacific free-trading regime may be advantageous to the United States and its ASEAN partners, provided such a formation remains open to nondiscriminatory trade with the rest of the world. In the meantime, AFTA should be judged as a means toward regional security, not regional economic integration. Also, in focusing on formal plans to cooperate, one should not overlook the rapid de facto spreading of economic transactions that in crisscrossing boundaries between countries help create security by implicating neighbors in each other's economies. The more such mutual implication occurs, the greater is the likelihood that one neighbor firing at another will hit its own foot. That logic is in part behind Singapore's effort to promote what could be termed a regionally industrializing core (RIC) between itself and the Malaysian and Indonesian territories of Johor and Riau to the north and south, respectively. Although much less developed, such a RIC has also been talked about for southern Thailand, west-coast peninsular Malaysia, and north-coast Sumatran Indonesia, and for eastern Malaysia, southern Philippines, and Indonesia's northern Sulawesi.

Another challenge for ASEAN in the rest of the 1990s will be to find ways of shouldering more of the burden for the old-fashioned military security of its region. The economic growth of the ASEAN states (the Philippines excepted) has enabled them to modernize their armed forces. Since 1990, Malaysia, Singapore, and Thailand, in particular, have rapidly increased defense spending. New acquisitions include sophisticated air and naval craft armed with advanced weapons. Force modernization in ASEAN has given rise to talk of an arms race.

Strengthening the incentive for ASEAN to take the initiative in helping to organize regional security in 1993 was the departure of the United States from the Philippines, an exit in 1992 sped by the explosion of a local volcano that rendered Clark Field unusable and by the unwillingness of the Philippine Senate to extend the U.S. lease on Subic Bay. Although the Bush administration signed separate agreements with several ASEAN members for low-profile ship visits and repair services, the association remained, for good reasons, unwilling to ally itself militarily with the United States. China could not play the role of protector. Too many in ASEAN saw it more as a potential predator, and China, in any case, still lacked the capacity to secure Southeast Asia. Nor could ASEAN ask Japan to replace the Americans. Too many Southeast Asians recalled the rapacity of the Japanese during World War II when Tokyo severely abused the region to supply its war machine, and even if Japan were asked to play such a role, Japan's own domestic opinion would still not allow it, except perhaps in careful, limited, and nonbelligerent association with, say, the United Nations, as in Cambodia.

That left ASEAN in 1993 with an opportunity to improve military coordination and cooperation among its members, including confidence-building measures of various kinds. Joint bilateral exercises were already common. Increasing the interoperability of military equipment could be another goal. Sharing facilities for military education and training could be a third.

In 1993 the ASEAN states had not counted out the United States. In a remarkable "Message from Asia" sent to President Clinton in February 1993, Singapore's elder statesman Lee Kuan Yew wrote, "It is stupid if we [in East Asia] do not go out of our way to help American investments come into our region and make it productive, to help American trade, and to buy American wherever possible. That is our *quid pro quo* for [a U.S. military presence to keep regional] peace and stability." Lee went on to argue that under such a swap — preferential market access for regional security support — the United States could easily eliminate its $70 billion trade deficit with East Asia within five years.[13]

The final challenge for ASEAN in the 1990s will be to manage its own expansion into Indochina. By 1993, Vietnam and Laos were allowed to observe ASEAN meetings and accede to its declarations but had not — yet? — become full members. In that same year, Malaysian Finance Minister Anwar Ibrahim, who hoped to succeed Mahathir Mohamad as prime minister, argued that ASEAN should try to make room for Burma, too, but Thai Prime Minister Chuan Leekpai cautioned that it might be difficult to fit the sheer diversity of all Southeast Asia into ASEAN or any other single format.[14]

Incorporating Indochina and, someday perhaps, Burma as well would strengthen ASEAN only if the resulting gain in its ability to represent the region and resolve regional problems were to exceed any loss in its ability to reach consensus. Factors potentially inhibiting success include Indochina's long history of struggle and war; the continuing commitment of Vietnamese and Laotian leaders to keep their still-Leninist polities closed even as they seek to open their economies; antagonism between Vietnam and China dating back centuries, reflected in the intensity of their dispute over the Spratly Islands; and the still uncertain future of Cambodia in relation to the ambitions of Vietnam and Thailand on the Southeast Asian mainland. Any decision to expand ASEAN northward would have to be carefully thought out if it were to succeed. Burma, long considered the region's "hermit state" because of its introversion and lack of interest in cooperating with capitalist Southeast Asia, seemed, in 1993, an even less promising would-be member of the association.

Ultimately, as in the past, the lesson of regional cooperation in Southeast Asia will be that nothing matters more than the political will of individual states to interact with one another and to compromise for the sake of shared interests. Even now, for all the synergy of RICs and international conferences, it is the ASEAN governments that hold political power, not ASEAN itself. ASEAN has succeeded, above all, because its leaders have kept this basic and ongoing reality in mind.

When he was still "living dangerously," Sukarno not only enjoyed abbreviating concepts but also abbreviating his abbreviations. In the spirit of his wordplay, if not his policies, one may do the same for ASEAN's Three Rs of Regional Cooperation — that is, reach out to each other while respecting one another's sovereignty and reassuring outsiders — by summarizing them under a fourth and most important R of all — be realistic.

NOTES

1. This and the next three paragraphs rely on the *Britannica Book of the Year 1965* (Chicago, Ill.: Encyclopaedia Britannica, 1965).

2. These were, respectively, Burma, Cambodia, Indonesia, Laos, Malaysia, the Philippines, and Thailand; North and South Vietnam; and British Brunei. ASA included Malaysia, along with the Philippines and Thailand, but not Indonesia. Singapore left Malaysia to become an independent country in 1965, North and South Vietnam were reunified in 1975–76, and Brunei reluctantly gained independence in 1984. Contributing to the Sultan of Brunei's anxiety over cutting his ties to London were his territorial dispute with Malaysia over Limbang, his worry that Malaysia might someday try to annex Brunei, and his memory of Indonesian support for a rebellion against him in 1962.

3. SEATO's other members were Australia, France, Great Britain, New Zealand, Pakistan, and the United States. By the time Pakistan withdrew in 1972, the organization was already moribund; it would be dissolved five years later. Technically, the underlying Manila Pact of 1954 is still in effect.

4. World Bank, *World Development Report 1992* (New York: Oxford University Press, 1992), pp. 218–29. The bank does not provide comparable data for hydrocarbon-rich Brunei, sometimes known as "the Shellfare state," which rode the roller coaster of oil and gas prices through boom and slump in the 1970s and 1980s, respectively. In its *Human Development Report 1992* (New York: Oxford University Press, 1992), p. 127, the United Nations Development Program estimated Brunei's per capita GDP in 1989 at $14,590, the second-highest in Southeast Asia (after Singapore). According to the same source , per capita GNP in 1965–80 grew on an annual average 0.6 percent in Indochina and 1.6 percent in Burma; the United Nations Development Program declined to make estimates for the 1980s (p. 175).

5. United Nations Development Program, *Human Development Report 1992*, pp. 127–28. Lack of space prevents discussion of the rejoinder that socialism in

Indochina or Burma would have succeeded if only capitalist countries such as the United States had allowed it to.

6. "Economic Indicators, Selected Asian Countries," *Far Eastern Economic Review* 10 (June 1993): 73.

7. Again, lack of space prevents discussion of the counteropinion whereby the United States, having bombed the Khmer Rouge in the countryside, bore responsibility for their viciousness once in power in the capital, Phnom Penh.

8. Sources are: on population and area, the *Asia 1993 Yearbook* (Hong Kong: Review Publishing, 1993), p. 6; on religious affiliation, *The 1993 Information Please Almanac* (Boston, Mass.: Houghton Mifflin, 1993), pp. 205 (Indonesia), p. 247 (Philippines), p. 272 (Thailand); and the Ministry of Communications and Information, Singapore, personal communication, November 2, 1989.

9. Sources are: on ethnic makeup, *Malaysia 1988 Yearbook*, p. 19, cited in Harry Aveling, "Perencanaan dan Kebijakan Bahasa di Malaysia," *Kritis* (Salatiga, Indonesia) 5 (October 1990): 21 (peninsular Malaysia; and *World Fact Book 1987* cited in Hans H. Indorf, *Linkage or Bondage: U.S. Economic Relations with the ASEAN Region* (Washington, D.C.: National Planning Association, 1988), p. v. (Singapore); on urban populations, World Bank, *World Development Report 1992*, pp. 278–79.

10. "Economic Indicators," p. 72.

11. Steven Greenhouse, "New Tally of World's Economies Catapults China into Third Place," *New York Times*, May 20, 1993, pp. A1, A6. As calculated by the World Bank using purchasing power parity, Japan and China had GDPs of $2.37 trillion and $2.35 trillion, respectively, in 1992.

12. My arguments for normal economic relations with Vietnam can be found in "Let's End the Vietnam Embargo," *The World & I* (March 1993): 86–91; "Vietnam: Time to End the Embargo," in *Pacific Policy Advisory* (Washington, D.C.: U.S. Member Committee of the Pacific Economic Cooperation Council, 1993). In January 1994 the embargo was finally lifted.

13. Richard Drobnick, "U.S. Security Leverage in Asian Trade Policy," *Pacific Economic Review* 1 (Spring 1993): 26–27.

14. "Thailand: Expanding ASEAN," in "Regional Briefing," *Far Eastern Economic Review*, March 4, 1993, p. 14.

V

EMERGING PLAYERS IN PACIFIC RIM REGIONALISM

17

Globalization and National Power in the Pacific

José Juan de Olloqui y Labastida

Recent developments in international affairs have emphasized the fact that economic activity influences international politics. In fact, the political influence and international activity of great powers have historically been supported by their economic vigor.[1] Without this, their capacity to influence international events diminishes sooner or later, as we have witnessed during the boom and decadence periods of the great powers.

Perhaps these changes indicate a more significant phenomenon that has not yet been sufficiently studied by academicians. I refer here to what we could call the necessary harmony among the elements that constitute national power. For example, territory and natural resources are frequently referred to as elements of power. However, even under the best of circumstances, these are merely potential elements if there is not a population large enough to exploit or protect them. Similarly, geographic considerations mean that the importance of these elements is reduced when they are not favorably located.

Notwithstanding their large size and considerable resources, Argentina, Australia, and Canada — to mention three typical cases — do not have the conditions to exploit their potential because of relatively small populations. Also, the lower levels of participation in world and southern hemisphere affairs of Argentina and Australia run counter to the expectations that might arise given their resources and per capita incomes.

Argentina's Atlantic coastline was of great importance for immigration and development, and it was also the window through which Argentina participated in world events. Australia, which used to be considered isolated in a dark corner of the world, is currently benefiting from growing commercial and financial flows in the Pacific Basin. Canada, which borders both oceans, is nonetheless limited by the inhospitable climate of most of its territory and the fragile political cohesion of its various population groups. This condition also applies to Brazil, which has every tool necessary to become a great power, including tremendous social contradictions among its people. To differing degrees, this factor is found in most developing countries.

Much more difficult to evaluate, but no less important, is national character as an element of power. National character may be defined as the will of a people to govern their own destiny and to determine the level of their international activity. It was their national character that allowed a small country like Ireland to become independent from a great empire at the turn of the century and to maintain neutrality in World War II, despite being pressed by its more powerful neighbor to join the battle against Germany. Similarly, although Finland possessed a small population, it was also successful in remaining independent in spite of the ambitions of a neighboring superpower, the Soviet Union.

From this viewpoint, it is interesting to note that national character is evidence, among other things, of the will of a country to participate in world events. For example, Italy and Great Britain show very different dispositions toward involvement and participation in international conflicts and decisions, notwithstanding the fact that they are countries with a similar domestic gross national product, perhaps due to their recent histories. Alternatively, it was only a few decades ago that different events confirmed that activism and the will to participate in international events can be counterproductive for a nation if a sound economy does not exist, as was the case for Nasser in Egypt, Nkruma in Ghana, and Sukarno in Indonesia. More recently, Libya and Iraq joined this list.

Furthermore, the disintegration of the former Soviet Union demonstrated, once more, what Turkey had already shown: that a great military power needs a strong economy. To some extent today, the United States is not able to fully display its capacities as a superpower — even though its only rival as far as political and military matters are concerned has disappeared — because of decreasing competitiveness, bulky deficits, and large external debts. On the contrary, the reconstruction and extraordinary economic growth experienced by Japan and the western European countries (especially Germany) following World War II have led to increasing importance and responsibility in the community of nations. This trend will undoubtedly continue to grow in the years ahead. It is not surprising, however, that in a climate of lesser political tensions, economic competition increases. This is the present trend, strengthened by the growing preference of many countries who have developed in the shadow of technological progress during the last decades to adopt open economic models in order to enter global markets competitively. This development model has been adopted by Mexico under the guidance of President Carlos Salinas de Gortari. It is also the most appropriate model to allow Mexico's geographic presence in the Pacific Rim to develop into a functional integration into the regional dynamic economic processes.

In the recent past, Mexico has implemented bold political, economic, and social reforms, led by the will to develop an increasingly efficient and democratic political system and an economy focused on international activity. This state of affairs will expand the options open to Mexico and achieve a higher level of development and well-being for the populace. Mexico provides extraordinarily favorable conditions to accomplish these tasks because it possesses an exceptional degree of what I call "multigeopoliticity," that is, possessing a geographic location that provides the opportunity to explore alternatives, as well as specific influences that allow full use of these alternatives.

THE MULTIGEOPOLITICITY OF MEXICO

Because Mexico borders the largest national marketplace in the world, it constitutes a bridge between this market and rest of the continent. Only Mexico and Canada are able to guarantee the United States surface supply of strategic raw materials, which is a reason why the United States considers Mexico a determining factor in its security and makes no concessions in this regard. Mexico is located in the northern hemisphere, which in terms of political geography is much more important than the southern hemisphere. Mexico is also part of, and one of the three major countries in, Latin America and the only nation in this region whose coastlines include the Atlantic, Pacific, and the Caribbean. In other words, Mexico belongs to the Atlantic world as well as to the Pacific Basin. It is located where the world's major events occur and the world's major markets are found.

Although Mexico's multigeopoliticity is increased due to the above factors, other factors like social lags and even the country's proximity to the world's most important power, have resulted in Mexico's inability fully to manifest its potential capacities. Specifically, Mexico has been cautious and defensive in foreign policy matters. At the same time, although the presence of the United States has helped Mexico assert its national identity and patriotism. This defensive spirit also explains Mexico's reluctance to get involved in the lobbying activities that occur in the U.S. Congress due to fears of providing reasons for reciprocal interference in Mexico's internal affairs. I consider this fear baseless, however, at least for the present time.

Similarly, and in contrast to the United States, Mexico's economic importance frequently goes unnoticed, even though Mexico is an outstanding member of the international community. Mexico currently ranks eleventh among the 160 members of the United Nations in population (82 million), thirteenth in terms of territorial size, and fifteenth in economic production. Mexico is also considered important because of its oil reserves and strategic raw materials. In spite of some sectoral lags, Mexico has diversified its industrial infrastructure and has achieved an important world ranking (twelfth) in indicators used to measure economic and social development such as the number of doctors, technicians, and engineers, and also the length of its highway network. No less important is the fact that Mexico retains its own national identity. More than a culture, Mexico is a great civilization with deep historical roots; it has also served as the introduction to the Latin American community for the United States.

LATIN AMERICA AND THE PACIFIC BASIN

The western coast of Latin America is frequently excluded when mention is made of the Pacific Basin. However, Latin Americans feel that they are potential members of the Asia Pacific community and should be viewed simply as countries on the opposite shore. The United States and Canada are usually considered to be on the eastern rim of the Pacific Basin, simply on the opposite shore from Japan and the economies of East Asia that are driving the region's economic growth. The omission of Mexico, however, is not accidental. Although similarities exist among nations on both sides of the Pacific, especially because economic development has been achieved without undue sacrifices of cultural values, broad differences still remain. In particular, each region has developed differently.

During the 1960s, the nations of the Asia Pacific region pursued export-oriented policies of development, while Latin America insisted on prolonging the life of import substitution strategies as a means to develop industrial bases. Latin America, therefore, closed its doors to foreign competition and concentrated instead on its modest domestic markets. The consequences of these development strategies were dramatic: Latin American nations, which had led the developing world in the 1970s, were trapped by the debt crisis of the 1980s. Dynamism was lost, and the Latin American nations were left out of the select group of nations that profited from the extraordinary expansion of international trade and surprised the world with their aggressive competitiveness and growth.

A superficial analysis of the most dynamic nations of East Asia versus those of the western Latin American coast shows a four-to-one ratio in the differences in economic growth rates. This disparity is apparent in all of the important economic indicators: investment, public finances, price stability, access to capital markets, international competitiveness, and, ultimately, social development. Despite having a territory similar in size to Russia and a population close to that of western Europe, Latin America's internal production rates are equal to those of Germany alone. This indicates both the potential and the challenges facing Latin America.

Latin America gained independence from the European powers a full century before many of the Asian nations, yet remained trapped by conflicts between liberals and conservatives — derived from the radical changes produced by the French revolution in Western political culture and thought — during its first 100 years of independence. In other words, Latin America lost 100 years of potential development in comparison with the nations of Asia. It is also true that Latin America achieved some considerable gains: it broke with the traditional agricultural and mining development model by adopting a projectionist strategy, it began its industrialization processes, and it recorded high growth rates. However, these seemingly temporary protection schemes for new industries were maintained over a much longer period and resulted in a highly inefficient industrial structure that was incapable of competing in foreign markets and remained highly dependent on the import of capital goods.

During the remainder of the 1990s, however, I would dare to predict that Latin America will experience an important economic change, barring unforeseen events like popular revolts, political instability, or international economic developments beyond control. We can speak of an American Pacific in the same manner in which we talk about the Asia Pacific. It would be impossible to understand the phenomenon of the Pacific Basin without looking at the close relationship between the dynamic economies of East Asia and those of North America. In the future, we will see an increase in the participation of the nations of Latin America in the Pacific regional dynamic. At this point, I would like to emphasize a geopolitical concept: it does not make sense to incorporate countries without coasts on the Pacific into the Pacific Basin regional organizations. Because of Latin American solidarity, current Latin American members of the organizations can be interlocutors for the other countries of the region, but this solidarity should not lead us to misconstrue the meaning behind the phenomenon of the Pacific Basin.

THE PACIFIC COMMUNITY

Despite the aforementioned differences and the concentration of economic relationships among East Asian and Latin American countries with the United States, many Latin American nations are very interested in strengthening their contacts with the Asia Pacific economies, including those Latin American countries that do not belong to the Pacific community and are, therefore, outside the existing regional organizations for the Pacific region, as in the case of Brazil and Argentina.

The attraction to the Pacific Basin phenomenon is such that there are nongovernmental entities, for example, transnational corporations, wishing to participate actively in the integration fora that have emerged in the region. Recently, at a Pacific Basin Economic Council international general meeting, an application for admission was received from a transnational corporation that, although not from the region, is more important in terms of Pacific Basin investments and trade than many of the small or less developed countries belonging to the Pacific community.[2]

At a national level, Japan tends to be the natural leader of the region in economic terms, and it will, therefore, acquire more political commitments (much as Germany will have to assume leadership responsibilities in Europe). The United States, though, will continue to play an important role in the foreseeable future, and there will be two great "natural" powers dominant in the Pacific at the beginning of the twenty-first century: Japan and the United States. These two nations will eventually be joined by China and Russia at a leadership level. In the next echelon are the so-called Four Tigers: South Korea, Taiwan, Hong Kong, and Singapore. These will be followed, in turn, by the "future tigers" of Indonesia, Malaysia, and Thailand.

The reality is that Latin America will have to participate in a more active manner in Pacific Rim trade to ensure that it is not merely a second-class member of the Asia Pacific community, due more to geography than to economic activity. Currently, the relationship between Latin America and the Asia Pacific region is poor. Latin America is neither an important supplier to, nor a purchaser of, goods from the nations of the Asia Pacific. This marginal economic participation must be reversed if Latin America wishes to benefit from the dynamism in the region.

I would like to point out that Latin American perceptions of the countries of the Asia Pacific region frequently have been incorrect. It must be realized that the nations of the Asia Pacific are not greatly interested in the political achievements of Latin America: democracy is not pursued as vigorously, and the Judeo-Christian values so dear to the West are not viewed as such in the East. For example, the Greek concept of democracy does not have the same roots in the Asia Pacific as in the West. The nations of the Asia Pacific seek functional governments, which will first represent their interests and then eventually lead to representative government. Stability, investment opportunities, and trade are the priorities. Relations between the two regions, therefore, should be based more on pragmatism and mutual economic growth.

POLITICAL OVERVIEW

As a consequence of its economic growth, Japan will gradually continue to acquire characteristics of an integral power, with growing political influence and increasing responsibilities in maintaining peace and stability in the region. In fact, Japan is already one of the biggest military powers in the world. Although it is not a nuclear power, some experts rank Japan as the third largest military power behind the United States and Russia on the state of the art of its weaponry. Likewise, the Japanese Diet has already begun to relax the limitations imposed on itself after World War II. If Japan expends 1 percent of its gross domestic product on the military, as it has been doing up to the present, it will be the most important military power of the region, with China as the only possible exception.

Let us also not forget that China is a great military power, a member of the "nuclear club" and in size, resources, location, and most importantly, population, a country with enormous weight in international affairs. China also intends to become a great economic power. In spite of the 1989 events at Tiananmen Square, I dare to assert that no deep differences exist among the Chinese elite on the issue of the economic strategies projected for the country or on the nature of these strategies. Differences certainly exist, though, related to the speed at which change can be carried out without disturbing stability and internal cohesion.

It is, therefore, possible to believe that China will not only achieve steady economic growth but also increase its political and military power, not only within the region, but also on a worldwide level. Hong Kong and Taiwan can play an important role for China as "windows" to the world and allow more access to foreign capitals and markets. These are among the objectives of China's foreign policy, for historical reasons, but they are not indispensable.

The smaller economies, such as Singapore, face an uncertain long-term future because of a lack of territorial reserves coupled with increased immigration from neighboring countries. The higher standards of living and greater opportunities of Singapore attract this immigration, and only a continued region-wide boom, or at least the development of other regions to which immigration is drawn, will diminish the risk of being destabilized by this massive influx.

South Korea is already an important player within and outside the region. Its Achilles heel can be political instability, but perhaps its economic successes will aid the stabilization of the political system. Unification with North Korea will initially result in problems but, once achieved, will produce a formidable regional player.

Russia is more European than Asiatic. Its eastern region is barely inhabited, its regional economy is rather weak, and most of its military power is permanently committed along the Chinese border. Thus, normalizing relations with Japan is a fundamental piece in the Russian strategy of modernization. This will allow Russia access to investment and trade while, at the same time, the opportunity to balance its position with China. This strategy, however, first requires an agreement on the Kurile Islands, which will not be easily reached.

On the Latin American side of the Pacific, we find interesting real and potential players. Presently, the most important nations are Mexico and Chile. Chile has a natural draw toward the Pacific due to its lengthy shores. It also has a strong maritime tradition and has advanced considerably in its economic reforms. Mexico exhibits similar characteristics vis-à-vis the Pacific, specifically in relation to the success of its economic reforms. Peru also has a clear attraction to the Pacific, but at the present time, it is experiencing serious economic and political problems that do not allow a more important kind of participation in the economic trends of the Pacific Basin. Sooner or later, Colombia will also join this region, even though it is not a participant in the Pacific phenomenon and, at present, struggles through internal difficulties provoked by drug traffic, among other things. The participation of Ecuador is likewise marginal at this time, because of its small size. This situation is even more evident for the Central American countries. Trade and relations between Central America and the Asia Pacific nations are conditioned by bilateral relationships with the United States more than anything else. This situation is also the case in Mexico, but to a lesser degree.

It is true that the United States and Canada have been the countries on the western side of the Pacific that have interacted the most with the Asia Pacific. However, it is important to note that the United States faces growing competition by its partners in the Asia Pacific, which will force, in turn, a painful reordering of the U.S. economy. This will have a negative effect in the economies of all the Latin American nations due to the size and importance of the U.S. market.

In view of European and North American integration processes and the dynamics of the Pacific Basin countries, it is not difficult to predict that the world soon will be ruled by three great economic powers, substituting the bipolarity previously established by the two Cold War military superpowers. In this scenario, total destruction of the earth due to nuclear war will be more remote, but daily coexistence also will be more difficult because of economic and commercial tensions. It is urgent, therefore, that Latin America recover its economic dynamism and participate actively in the major world markets. It is in this environment that Latin Americans have to struggle for legitimate places as emerging powers. Latin Americans should not accept limitations imposed by unipolarity, bipolarity, or tripolarity but, instead, decide their destinies autonomously. I am not excluding Mexico from these emerging powers, even though Mexico will be participating in the North American Free Trade Agreement (NAFTA).

MEXICO AND THE PACIFIC BASIN

Since NAFTA has been ratified, the new "outward oriented" development strategy that Mexico has begun will gradually be consolidated. This, I believe, has been the best strategy for the new conditions of the world economy. Although the Uruguay Round of the General Agreement on Tariffs and Trade negotiations has been successfully concluded, we should be warned about changes in the world scene that may affect the future of free trade.

First, the Pacific Basin countries that adopted free trade strategies at the end of the 1960s and beginning of the 1970s were very successful, but we must not forget that this required considerable discipline and sacrifice on their part, sacrifices that Latin America should also be willing to assume. Second, although this success was due partly to the export-oriented economies in Asia that were able to take advantage of the growth of the U.S. marketplace, Latin American countries, on the contrary, went into debt during the 1980s and, therefore, did not have the competitive capacity to export to the United States. This resulted in a "lost decade" for Latin America when Asia was experiencing tremendous growth. Third, it was easier for the Asia Pacific countries to conquer the greatest market of the world, the U.S. market, at the time when they were the only followers of that development strategy. As the number of countries competing for the large markets becomes greater, the profit margins will be lower and the risks will increase. Fourth, the 1990s will undoubtedly see a strong adjustment in most of the significant markets in the world, that is, the United States and the European Community. The former needs to correct its commercial deficits and reduce external debt, while the latter faces demands presented by the break-up of the former Eastern bloc. Needless to say, as trade flows are liberalized, capital mobility will be favored, economic growth increased, and new markets opened. Not all of this will be as attractive or profitable as before, and the climate of international competition will be much more intense. In other words, I believe we are heading in the right direction, but we must not consider the opening as a panacea or think that economic achievements can be accomplished without considerable effort.

Latin America must learn to compete, and to compete in more demanding surroundings with rivals who, in some cases, have a considerable advantage in technological development. This, in turn, will increasingly be the main determinant of the comparative advantages of nations. Mexico is a very special case due to multigeopoliticity. This multigeopoliticity has opened the path to negotiate the NAFTA agreement with the United States and Canada and to form the largest market in the world. Because of this multigeopoliticity, Mexico sees NAFTA as market opening, not market closing, and Mexico hopes to take advantage of all of its options. This is why Mexico is making parallel efforts to approach other markets, evident by the execution of the Framework Agreement of Cooperation that Mexico entered into with the European Community and bilateral agreements with other countries of Latin America. Also, for this reason, Mexico is a member of the Pacific Basin Economic Council and of the Pacific Economic Cooperation Council and has recently joined the Asia Pacific Economic Cooperation forum in accordance with the final deliberations of the annual meeting of the Asia Pacific Economic Cooperation held in Seattle in November 1993.

It is also important to emphasize Latin American integration. Although it is true that Mexico intends to develop its own options, Mexico also includes Latin America in its planning because Mexico believes it is one of the three most important countries of the region and feels a sense of special responsibility. Mexico is pursuing the execution of similar trade agreements with several Central American countries such as Costa Rica; the negotiation for a trade agreement with Colombia and Venezuela has been finalized, and the agreement with Chile is already in force. All of these initiatives attest to Mexico's wish to see Latin American nations succeed.

CONCLUSIONS

Undoubtedly, history is changing as the postwar bipolar division, ideologies, and strategies for economic development seem to be crumbling, and economic activity is being globalized and regains importance.

New demands will appear and new opportunities opened only to those countries willing to commit their efforts in the development of all possible potentials for growth and development. Mexico is destined to see that the greatness of its people and the nation is achieved. Therefore, Mexico has taken the steps that will allow the use of the advantages offered by its exceptional multigeopoliticity. Mexico is conscious that, in its turn, economic growth will go hand in hand with greater political influence and international responsibility.

Truly, the experience of great powers clearly shows the need to maintain a harmonious balance between economic growth and political and military power. Likewise, the experience of Japan and Germany shows us that economic growth leads to an increase in political importance. At the end of the Cold War with the emergence of new powers, there will be increased international competition in the economic field. Therefore, and as a result of the economic growth of East Asia, it does not seem exaggerated to assert that the beginning of the twenty-first century shall be dominated by the Pacific Basin. Mexico will play an important role in this scenario.

NOTES

1. I stated this in the Twenty-fourth International General Meeting of the Pacific Basin Economic Council, held in Guadalajara, Mexico, in May 1991.

2. The Pacific Basin Economic Council, in which I participate as international counselor, has not, as yet, decided in this respect, although, in my opinion, we cannot accept this application because a corporation could participate only as a member of a national delegation. This incident is indicative of the actual forces that operate in the Asia Pacific region.

18

Russia on the Pacific: Beyond Communism and Confrontation

Vladimir I. Ivanov

For the first time in its modern history, Russia finds itself almost in an ideal security environment in Northeast Asia. Its eastern borders are stable. Siberia and the Russian Far East are the only parts of the Old Russian Empire and of the former Soviet Union where the shape of the country has not been changed. There is no more conflict of ideologies or strategic interests with the United States. China is an emerging economic and political partner. Moscow has a potential diplomatic advantage in its relations with both Koreas. Relations with Japan, if viewed in historical perspective, are better than at any time in this century.

Since the dissolution of the Soviet Union, a reevaluation of Russia's posture and interests in the East Asia and Pacific region is complicated, yet more promising. The promise lies in achieving greater security, stable and positive political relations, and access to Asia Pacific markets and sources of economic dynamism. The difficulty consists in formulating a new foreign policy and national security doctrine that will not contradict but instead facilitate the implementation of the main goal of economic and social renovation. A nonthreatening, prosperous, cooperative Russia on the Pacific could contribute to positive long-term changes and would enhance regional stability and cooperation.

RELATIONS WITH WASHINGTON

For Russia, new relations with the United States and Japan in Northeast Asia constitute both a source of opportunity and a major foreign policy challenge. The combination of political support on the part of the United States and the financial power of Tokyo could be two of the most decisive external factors in Russia's modernization. Full-scale economic cooperation in this triangle could be greatly facilitated through a comprehensive security accommodation. Without deep structural changes in Moscow's security relations with Washington and Tokyo, it is difficult to envision the emergence of genuine political or economic partnership.

Ironically, even after the fall of communism, Moscow's and Washington's fundamental values, broad economic interests, and security aspirations are still in conflict with the inertia of the nuclear strategic posture. Japan is in the midst of the same strategic dilemma as a hesitant third party, indirectly involved in the northwestern Pacific residual military stand-off. Furthermore, the inertia of the defense posture and bureaucratic constraints have a potential to prevent all three countries from looking beyond nuclear deterrence and the balance of power scenario. The typical view of Russia on the Pacific is still negative and linked to its military power and nuclear posture, which is suspected to become a source of tension in the region again due to domestic instability or reverse developments in foreign policy in Moscow. Democratic changes in Russia thus far are not a factor in the analysis with respect to their impact on Asia.

Currently, Russian security and strategic posture and thinking are in transition, and Moscow gets stuck between two polar patterns vis-à-vis the United States in Asia: it is neither a principal military adversary as in the 1980s, nor is it yet considered as a potential partner, although more than any other nation in the region, Russia needs a good relationship with the United States in Asia. An expectation prevailed that the United States, after the reconciliation with Moscow in Europe, would initiate changes in the northwestern Pacific and, thus, among other things, indirectly help Russia's accommodation with Japan in particular, but until recently, Russia was not even mentioned when U.S. security and political posture in Asia were discussed.[1] Sometimes, Russia is not even considered as a part of Northeast Asia.[2] Very few U.S. experts on Asia and Pacific affairs tend to see recent developments in Russia in terms of systemic shifts affecting Asia's transition to democracy, while others indicate that after the collapse of communism, Russia in Northeast Asia remains, at best, a "distant third-tier state."[3]

The Clinton administration, with inherited lack of consistent political attention to Asia and limited high-level contacts with Asian leaders, faces the "Russian question" in its emerging Asian policy. It is absolutely new, because the goal of building positive relations with Moscow was related more to global and European affairs than to Northeast Asian regional goals.[4] For Moscow, creating U.S. regional leadership could be a key factor in helping Russia to find its proper role in regional relations. Without positive interaction with the United States, Russia will remain in isolation from the regional community, and the possibility of new mistakes and misunderstandings will persist.

The problem of motives looms large for Japan, which, when compared with the United States and Germany among its Group of 7 partners, does not gain any immediate security or political advantages from assisting Russia in its transition. There is very little that the current U.S.-Japanese security agenda or loose consensus within the Group of 7 on Russian reform process could provide to fill this gap. Japan is expected to play the role of major donor comparable to Germany, but there is no clear understanding about how Tokyo will be able to influence the process it is supposed to finance. In the opinion of many Japanese experts, billions of dollars in economic aid cannot effectively work without a system of specific economic and administrative measures implemented by the Russian government. They also insist that Japan should be given a much greater role in advising the Russian government on the problems of economic policy.

Japan's economic philosophy is different from that of the United States and of the International Monetary Fund. Although the International Monetary Fund program adopted by Russia is aimed at macroeconomic stabilization, Japanese experts maintain the view that it is not enough and that measures should be taken to revitalize production. They say that market mechanisms cannot be almighty and that Russia should adopt some forms of wage and price control to preserve economic stability. Japanese economists have encouraged targeting of strategic industries, in Russia's case, oil. They propose low-interest development loans and breaking up state monopolies to promote domestic competition·[5] Among preconditions for success of the reform process in Russia and other republics of the former Soviet Union are reliable transport links, normal functioning of communication and information systems, a continuous emphasis on the process of new technologies development, and normal legal and business environments compatible with world-wide standards. The reform plan should concentrate on industrial restructuring, including promotion of competition, coordinated approaches to mineral and energy resources development and utilization, and environmental protection and security of nuclear power plants. From the Japanese standpoint, the process is more important than the final goals or formal targets in building a market economy in Russia.

A special report produced by the Japanese Ministry of International Trade and Industry (MITI) on Russian reforms stresses the importance of centrally guided policies based on established long-term goals, contrary to beliefs in market principles only.[6] Experts from MITI suggest that the Russian government should take emergency measures to halt the output decline and encourage competition among domestic producers by dividing state monopolies into competing companies. MITI also proposed that Russia learn how to channel funds through government institutions and private banks to encourage capital accumulation through preferential taxation schemes and to establish "priority production programs" to ensure the supply of essential industrial goods. Japan has proved that it is "possible to breed bureaucrats who understand how the price mechanism works and how to act as standard bearers for a free-market economy," say the authors of the MITI report. The "Japanese model" provides an approach where improvements to the structure of the economy — for instance, the privatization of the defense industry and rebuilding of the basic industries — are taken care of in a gradual manner first, followed by moves toward liberalization.

In addition to some differences with the United States in advising Russia on its style of development, the Japanese do not feel comfortable in terms of their involvement because Russia is still a major source of residual security concerns for Japan, and this is an issue that cannot be addressed successfully without the participation of the United States.[7] The greatest contribution that Russia can make to regional security, as well as its own security and economic reforms, is to provide incentives for Japan to continue to be "a prototype of global civilian power unique in world history."[8] After all, how many weapons does Russia really need in the North Pacific and for what purposes? How advanced should these weapon systems be and how relevant is the possible use of nuclear devices in an "era of amorphous threat" and new security concerns that are quite different in nature?

Serious strategic complications also emerged in the 1980s related to the problem of the Northern Territories. Compromise with Japan, based on new security relations and followed by a peace treaty, should allow the territorial dispute to be viewed in the broader context of developing a new, long-term relationship based on partnership. This will be easier to achieve if it provides political "breathing space" to both Russia and Japan and is designed to be acceptable to domestic political forces and the public in both countries.

The process of resolution of the problem must be synchronized with an agreement on the cooperative security relationship between Russia on the one hand and the United States and Japan on the other. The involvement of the United States as a guarantor in this scenario could be an important factor. A trilateral process could be initiated by a trilateral summit as a starting point for building a new nonconfrontational regional security and political environment,[9] as well as a wider regional security structure.

SEA OF OKHOTSK BEYOND START II

A Cold War concept of nuclear strategic stability still has an overwhelming influence over Russia's relations with the United States and Japan. It could continue to be a negative factor in the future if nuclear strategy considerations still dominate the regional security agenda. Russian Fleet Ballistic Nuclear Submarines (SSBNs), theoretically capable of hitting their targets from the "home waters" of the Sea of Okhotsk, U.S.-Japan antisubmarine warfare (ASW) efforts, anti-strategic submarine warfare, and Russian conventional forces deployed to protect SSBN bases still constitute the only stage for U.S.-Japanese quasi-hostile security interaction with the Russian Navy, which is forced to follow a bastion strategy for protection of its SSBN fleet.

In order to provide protection for 22–24 SSBNs (only 3 or 4 were deployed at any given time), Moscow had to deploy about 40 nuclear-powered attack submarines and more than 150 naval aviation aircraft, as well as the country's largest surface fleet. These forces, related to the security of the Sea of Okhotsk and the Russian far east, posed a potential threat to Japan and exposed Tokyo to new U.S. requests for a more active military role. By 1991 Japan had almost 90 percent as many ASW aircraft as the United States in the entire Pacific and Indian oceans, more tactical fighter aircraft than the U.S. Air Force had in Japan and Korea combined, and a rather sizable, potent, and very modern navy with 50 destroyers and destroyer-type ships suitable for ASW.[10]

Under the Strategic Arms Reduction Talks (START II) provisions, Russia could retain 1,730 nuclear strategic warheads on its Typhoon, Delta III, and SSBNs by the year 2003. The total number of Russian SSBNs is expected to be reduced from the current 59 to 18 in ten years. If 22–24 Russian SSBNs are currently deployed in the Pacific, how many of them should be kept there toward the final stage of the START II agreement, for what purpose, and at what political cost? Even if Moscow decides by the year 2003 to retain all of its remaining SSBNs only in the Bering Sea, the role of the northwestern Pacific will be uncertain at least for another decade, with nothing but negative implications for Russo-Japanese and Russo-U.S. relations.

A narrow definition of strategic stability prevented analysts from appreciating the fact that Russians felt acutely menaced by U.S. submarine-launched ballistic missile and ASW capabilities, and military secrecy caused analysts to minimize the extent to which submarine-launched ballistic missiles have been targeted against the Soviet nuclear strategic forces, and not just the command and communication centers. SSBNs are more vulnerable to attack than is generally acknowledged. In time of peace, only about half of the U.S. SSBNs and less than one-fourth of the Russian fleet are deployed at sea. Even at high alert, 20 percent of U.S. and 40 percent of Russian SSBNs are vulnerable to attack at their bases. However, START II could also open a window of opportunity for new relations in the region, depending on the process of rethinking the concept of strategic stability and changes in the concept of nuclear deterrence.[11]

MULTILATERAL BILATERALISM

Dramatic changes that took place in 1991 and 1993 opened the opportunity for much greater positive security cooperation between the United States and Russia and also created a new situation for Moscow and Tokyo. In fact, the only realistic scenario is for the latter two to change their security relations. From the Russian standpoint, discussion of the future of the U.S.-Japanese security alliance is tied to reassurances that Japan's role will not extend to the creation of an offensive or nuclear military capability[12] and that Russia will not be a target of the U.S.-Japanese security treaty. To some extent, the answer to these problems lies with the structuring of Russian Far Eastern forces and the reevaluation of regional security doctrine for the United States and Japan. The continuation of their relationships in the present form is neither desirable nor necessary, because the north Pacific is becoming far less important as an area for potential Washington-Moscow interests. For Russia, as well as for the United States, the problem is to complement disarmament efforts, which have remained fixedly Eurocentric, through initiatives that will ease the security environment around Japan. By no means will this lead to a policy of isolating China. Moreover, any design for a multilateral security process in the north Pacific will not be effective unless all four major powers cooperate. Normal trilateral relations between Russia, the United States, and Japan are a major precondition for region-wide dialogue on security, stability, and cooperation in the northwestern Pacific/Northeast Asia regions. Without cooperative relations within this triangle, it is unlikely the wider regional structure will evolve.

NONPROLIFERATION: A COMMON AGENDA

"Why should we work for creation of something additional to the current security linkages in the absence of a clear source of threat?" critics of the idea of multilateralism for the north Pacific ask. "Why should we risk the existing bilateral security relations, which have proved to be efficient and are tested by decades of cooperation? With North Korea continuing to play its own version of NCND policy, the problem of nonproliferation of nuclear weapons and the future of the Nonproliferation Treaty (NPT) must be foremost on the agenda of U.S.-Japanese-Russian trilateral relations. Another important issue that should be discussed by the United States, Japan, Russia, and China is the extension of NPT. No-first-use of nuclear weapons or negative security assurances should be considered as a possible way out, not only from the current deadlock with the suspected nuclear weapons program of North Korea but also as a broader conceptual basis for the nonproliferation regime. An international convention on no-first-use could be a diplomatic way out for the United States not only to prevent North

Korean withdrawal from the NPT but also to preempt possible demands of negative security guarantees from other potential violators of the treaty, even though disagreement exists about such an idea in the defense community.[13]

A phased withdrawal of nuclear strategic and attack submarines and strategic and tactical nuclear weapons from the north Pacific and Russian far east could effectively facilitate security cooperation and, at some point, might lead to the establishment of a north Pacific nuclear-weapon-free zone (NPNWFZ). Moscow can initiate radical changes in the regional security and strategic situation. START II and Moscow's new relations with Washington, in particular, should help the large-scale deactivation of strategic and tactical nuclear arsenals, including sea-based systems, and could facilitate an improvement in Russo-Japanese relations as well as decrease residual military tensions in the Sea of Okhotsk and the Sea of Japan.

In the newly emerging global context, the idea of a north Pacific nuclear-weapon-free zone is becoming a realistic and desirable option directed at building new relations with both Washington and Tokyo. The denuclearization of the north Pacific will position Moscow for partnership relations with the United States and Japan. It will also substantially improve the climate for keeping the Korean peninsula and other parts of the Asia Pacific region free from nuclear weapons. As a relatively long-term goal for trilateral and multilateral relations in the northwestern Pacific, the idea of denuclearization of the region could help to deal with the problem of the dumping of nuclear waste. A total of 23 dumping grounds designated by the former Soviet Union authorities in the northern parts of the Sea of Japan have been in use since 1995. They include two old nuclear reactors and 38 boats with nuclear waste material.[14]

In addition, a multilateral approach to security problems could facilitate transparency in defense activities, military spending, and technological developments.[15] It could help to introduce confidence building and strategic reassurance measures and deal with potential conflict on the Korean peninsula and the future regional posture of China, including Beijing's policy toward Taiwan. Finally, it could help to create a framework for continuous security involvement of the United States in regional affairs.

CHINA AND THE KOREAS

Relations with China is Russia's most important test ground for its new policy of future partnership with the United States, as well as an indicator of the maturity of Moscow's Asian policy in general. There is no doubt that China has the potential to become a leading export market for Russian goods and raw materials. Therefore, the temptation to jump into close business and political relations could be overwhelming.[16] The real problem is not just to turn a blind eye to the Chinese political system but also to evaluate carefully the long-term strategic interests of Russia.

By any measure, compared with the status of affairs in 1991 or even 1989, China is much stronger politically and more active diplomatically than Russia throughout Asia. Russian weapons are far superior to those available to China from the former Third World and less costly than Western military products. If purchased in sufficient quantity, they will enable China to leapfrog into the modern era, especially if we consider the indirect spin-off of the Chinese potential to project power[17] and, by advancing its missile technology, gradually become a regional superpower. As Russian foreign policy analyst Vikentii Matveev indicates, "The problem is that the nature of [Russian] arms sold to China upgrades its offensive, not defensive, potential and that creates concern for several countries of the Asia Pacific region."[18]

Expanded Sino-Russian military cooperation poses a potential challenge to Japan, which felt isolated after President Yeltsin abruptly canceled his trip to Tokyo and then visited Seoul and Beijing shortly thereafter. Moreover, Sino-Russian cooperation annoys the U.S. defense community, which has prompted the Clinton administration to reevaluate China's future military potential and strategic posture. For the first time, in the 1993 National Security Strategy report, there was an indication that it is necessary to carefully watch the emergence of China onto the world stage and support, contain, or balance this emergence as necessary to protect U.S. interests. Probably no provisions should be made for Russian arms in these changing relationships, at least not without prior careful assessment.

By the same token, Russian relations with South Korea should serve the purpose of an integrated Russian Northeast Asian policy and not just bilateral relations with the Republic of Korea. For example, being primarily a list of scheduled diplomatic events, the Memorandum of Understanding on military exchanges between Russia and South Korea conveyed a negative impression to some Japanese, who were concerned that there could be something more in those military-to-military negotiations than simply an exchange program. Even though the positions of Moscow and Seoul converge on the idea of a multiparty dialogue and formal security cooperation in Northeast Asia, as two less than influential parties, Russia and South Korea alone cannot successfully advance this idea even if it is good and even if their views coincide.

Contrary to the spirit of multilateralism, Moscow is succeeding in throwing away its slim chance to be a partner of South Korea, the United States, and Japan in Korean affairs by shutting the door to possible future contacts with North Korea. Bilateral political relations that never were warm or trusting sank to their lowest level after Eduard Shevardnadze failed to meet the North Korean leader in September

1990 and after Russian diplomatic relations were established with Seoul. Diplomacy toward North Korea was emotional and lacked pragmatism, considering the limits of Russia's influence on Korean affairs or its diminishing importance as a player in Northeast Asia. Instead of trying to position itself as a potential mediator, or at least the country that could play this role with "North Korea versus the International Community" in connection with its adherence to the NPT, Russia went too far in leaning toward South Korea. There was very little understanding that it is exactly that policy that would make Russia's role in Korean affairs almost irrelevant. Moscow's policy toward North Korea significantly diminishes its influence as a potential participant in Northeast Asian security processes, nonproliferation issues, and even as a potential partner for regional cooperative efforts with Washington and Tokyo.

An almost final and intended rupture of relations with one totalitarian and isolated communist state — North Korea — was complemented by praise of China's economic and social experiment and, at the same time, provides for military equipment and advanced technology transfer to the state that only four or five years ago was one of the main sources of security concerns. In one Northeast Asian capital, the call was made for partnership in the quest for the shared ideals of peace, prosperity and human dignity, and in another, for respect of each others' choices and differences in social system and ideology, but in the third case, the concern over the human rights issues was emphasized. The statement that "Russia needs no revolution and no cataclysms either," has also been made in connection with China's 14-year success story of gradual reform. Total conceptual paralysis occurred in dealing with strategic nuclear arsenals developed and designed by the Soviet regime to deal with exactly the same countries with whom Russia wants cooperative relations.

It should be noted here that despite high-level visits to Seoul and Beijing in November and December 1992, Russian Northeast Asian summit diplomacy did not help much to advance Russia's own interests, either strategic or regional. It was nothing more than a semiradical diplomatic exercise, which dealt primarily with peripheral or already resolved issues. The core precondition for the success of Russian reforms and its new positive security and political role in Northeast Asia is cooperative relations with the United States and Japan. President Gorbachev, despite his bold initiatives, was unable to change the main pillars of relations with Tokyo and Washington as far as Northeast Asia was concerned. After he visited Japan in 1991, it became crystal clear that bilateral relations with an eastern neighbor cannot be different without a common approach accepted by Japan and the United States to Russian reforms and long-term security relations with Moscow. Are there any hopeful indications that President Yeltsin could do somewhat better?

Domestic political turmoil creates new constraints on diplomacy. Economic chaos limits even modest hopes for closer economic interaction with the region. It is also true that attempts to dismantle the old economic system, as well as domestic instability and problems within the borders of the former Soviet Union, made Russia almost an irrelevant element of regional relations in Asia. However, if isolated, Russia may be an obstacle to the construction of higher order security and economic regimes in the region. The approach the United States and Japan have to take collectively to Asia's future must include Russia as an essential regional actor.

NOTES

1. Lonnie S. Keene, "New Dimensions in Political and Military Postures in Asia: Security Dialogue and Preventive Diplomacy," paper presented at the UN Office for Disarmament Affairs-sponsored conference, "National Security and Confidence Building among Nations in the Asia Pacific Region," Katmandu, Nepal, February 1–3, 1993, pp. 6–10. To be precise, there is brief mention of the territorial dispute between Russia and Japan (p. 5) and of Russia as a part of "a broader consensus on the nuclear issue" on the Korean peninsula (p. 8).

2. "America's Role in Asia: Interests and Policies," report of the Working Group convened by The Asia Foundation's Center for Asia Pacific Affairs, January 1993.

3. Richard F. Ellings and Edward A. Olsen, "A New Pacific Profile," *Foreign Policy* 89 (Winter 1992–93): 123–24.

4. "America's Role in Asia: Interests and Policies," p. 14.

5. "Japanese Tout Their Brand of Capitalism," *Wall Street Journal*, July 20, 1992, p. 35.

6. See Fusac Ota, Hiroya Tanikawa, and Tasuke Otani, "Russia's Economic Reform and Japan's Industrial Policy," paper presented at the Symposium on Unification of Europe, June 1–2, 1992; Yonemura Noriyuki and Tsukamoto Hiroshi, "The Role of Industrial Policy in Post World War II Economic Development in Japan," MITI, March 1992.

7. Hamanouchi stated "Arms reductions in North East Asia is a possibility only under the following extremely hypothetical condition: that a major breakthrough in START II leads to the downplaying of nuclear strategy to the degree that the deployment of SSBNs is limited, for example, to the North of Barents Sea and Arctic Ocean ice cap, and the Soviet Union be willing to risk negotiations of conventional-arms reduction" in Yashuhide Hamanouchi, "Japan's Security Policy and Arms Control in North East Asia," IIGP Policy Paper 60E, October 1991, p. 9.

Nishimura writes "And there is unlikely to be any change in this situation as long as the Soviet Union continues to deploy SSBNs in the Sea of Okhotsk. In consequence, during the 1990s there will be absolutely no change in the importance of maintaining the U.S.-Japan joint deterrent strategy directed at the Soviet Union. Instead of taking the situation of the Soviet strategic forces deployment in the Sea of Okhotsk as an established fact indifferent to the threat to Japan's national security . . . a double-track approach should be followed: pursuing the neutralization of Soviet strategy, while at the same time, conducting negotiations to bring about a change in the deployments of Soviet SSBNs" in Shigeki Nishimura, "Transformation of the U.S-Japan Defense Posture: The New Soviet Challenge," IIGP Policy Paper 65E, October 1991, p. 18.

8. Yoichi Funabashi, "Japan and America: Global Partners," *Foreign Policy* 86 (Spring 1992): 26.

9. "On September 1967, Senator Mike Mansfield of the U.S. attracted a great deal of attention when he attended the Shimoda conference of Japanese and American scholars and politicians. At the conference, he suggested that the solution to the northern territories dispute will only be resolved in the context of some more general settlement dealing with Japanese, American, Chinese, and Russian defense relations." From F. C. Langdon, *Japan's Foreign Policy* (Vancouver: University of British Columbia Press, 1973), p. 134, 137; M. Mansfield's proposal was published in *Mainichi Shimbun*, September 16, 1967, pp. 1, 3 (morning edition), p. 1 (evening edition).

10. Japan already has a substantial and very modern naval force, including some 120 maritime aircraft, 56 major surface combatants (39 destroyers and 17 frigates), and 14 submarines. It was planning to acquire tanker aircraft to extend the range of its air coverage and was considering the acquisition of "defensive" aircraft carriers.

11. "More and more political and military leaders accept the idea that basic changes in the world's approach to nuclear weapons are required. Many have endorsed an idea of returning to a non-nuclear world, among them Les Aspin in his speech at the Massachusetts Institute of Technology in June." Robert S. McNamara, "Nobody Needs Nukes," *New York Times*, February 23, 1993.

"Multilateral arms control also faces new challenges that will require rethinking of past assumptions. It may be necessary to expand the scope of existing nuclear safeguards agreements, for instance, to cover weapons-related equipment as well as nuclear material and to accommodate challenge inspections of both civilian and military installations." Edmund Piasccki and Toby Trister Gati, "The United Nations Disarmament," a report of the United Nations Association of the United States of America, New York, 1992, p. 18.

See also Michael J. Mazarr, "Military Targets for a Minimum Deterrent: After the Cold War How Much Is Enough?" *Journal of Strategic Studies* 15 (June 1992): 147–71.

12. Shigeki Nishimura, a colonel in Japan's Ground Self-Defense Forces, suggests that "it is, in fact, impossible for Japan to maintain an exclusively defensive posture except within the framework of the U.S.-Japan security system, in which U.S. provides the supplementary offensive capability" and that "a separate Japanese defense capability would require nuclear arms." *Far Eastern Economic Review*, August 2, 1992, p. 23.

13. See George H. Quester and Victor A. Utgoff, "U.S. Arms Reductions and Nuclear Nonproliferation: The Counterproductive Possibilities," *Washington Quarterly* 16 (Winter 1993): 137.

14. *The Korean Herald*, April 16, 1993.

15. See Mikhael Moodie, "Transparency in Armaments: A New Item for the New Security Agenda," *Washington Quarterly* 15 (Summer 1992): 75–82; George Segal, "Managing New Arms Races in the Asia/Pacific," *Washington Quarterly* 15 (Summer 1992): 83–102; Douglas M. Jonston, "Anticipating Instability in the Asia-Pacific Region," *Washington Quarterly* 15 (Summer 1992): 103–12.

16. "We are prepared for cooperation in all fields, including the most sophisticated weapons and armaments." Experts from Yeltsin News Conference in Beijing, December 18, 1992, FBIS-CHI-92-244, p. 9.

17. Banning Garrett and Bonnie Glaser, "Yeltsin's China Mission," *Far Eastern Economic Review*, December 17, 1992, p. 24.

18. Vikentii Matveev, "Bananas for 'Kalashnikovs,' What Kind of Weapons Should We Sell to China?" *Nezavisimayay Gazeta*, January 29, 1993.

19

Redefining the Pacific: The New Architecture of Economic Regionalism

R. Sean Randolph

The success of Pacific economic regionalism in the 1990s will require a reconsideration of what constitutes "the Pacific." This has been necessitated by an expansion in the membership of the "Pacific club" and by the advent of a host of bilateral and subregional trade agreements within the Pacific area.

AN EXPANDING CIRCLE

One of the earliest challenges faced by proponents of Pacific regionalism was the problem of definition: in a region as large and diverse as the Pacific, could interests be identified that were widely enough shared to justify the creation of a regional cooperative framework? Cultural and historical differences were compounded by geographic distance. Wide variations in the size of national economies and levels of economic development also make a close association problematic. The one point on which agreement existed was that many of the region's economies were linked by rapidly expanding trade and investment and that these relationships needed to be developed and nurtured.

At its inception in the late 1960s, the circle of participants in the Pacific movement was small. The Pacific Organization for Economic Cooperation and Development industrial states — the United States, Canada, Japan, Australia, and New Zealand — both conceived and largely defined the regional cooperation movement.

Over the 20 years form approximately 1968 to 1988, the newly industrialized economies and the balance of Southeast Asia also joined the process. This occurred as nearly all Asian economies registered strong economic growth and successfully pursued development strategies based on exports. For purposes of regional cooperation, the working definition of "Pacific," therefore, advanced from an industrial/Organization for Economic Cooperation and Development framework to one broadly based on outward-oriented market economies.

This period also coincided with the closing phase of the Cold War. By definition, the "market economies" did not include the Socialist economies of Russia and Indochina (China being a special case that in economic terms bridged the market and socialist systems). By associating "the Pacific" with rapidly growing market economies having strong trade and investment ties, economic strategists accurately identified the criteria that made the Pacific an economic zone with increasingly interrelated interests. The extent of interests with Russia and its allies was minimal at best. Coincidentally, the exclusion of the Socialist bloc from the Pacific framework paralleled with U.S. strategic interests, which, at the time sought to restrict Soviet involvement in the region.

NEW PLAYERS

Two recent developments have redrawn the Pacific landscape. The first is the end of the Cold War and the emergence of Russia (and soon Vietnam) as an economic and political player. The collapse of Soviet communism and the economic reforms initiated by Mikhail Gorbachev and Boris Yeltsin have opened Russia's door to foreign investment, including investment from Asia, and have expanded the potential for foreign trade as well as having given Russia, which once considered Pacific regionalism an anti-Soviet subterfuge, political respectability.

Political uncertainty, currency instability, shortcomings in the legal system, and other constraints have, until now, restricted economic activity between Russia and the Pacific. The continuing dispute over the Kurile Islands has also dampened the prospects of any large-scale capital infusion from Japan. However, the end of ideological confrontation has brought with it political acceptance and Russian membership in nongovernmental regional bodies such as the Pacific Economic Cooperation Council (PECC). Russia's potentially large consumer market and the rich natural resources of the Russian far east hold a particular attraction for many Asian corporations, particularly in neighboring Japan and Korea. If and when economic stability is achieved, Russia is likely to emerge as an economic as well as political factor in Northeast Asia.

Latin America has also begun to make its presence felt in the Pacific. Following a "lost decade" of debt and economic stagnation in the 1980s, many Latin nations have adopted economic reform policies embracing privatization, deregulation, the reduction or elimination of tariff and nontariff barriers, promotion of exports, and increased openness to foreign investment. These policies have, in most cases, been paired with budget discipline and a commitment to control once-rampant inflation. The result has been a resumption of growth and a revitalization of economies throughout Latin America.

This process has been led by two Pacific Latin American nations, Chile and Mexico. In 1992 Chile achieved 9.7 percent growth, the world's second highest growth rate after China. This followed annual growth in the 6–10 percent range from 1988 to 1991 (except for 1990, when growth was 2 percent). Chile's growth is based on an effective combination of domestic consumption and investment, foreign investment (averaging $1.1 billion annually during the 1990–93 period), and exports. As part of its policy of global economic integration, it has successfully diversified overseas markets, with special emphasis on the Pacific. As a result, in 1991, Japan overtook the United States as Chile's leading export market. Since 1985, exports to and imports from nearly all Asia Pacific markets have experienced growth rates of 300 to 1,000 percent.

Mexico presents a similar case. Building on groundwork laid during the administration of President Miguel de la Madrid (1982–88), Mexico's President Carlos Salinas de Gortari has pursued an ambitious policy of economic reform, including many of the measures earlier undertaken by Chile. Although Asian investment in Mexico remains relatively small (Japan is the fifth largest foreign investor, with a total stock of $1.9 billion), many Asian corporations — particularly from the electronics industry — have invested in the maquiladora (in-bond) sector. Continued economic growth and a domestic market of 82 million consumers with rising incomes will, in the coming years, make Mexico an increasingly attractive market and site for Asian investment.

Mexico enjoys a special advantage in its bid for membership in the Pacific club by virtue of its proximity to the United States. The North American Free Trade Agreement (NAFTA) has definitively placed Mexico within the Pacific framework, politically and economically. In economic terms, the formal linkage of Mexico's economy to that of the United States and Canada situates Mexico as a full partner in an integrated North American trade and investment system that is highly integrated and centered on the United States, the single most important trading partner for most Asian nations. Given a continuation of successful reform and a strengthening relationship with the United States, Mexico is likely to emerge as both a significant market and possibly even a competitor for Asia.

The emergence of Chile, Mexico, and Peru as nations with a Pacific as well as hemispheric identity is reflected in their membership in key regional groupings. All three have joined PECC and the Pacific Basin Economic Council (PBEC). Colombia has been provisionally accepted as a PBEC member. Most importantly, Mexico was accepted as a member of the Asia Pacific Economic Cooperation (APEC), a forum of Asia Pacific governments, at its meeting in November 1993, and the same meeting formally opened the door to Chilean membership in 1994.

NEW SYSTEMS

The traditional concept of the Pacific is also being challenged by a range of bilateral and subregional free-trade agreements.

Of these, NAFTA has attracted the most attention because it links a large developing economy with the world's most advanced one. Elsewhere in the Western Hemisphere, economic integration is also proceeding rapidly. Mexico and Chile concluded a free-trade agreement in 1991. Chile has also signed free-trade agreements with Venezuela, Colombia and Bolivia, and is the next nation in line for free trade with the United States. The Mercosur agreement (1990) aims for full economic integration between Argentina, Brazil, Paraguay, and Uruguay, and advanced trade liberalization agreements are in place between Colombia and Venezuela; the Group of Three (Mexico, Colombia, and Venezuela); Colombia, Venezuela, and the Central American Common Market; and within both the Central American Common Market and the Andean Pact. Although the formula and timetable for liberalization vary from agreement to agreement and some, such as Mercosur, face significant internal problems, the process has, by and large, been greeted with enthusiasm and in many cases is already generating substantially increased trade volumes.

These developments, while significant in themselves, are of added importance because of the interest expressed by most Latin American nations in free trade with the United States. The Enterprise for the Americas Initiative, launched under former President Bush, envisages a regional free-trade framework linking the United States and Latin America on a hemispheric basis. The concept of the Enterprise for the Americas Initiative has subsequently been endorsed by the Clinton administration, which has also promised more free-trade agreements in the region. This prospect of a Western Hemisphere trading bloc, although highly speculative, has caused particular concern in Asia and underlies some part of Asia's concern regarding NAFTA.

Subregional integration is also underway in the western Pacific. The closer economic relationship between Australia and New Zealand has already forged a successful integration of those two countries' trading systems. In Southeast Asia, the Association of Southeast Asian Nations Free Trade Agreement, launched in 1992, anticipates free trade among members of the Association of Southeast Asian Nations within 15 years.

Malaysian President Mahathir's call for an East Asian Economic Group has touched sensitive nerves on both sides of the Pacific by calling for an East Asian forum that excludes the United States. Although the original concept of an East Asian Economic Group was later repackaged as a loose, lower-profile consultative forum (the East Asian Economic Caucus), it continues to produce unease among those who fear the political implications of drawing sharp regional lines and doubt its economic advantages. The East Asian Economic Caucus has attracted a degree of support, however, from others who welcome the idea of a forum exclusively devoted to Asian interests. For the present, the proposal is inactive, but a failure of the Uruguay Round or the perception of a protectionist surge in the United States could revive its prospects.

MAKING THE PIECES FIT

The challenge facing the Pacific Economic Cooperation movement is how to make these seemingly disparate pieces fit into a coherent framework that embraces the entire Pacific region.

One element in that process has already been simplified. The failure of Soviet communism and the general retreat of the socialist economic system has eliminated ideology as a factor and placed market economics center stage as the preferred vehicle for growth. This principle is now shared not only by the traditional market economies but also by Russia, China, and Vietnam.

How to manage bilateral and subregional trading groups is more challenging. By definition, these are preferential units, designed to create internal advantages even if they do not create overt barriers against outside partners. This discrimination is not, however, inconsistent with the General Agreement on Tariffs and Trade (GATT), which explicitly allows free-trade arrangements on the condition that they cover substantially all trade and do not erect new barriers against nonparticipating countries. As former GATT Director Arthur Dunkel has pointed out, GATT's founders foresaw the need to accommodate groups of nations that were prepared to pursue liberalization on a more accelerated basis than could be achieved through global negotiations.

It is essential, at the minimum, that current and future free-trade agreements meet these GATT criteria. It is no less important, however, for nations participating in such agreements to recognize that free trade with one country or a group of countries, no matter how beneficial, cannot fully substitute for access to an open global market. This suggests that countries participating in free-trade arrangements should in no way reduce their commitment to GATT's multilateral framework. It also suggests that even as internal barriers are lowered between members of free-trade groups, participating nations should pursue unilateral trade liberalization with outside countries as well.

Development of bilateral and subregional trading systems in the Pacific must, therefore, be combined with a reinforced commitment to the GATT and the enhanced access to global markets that it provides and should be linked with an enhanced commitment to economic cooperation on a Pacific basis.

With flexibility, Pacific economic regionalism can accommodate the new subregional systems. To do so, however, a new paradigm is required that redefines the Pacific as a geoeconomic zone and articulates a rationale for how and why nations participating in subregional agreements can also benefit from participation in a wider regional framework.

Most market economies in the Pacific have greatly benefited from access to multiple overseas markets and investment partners. This holds true for the United States and Japan (which are, by definition, global economies) as well as for the newly industrialized economies and the rapidly developing economies of Southeast Asia. An exclusive concentration on a single market or subset of trading partners will needlessly limit market opportunity and inhibit new foreign investment.

The foundation of Pacific economic regionalism continues to be the extensive and broad-based trade and investment relationships that have developed in the area over the past 30 years. Within that framework, the United States and Japan predominate as markets, as exporters, and as investors. Since 1986, the share of Asian exports going to the United States has fallen from 35 percent to 25 percent, while intra-Asian exports have risen from 30 percent to over 40 percent. Although the importance of the United States as a market relative to internal Asian markets has declined, it, nevertheless, remains the single most important export market for most Asian economies and will remain a vital regional market for the indefinite future. Conversely, the strong economic presence established by Japan throughout the Pacific in the 1980s is welcomed by its neighbors, but not to the exclusion of a significant, counterbalancing U.S. presence.

Because it embraces trans-Pacific interests as well as those specific to Asia and the Western Hemisphere, Pacific regionalism bridges the area's diverse economic interests. In the absence of such an umbrella, the risk of exclusively defined economic blocs would be significantly greater. By blurring those lines, Pacific regionalism contributes needed flexibility to a trading system that is undergoing rapid change and is experiencing increasing economic and political pressure.

In contrast to Europe, Pacific economic regionalism has evolved in a bottom-up fashion, based not on ambitious government master plans but on the independent processes of the private sector. Private sector organizations such as PECC, PBEC, and the Pacific Trade and Development Conference have led that process. Now, however, the advent of the intergovernmental APEC forum promises to take Pacific regionalism in a new direction. Its success or failure in doing so will determine the future of the Pacific cooperation movement and will, indirectly, have a major influence on the global trend toward regional trading systems.

Launched in Canberra in November 1989, APEC was created as a forum for Pacific governments to consider issues of common economic concern. Its early meetings — an annual conference of trade and foreign ministers supported by periodic meetings of senior officials — necessarily focused on procedural and definitional matters such as structure and membership. A series of working groups was also established to consider concrete cooperation in fields such as transportation, marine resources, investment, and human resource development. Since 1992, when a permanent international secretariat was established in Singapore, APEC has begun to assume the shape of a more formal international organization.

If developed and supported, APEC can play an important future role as a bridge linking both private sector and government interests in the region. Its immediate challenge is to construct a program that is sufficiently concrete to merit serious investment by its member governments. This will be particularly important as local subregional processes compete for government time and resources. If this can be accomplished, APEC may provide an alternative model for economic regionalism that is more open and flexible than other regional systems to date.

APEC's Working Group on Regional Trade Liberalization is central to this process. By building on the GATT and accelerating (or going beyond) its reforms regionally, APEC can produce concrete benefits for regional economies while strengthening the global trading system. Topics now under review include harmonization of customs procedures and improved transparency regarding investment procedures and nontariff barriers. Ultimately, APEC should aim to serve as a forum for the negotiation of regional economic agreements that generate common data and standards and reduce regional barriers to trade and investment.

It is essential that APEC's program be developed in close partnership with the private sector and avoid creating large administrative structures or bureaucracies. To achieve a maximum result in economic terms, it must retain the orientation toward the private sector that has defined Pacific regionalism to date. This will require interaction with the business community and a responsiveness to its needs and priorities. This also suggests that APEC's programs be designed in consultation with the private sector and that its products be openly disseminated to and accessible by businesses and private researchers inside and outside the region.

Finally, mechanisms must be found to accommodate the new economic actors on the Pacific Rim. Nongovernmental bodies such as the PECC and PBEC can play an important transitional role by accommodating and giving expression to the regional aspirations of Russia and Latin America. As private sector entities, they are less burdened by the political and diplomatic baggage of governmental institutions and are more directly connected to the realities of international business. A rapid expansion of APEC's membership may not be advisable until its institutional framework and objectives are settled, but that time is not far off. For their part, applicants must demonstrate a willingness and ability to contribute to those objectives. Ultimately, however, APEC must prove itself flexible enough to absorb these new members and their perspectives.

CONCLUSION

In the end, the movement toward economic organization in the Pacific must accommodate new economic forces, both national and institutional, and produce concrete economic benefits. To achieve this, a flexible structure and a close relationship between the government and private sectors is essential. Given the development of the Pacific Economic Cooperation movement so far, there is solid reason to believe that this can be achieved.

20

A Vision for the Asia Pacific Economy in the Year 2000 and the Tasks Ahead

Ippei Yamazawa

The East Asian economies have achieved spectacular growth during the 1970s and 1980s. These include the Asian newly industrialized economies (NIEs), the six member nations of the Association of Southeast Asian Nations (ASEAN), China, and Japan, with much lower growth. As regional economic integration proceeds in Europe and North America, several proposals for regional grouping have been made for East Asia. Regional groupings, however, should not be based on either rivalry or bandwagon motives. If we study the East Asian economies objectively, we see that the regional integration of the European or North American type is neither feasible nor desirable for East Asia: not feasible because the East Asian economies are diverse in size, resource endowments, and stages of development, and they are less experienced in regional integration, and not desirable because the East Asian economies have already achieved rapid growth without any institutional integration.

Nevertheless, loose forms of institutionalization for economic cooperation are now sought in order to maintain current growth rates by mitigating trade frictions, facilitating trade and investment expansion, and resolving bottlenecks in industrial infrastructure and human resources. The area this cooperation would cover has grown now to encompass the Asia Pacific region as a whole, including North America and Oceania, because of East Asia's close link with the latter two regions. The Asia Pacific Economic Cooperation (APEC)/Pacific Economic Cooperation Council process fits this purpose. The APEC forum is the annual meeting of the foreign and trade ministers of 15 Asia Pacific economies. The Pacific Economic Cooperation Council is a nongovernmental meeting series that includes businesspeople, academics, and government officials from 20 Asia Pacific nations acting in their private capacities.

In early 1993, Japan's Ministry of International Trade and Industry (MITI) organized a study group to map a vision for the Asia Pacific economies in the year 2000. The group reflected a typical MITI approach to policy implementation for industrial development at home. In the 1960s, 1970s, and 1980s, MITI produced a vision for Japanese industrial development that provided a basis for the formation of a national consensus on the future direction of industrial development and enabled the implementation of policies conducive to Japan's industrial development. The 1992 study group followed a similar format, intending to provide a consensual basis for Asia Pacific industrial development. Intended for Japanese audiences, the study group was also targeted to appeal to other APEC members. It was composed of Japanese business people, academics, and government officials and produced a report following an intensive four-month study. The report was first submitted to a gathering of experts from the APEC member countries for their comments and revision and then was presented in final form to the APEC Ad Hoc Economic Group Meeting on August 10–11, 1992 in Tokyo and adopted by the APEC Ministerial Meeting in September 1992.[1] This chapter is based on a summary of the report's recommendations for the tasks ahead in Pacific cooperation.

GOALS OF THE REPORT OF THE MINISTRY OF INTERNATIONAL TRADE AND INDUSTRY

The MITI report had three aims. First, it attempted to measure the increasing interdependence among the Asia Pacific economies. Asia Pacific economies vary significantly in size, resource endowments, and developmental stages, as well as in growth of production, trade, and investment. Interdependence among member economies has increased steadily within this context of diversity. Many economists talk about the increasing interdependence in the region, but no serious efforts have been made to quantify it. The MITI report attempted to measure the degree of interdependence among the member economies in commodity trade, services trade, foreign direct investment, workers and other personnel movements, and so forth. The report estimated a matrix for each type of intraregional flow, specifying both sources and destinations. However, the limited availability of reliable data, particularly for service, trade, and personnel movements, inhibited these efforts.

Second, the report was to clarify the mechanism underlying the increasing interdependence in the Asia Pacific. Three factors were identified: the open economic policies adopted by APEC member governments, active transfer of industries from "early starter" to "latecomer" economies in the region, and the activities of multinational enterprises (MNEs) in the Asia Pacific. MNEs took advantage of the open economic policies and were active agents in industrial transfer, specifically affecting local enterprises. However, the conventional identification of local firms and MNEs by their country of origin no longer holds. Instead, the current distinction reflects different developmental stages of individual firms. In other words, every firm begins as a small local enterprise with its business horizon limited to its home market. As the firm develops, it will begin to operate across national borders, thereby becoming an MNE if it is properly endowed with sufficient entrepreneurship and the production of comparative advantage. MNEs also are not restricted to developed countries. Many firms in the NIEs can now be considered MNEs. The same holds true in the ASEAN countries. However, the MITI report confined its analysis to the MNEs originating from the United States and Japan because comparable foreign direct investment data were available only for these two countries.

Third, the MITI report was to provide the APEC member countries with a vision of APEC economies in the year 2000. The year 2000 is no longer in the distant future. It should, therefore, be possible to continue revising the performance trends of the 1980s to paint an image of the Asia Pacific economies in the year 2000. The report concluded with a list of the tasks ahead to achieve such a vision. It is imperative to maintain the current growth performance of the region up to the year 2000, and the report emphasizes that consultation and cooperation among the APEC member governments is needed to facilitate further expansion of trade and investment, conduct regular policy dialogues, resolve bottlenecks to further industrial development, and conclude the Uruguay Round and strengthen the General Agreement on Tariffs and Trade (GATT) regime.

INCREASING INTERDEPENDENCE IN THE ASIA PACIFIC ECONOMY

The Asia Pacific is rich in diversity, a fact that is evident in the region's natural resource endowments, population, developmental stages, and income levels. This diversity has been harnessed to increase economic interdependence and to maintain the high growth of the region as a whole. In the 1960s, the United States, Japan, and the other developed countries enjoyed high growth. However, in the 1970s, the high growth rate in these countries slowed, and conversely, it was the Asian NIEs (Hong Kong, Korea, Singapore, and Chinese Taipei) and the remaining ASEAN countries (Brunei, Indonesia, Malaysia, the Philippines, and Thailand) that achieved high growth. The expansion of trade and investment in the region in the 1980s stimulated growth in the Asian NIEs and the ASEAN countries. The rapid growth of China has been achieved through active economic exchange with the market economies within the region, which, in turn, has contributed to the growth of the region.

Growth in manufacturing has exceeded gross domestic product growth rates in the high growth countries of the Asia Pacific region. This trend indicates that rapid industrialization was the main mechanism underlying the high growth in the region. Rapid industrialization was accompanied by changes in the industrial structure. The process of industrialization usually begins with existing food processing and easily accessible resource processing. Consequently, if there is a scarcity of mineral and foods resources, labor-intensive manufacturing develops, progressing in the next stage to capital-intensive manufacturing and machinery production. The high growth rate of Asian NIEs and the ASEAN countries has followed this path. Although the market share of machine products has declined in all the developed countries with the exception of Japan, the Asian NIEs have rapidly expanded their market share of machine products and the Asia Pacific region is now becoming the world's source of supplies for machinery.

Through the open economic system of the Asia Pacific region, changes in the structure of industrial production are directly reflected in the export structure of each country and area. Initially, the Asian NIEs and the ASEAN countries raised their export share of labor-intensive manufactured goods and became a world supply center. Subsequently, these countries have increased their export share of capital-intensive manufactured goods and machinery while retaining a high import dependency on parts and intermediate goods. The progress of international specialization within certain industries is striking.

Measurement of Increasing Interdependence

A matrix analysis of various economic transactions of the Asia Pacific region indicates increasing interdependence. In the area of trade, an examination of the commodity trade matrix indicates increasing interdependence within the region. The average annual growth rate of trade overall in the Asia Pacific is 14.2 percent, which only slightly exceeds the total world trade growth rate. However, within the trade matrix, certain bilateral trade relationships have shown remarkably high growth rates. Countries with high growth rates, such as the Asian NIEs and the ASEAN countries, have realized trade expansion in both imports and exports that greatly exceeds the average figures. By the mid-1980s, Pacific trade surpassed Atlantic trade for both the United States and Canada. Thus, in 1990, APEC's overall intraregional trade ratio (measured by imports and exports) expanded to 60 percent.

The expansion of service trade is an important aspect of the increasing interdependence. In 1990, the APEC region's overall service trade reached $55 billion, which corresponds to two-thirds of the APEC members' total commodity trade of $83.2 billion for that year. Service trade in the region is expanding at a rate of 15 percent annually, exceeding the world average by 1.5 percent. This expansion is particularly striking in East Asia, where Japan, the Asian NIEs, and the ASEAN countries have expansion rates reaching 20 percent annually. It was not possible to create a matrix for total service flow in the MITI report, but the matrix of air transport and international telecommunications in the Asia Pacific region was presented. Japan and the Asian NIEs show striking growth in both categories. Expansion also occurred in service trade across the Pacific between the Asia Pacific countries noted above and North America.

Foreign direct investment ranks alongside commodity and service trade as a driving force in the increasing interdependence within the Asia Pacific region. A foreign investment flow matrix of the Asia Pacific region for 1980, 1985, and 1989 was prepared, combining statistics of incoming and outgoing direct investment for each country and region. However, because the arrangement of these statistics differs from country to country and because the statistics are based primarily on reported figures for admission, which differed from actual investments, this matrix presented numerous problems. It was, nevertheless, a first attempt at preparing a matrix for foreign investment flows that included the European Community (EC) and indicates some special characteristics of foreign investment in the Asia Pacific region.

First and foremost, the total amount of foreign investment received by the Asia Pacific region in 1989 reached $100 billion, 2.6 times the EC total. The main recipient of this investment was the United States with three-fourths of that total, followed by the ASEAN countries with $15 billion, Oceania with $6 billion, and the Asian NIEs with $5.5 billion. The main providers of the investment were Japan and the United States. In the second half of the 1980s, investments in the ASEAN countries expanded at a greater rate than in the Asian NIEs. The main investing countries were Japan, the Asian NIEs and the United States, in that order. On the other hand, the amount of investment from Japan and the United States was almost identical for the Asian NIEs and Oceania.

In addition to the flow of commodities, services, and capital, the personnel movement in the Asia Pacific region was significant. Exchanges included laborers, students, trainees, and tourists. It was possible to prepare a flow matrix for each group, allowing for the fact that many limitations were encountered in the data dealing with laborers. In the Asia Pacific region, the main recipients of foreign laborers are the United States and Japan. Each year the United States received 80,000 laborers from the ASEAN countries (mainly from the Philippines) and 60,000 from the Asian NIEs. Japan received 20,000 laborers from the ASEAN countries. From the student matrix, it is apparent that APEC members accepted 230,000 students from within the APEC region (1988), with three-fourths of that figure representing the United States, followed by Japan, Australia, and Canada, in that order. Japan was enthusiastic about accepting technical trainees. In addition, the Asia

Pacific region received 88 million tourists in 1989; a 2.4-fold increase over 60 percent (56 million) came from within the region. If we look at this in the matrix, we see that the flow of tourists to the United States, Japan, the Asian NIEs, and the ASEAN countries is large.

Bilateral Official Development Assistance (ODA) by the Development Assistance Committee of the Organization for Economic Cooperation and Development to developing countries in the region also contributes to the increasing interdependence. The Asia Pacific region received $4.5 billion in 1989, which is about three times the total of 1980. The share of the total bilateral ODA supporting the region in-creased to 14 percent in 1989, which is 5 percent higher than in 1980. Of the total of $4.9 billion, 60 percent was provided by Japan, and when we add North America and Oceania, 75 percent of ODA for this region was provided by the developed countries within the region. On the other hand, South Korea provided about $230 million of bilateral ODA in 1989, transforming itself from a receiving country into a donor country.

Toward Greater Trans-Pacific Transactions

The preceding analysis shows a rapidly increasing interdependence within East Asia. This interdependence is the result of the rapid expansion of the Asian NIEs and the ASEAN economies and of their trade with neighboring economies. However, we should not overlook the fact that these economies have expanded their trade with other parts of the Asia Pacific region, especially North America and Oceania. In fact, trade between East Asia and North America and Oceania has been expanding far more rapidly than trade with economies outside the region. Let us review trade and other transactions between East Asia, North America, and Oceania, that is, trans-Pacific transactions.

With regard to trade, trans-Pacific trade (total trade between North America and the other APEC members) was only slightly greater in 1980 than trans-Atlantic trade (total trade between North America and the EC). However, it had expanded to 1.5 times that of trans-Atlantic trade in 1990. With regard to foreign direct investment, trans-Pacific investment in 1980 was only 19 percent of trans-Atlantic investment. However, due to the increasing investment of other APEC members in North America, that ratio increased to 57 percent in 1989. From 1980 to 1989 the ratio of trans-Pacific travelers to trans-Atlantic travelers increased from 26 to 44 percent. Trans-Pacific transactions will continue to expand throughout the 1990s and add to the increasing interdependence in the Asia Pacific.

STRUCTURAL CHANGES IN THE ASIA PACIFIC REGION

From this analysis we see how increasing interdependence of the Asia Pacific region has proceeded in the areas of commodity trade, service, trade, direct investment, and personnel movements. What is the mechanism promoting these aspects of interdependence? It is possible to suggest various causes, starting with the dramatic progress in transportation and communication technology in recent years that makes it possible to conduct economic exchange across the vast Pacific Ocean. However, the remainder of this chapter will focus on the following three factors: first, increasing interdependence in the open economic policies of the countries in the Asia Pacific region and their macroeconomic performance; second, the ways in which new industries, especially manufacturing, have been introduced to the developing countries in the region and how these industries have developed; and, third, the operations of MNEs in the Asia Pacific region. These three factors are interrelated, and, obviously, all three contribute to the increasing interdependence of the region. The first two factors have been discussed on the national level; the third differs in that it takes the perspective of MNEs. Thus, the study of MNEs may represent a new approach.

Economic Interdependence and Macroeconomic Performance

The diversity of the economies of the Asia Pacific region is a reflection of each country's competitive advantages in different fields of production. This diversity has led to a complementary pattern of trade. The macroeconomic performance of the developing countries in the Asia Pacific has been spectacular, and each country has realized high rates of growth. These high growth rates have stimulated even higher export growth rates, low inflation rates, increased savings rates, and high investment efficiency. It is noteworthy that although the developed countries in the region demonstrated growth rates of 3–4 percent, the high growth of the region's developing countries was largely due to active trade and investment with developed countries, such as the United States and Japan.

Prudent economic policy has formed the foundation for achieving such high growth rates in the developing countries of the Asia Pacific region. In the 1980s, most developing countries of the region were exposed to large fluctuations in both income and price. They suffered from imbalances in international balances of payments, fiscal revenue, and expenditures and from the gap between savings and investment in the private sector. These imbalances have carried over into the 1990s. Because of their export-oriented economies, both the Asian NIEs and the ASEAN countries were prone to external shocks. They, nonetheless, deserve praise for achieving economic stability through the administration of prudent fiscal and financial policies and exchange rate regulation.

The importance of structural adjustment policy in the broad sense of the term ranks with that of macroeconomic policy and includes all measures taken to strengthen the supply side in the mid to longer term: trade policy, financial reform, and fostering of human resources. Of course, the measures taken in each country of the Asia Pacific region reflect that country's state of development and economic scale and, thus, are in no way uniform. However, there are some common elements. In order to alleviate trade frictions, the Asian NIEs promoted active trade liberalization and privatization of public enterprises. Wage increases and raised exchange rates forced changes in industrial policies centered on raising the level of sophistication of the industrial structure and on the development of technology. Trade and financial liberalization and the privatization of public enterprises are common to the policy of all the ASEAN countries. An analysis of the early stages of industrialization indicates that the industrial policies of these countries are characterized by promotion of industrial product exports, development of domestic infrastructure, fostering of small and medium-sized enterprises, and active introduction of foreign capital.

The Patterns of Transfer of Industries

One of the main mechanisms supporting the increasing interdependence in the Asia Pacific region is the transfer of new industries, particularly manufacturing industries. In fact, a shift has occurred in the countries that have achieved international competitiveness in exports from mature industries, such as textiles and steel, from the United States and Japan to the Asian NIEs and from the Asian NIEs to the ASEAN countries. This phenomenon is known as the "flying wild-geese pattern" of industrial development and has served as a catalyst for the deepening interdependence in the Asia Pacific region. The pattern has already extended to the point of developing the electronics and automobile industries in the ASEAN countries. The continued success of industrial transfer in the future is the key to predicting the future success or failure of industrialization in ASEAN and the probability of increasing interdependence in the Asia Pacific region.

Two types of enterprises have promoted the flying wild-geese pattern of industrial development. The first group consists of local enterprises in the developing countries that have been the recipients of industrial transfer. Their entrepreneurial spirit makes them eager to acquire new technology to catch up with the leading companies and, thus, makes them a prime mover in import substitution. The second group is composed of MNEs in the developed countries, which are the source of the industrial transfer. After choosing the most appropriate country, these multinationals begin the transfer of new technology. Then the local enterprises follow the typical development pattern of the Japanese industries in their attempt to catch up with the technologies in the developed countries.

The MNEs present the product cycle theory applied to the pattern of foreign investment displayed by U.S. enterprises. The type of enterprise that becomes the main catalyst in a given country is dependent on both the industry and the particular "follower country" receiving the new industry. The catch-up activities for industries such as textiles and steel that are technologically mature are carried out primarily by the local enterprises of the developing country. However, in industries such as electronics and fine chemicals where new products and technologies often emerge, the role of MNEs inevitably becomes larger. Further, recipient countries blessed with an entrepreneurial spirit are capable of catch-up development led by local enterprises. However, when demand for new products is limited in the domestic market, export orientation is necessary from the very beginning. Thus, dependence on the MNEs becomes necessary, because they are familiar with overseas markets. Some cases exist where both catalysts actively work together in industrial development.

The introduction of new industries into the ASEAN countries is striking, particularly into Indonesia, Malaysia, and Thailand. In the second half of the 1980s, the industrial growth rate of these three countries was the highest in the region at 11–14 percent, with the percentage of manufacturing in total domestic production in 1990 expanding to 19 percent in Indonesia, 27 percent in Malaysia, and 25 percent in Thailand. The transfer of selected new industries stands out, such as electrical machinery and parts, precision machinery, and chemicals.

The export orientation of these new products has begun, with the percentage of industrial products in total exports reaching 46 percent in Indonesia, 60 percent in Malaysia, and 75 percent in Thailand. This rush of new industries is characterized by the participation of MNEs, particularly in areas that are considerably export oriented. The Asian NIEs rank alongside Japan with their large number of MNEs in the ASEAN countries, and U.S. MNEs also have begun to increase. The international development of these enterprises represents attempts to confront rapid adjustments in the exchange rate, wage increase, and labor shortages.

What was the relationship between local enterprises and MNEs when these new industries began? The textile industry matured in the 1960s and 1970s through joint ventures between local enterprises and MNEs, and import substitution had already been accomplished by the end of the 1970s. In the 1980s, we observed a shift to export orientation, and in many cases, local enterprises became relatively dominant. The electrical appliance industry began import substitution through joint ventures, but before this was accomplished, 100 percent foreign capital export-oriented industries began independently along new lines and began to expand rapidly. The automobile industry also began through joint ventures and is currently in the process of import substitution. This industry displays the type of industrial development mentioned above, namely, through MNE leadership, yet growth in the automobile industry is also due to special incentive policies stressing exports that are often implemented by the recipient countries.

Following the typical development structure of Japanese companies, the MNEs bring with them the newest processing and assembling equipment when entering a country, and they have a high degree of dependence on imported parts in order to maintain high product quality. In addition, parts of companies have also entered the local market, forming a parts-procurement network. The issue recipient countries now face is how best to include local companies in these export-oriented new industries. As local production increases, the share of local parts procurement will also increase and local companies will be brought into the local parts-procurement network. The localization of the new industries themselves will progress when expertise and management personnel are localized and the number of parts developed locally begins to increase. This leads to increased participation of local companies in the new industries. Thus, it is more effective in the mid to longer term to provide inducements through supporting engineers and development by MNEs rather than by creating adverse effects by placing various performance requirements on MNEs through regulations.

Activities of Multinational Enterprises

In the Asia Pacific region, many economic activities, such as direct investment and trade undertaken by MNEs, are contributing to increasing interdependence in the region. The activities of MNEs literally transcend national borders and reflect a dramatic change from the now outdated perspective of an era when national boundaries formed the basis for analysis. This chapter will now examine the behavior pattern of MNEs whose activities cross borders by looking at U.S. and Japanese MNEs. For these two countries' MNE groups, the U.S. Department of Commerce and MITI have published virtually comparable large-scale surveys, conducted every three years during the 1980s. In addition to Japan and the United States, Asian MNEs were also very active. However, due to data limitations, we were unable to compare Asian MNEs with those of the United States and Japan.

Although U.S. and Japanese MNEs display differences in their patterns of specialization in individual industries and the contributions of trading companies (Japanese companies have historically been very active), they demonstrate recognizably similar patterns of activity. The MITI and U.S. Department of Commerce studies examine the sales and purchasing patterns of the subsidiaries of U.S. and Japanese MNEs in Asia (Asian NIEs, the ASEAN countries, and China). Although these studies exhibit statistical limitations, they found that the percentage of exports in total sales was the same for both groups. However, although the export ratio of U.S. MNEs does not differ between Asia and other regions, Asian subsidiaries reflect export ratios substantially higher than other regions in the case of Japanese MNEs. Differences can also be seen in the purchasing patterns of the two groups. U.S. MNEs exhibit a low dependence on purchasing for the home country, and the weight of both local procurement and third-country procurement is great. However, for Japanese MNEs, the procurement ratio from the home country is high, although the percentage of procurement from the home country for Japanese MNEs tended to decrease during the 1980s. This statistic reflects the fact that as experience in overseas operations accumulates and the procurement network expands, technological transfer to local companies progresses and improvement in the quality of parts is achieved.

Vigorous intrafirm trade is apparent between the headquarters and the overseas subsidiaries of all MNEs and among the overseas subsidiaries themselves. The world-wide business strategy of MNEs has been to produce in places most suitable for products and to sell widely throughout the world. Thus, parts, intermediate goods, and finished products, as well as new technology, designs, and market information, must be actively traded. Not much difference is evident in the intrafirm trading patterns for purchasing between U.S. and Japanese MNEs. However, the U.S. MNEs have a high percentage of interfirm trade in their sales, and their share of exports for home country sales is particularly high.

The overall weight occupied by all MNEs, including MNEs from countries other than Japan and the United States, in the economic activity of Asian NIEs and the ASEAN countries is significant. This is especially true in the secondary industries in Singapore, Thailand, Malaysia, and the Philippines (the core of which is manufacturing), where the share of MNEs in total employees, sales volume, and added value has reached 30–50 percent. For Indonesia, Korea, and Taiwan, this share is approximately 20 percent. The export ratio to Japan of Japanese MNEs in Asia was 44 percent in 1989, which was nearly four times the 12 percent for all Asian exports in manufacturing industries. Thus, we can see that Japanese enterprises have played a leading role in the expansion of exports of Asian industrial products to Japan.

THE VISION OF THE ASIA PACIFIC REGION IN THE YEAR 2000 AND TASKS AHEAD

Past Trends and New Challenges

The year 2000 no longer lies in the distant future. It should, therefore, be possible to continue revising the performance trends of the 1980s to paint an image of the Asia Pacific economy in the 1990s. Over the past few years, we have witnessed drastic changes in world politics and economies. The most notable changes are the near collapse of the socialist economies and the resulting end of the Cold War. This state of affairs presents us with both blessings and challenges. On the one hand, the world economy has been freed from the burden of the Cold War regime of the past 40 years. On the other hand, the global economy has inherited the burden of assisting the malfunctioning economies of former socialist regimes.

The challenges facing us will, no doubt, lead to many problems in the Asia Pacific region, and a common program will be necessary to contend with the consequent problems. Yet, time remains before the year 2000 is upon us, time that permits us to tackle both new and old problems through active readjustment rather than taking simple stopgap measures.

As discussed earlier, the continued growth of the Asia Pacific region is based on the diversity of the region's economy and increasing interdependence. As we approach the year 2000, this growth should continue, probably expanding to South Asia and Central and South America. In this process, it is possible that APEC members may face trade and investment frictions and other difficulties that may act as a brake on the increasing interdependence of the region and obstruct the region's continued growth. In view of this, the Asia Pacific region must prepare to face new challenges and devise measures to overcome difficulties and realize continued growth beyond the year 2000.

Tasks Ahead

The economic development of the Asia Pacific region is based on interdependence, and to maintain this development as we head into the twenty-first century, we must deal collectively with the following tasks.

Maintain and Strengthen the Free Trade System

As we have seen, the key factor that has supported the development of the Asia Pacific region has been the open trade system in each country. In the future, it will be essential to maintain and reinforce the free, multinational trade system in order to maintain the high growth potential of the area. In order to accomplish this, countries in the region need to maintain their open markets without resorting to protectionism. Similarly, it is desirable that APEC members continue to make full use of open, nonexclusive cooperation and contribute to the maintenance and strengthening of the GATT system. It is also necessary for APEC members to use their experience to help expand the region's free market system to include countries currently in the process of shifting to market economies.

Expand Trade

Throughout the 1980s, the Asia Pacific region recorded a high rate of overall economic growth. The expansion of international trade and investment in the region by Japan and the United States contributed greatly to realizing economic growth. In the first half of the 1980s, exports from this region, especially from the Asian NIEs, expanded rapidly.

As we have already seen, in the second half of the 1980s, with the adjustment in foreign exchange rates based upon the Plaza Accord, exports from Asian NIEs and the ASEAN countries to Japan and the United States grew steadily, and the economic growth achieved in these countries was supported by overseas market demand.

In order for the Asia Pacific to maintain the sort of economic growth achieved in the 1980s, it will be important for nations in the region to make efforts toward further deregulation of trade and to maintain an even freer flow of goods. To this end, it is necessary for the countries of the region to maintain open trade policies. Asia Pacific economies must also redouble their efforts to remove import regulations that interfere with free movement of goods and to reduce tariffs, border measures, and other nontariff regulations. Moreover, in order for the Asian NIEs and the ASEAN countries to maintain growth based on exports, they will need to secure new markets and will be expected to play such a role in accordance with their economic growth.

A survey of imports in the region shows that the Asian NIEs and the ASEAN nations reached a high import level in the 1980s (mainly in manufactured goods) due to advances in intraindustry specializations. Areas remain where import substitution measures, such as domestic parts procurement, should be advanced gradually in order to continue growth.

Secure a Freer Flow of Managerial Resources and Capital

A key factor in promoting the high rate of economic growth in the region, especially with Asia, has been the active overseas direct investment by the United States, Japan, and the Asian NIEs. In the first half of the 1980s, U.S. business enterprises carried out active overseas investments supported by a strong dollar, while in the second half of the 1980s, manufacturing sector investments were maintained by Japan in the ASEAN countries and the Asian NIEs. Direct investment serves the role of transferring not just capital but also managerial resources, managerial expertise, technology, and services of the investing country in an integrated form to the receiving country. This kind of mutual exchange through direct investment is spreading throughout the Asia Pacific region. Both the investing country and the receiving country benefit from an industrial division of labor within the region and through the effective allocation and utilization of resources.

The main bearers of direct investment are the MNEs. In this region, despite various types of obstacles and impediments, the activities of MNEs have become increasingly vigorous. As has been shown, MNEs have made large contributions to the development of local economies through technology transfer, creating additional employment in local communities and expanding exports to overseas from within the region.

To enhance the vigor of MNE activities, it is necessary to remove the obstacles that hamper the development of borderless movement of investments and business activity. From this viewpoint, it is necessary to ease regulations on investments, ease controls on the activities of MNEs, and implement measures that strengthen protection of intellectual property. At the same time, it is important for MNEs to make the necessary efforts to expand the ranks of locally hired employees.

Nurture Supporting Industries

Although MNEs, primarily those of Japan and the United States, have clearly contributed to the economic growth and sophistication of local industries, problems persist, such as the gaps between these MNEs and local industries; weak linkages in areas such as procurement of parts; and excessive dependence upon imports related to parts and materials. In the future, if sustained development is to continue in the developed countries, it is necessary to maintain an open stance toward investment and trade and to actively nurture local industrial capital and supporting industries to support main industries. In this way, we can anticipate such effects as the expansion of local procurement and a decrease in the import ratio of raw materials.

Develop Human Resources

In the course of rapid economic development in the Asia Pacific region in recent years, a shortage of talented personnel has emerged as a problem. Human resources development is an urgent task to be tackled if the region is to continue sustained economic growth in the future. Especially critical are the shortage of management personnel who will shoulder localization of foreign businesses and development of local businesses; the shortage of industrial engineers to support productive activities and promote research and development of products; and the shortage of experts in economic development to plan and design industrial policies, such as the development of supporting industries. Overall development of human resources is vitally needed and must be fostered through promoting local education and training programs as well as training of prospective personnel in developed countries.

Develop Industrial Infrastructure

The continued progress of the developing countries in the Asia Pacific region is dependent on the growth of MNEs and local business enterprises. However, social and economic infrastructure, including electrical power, water works, roads, communication facilities, and ports and harbors, which serve as the foundation for industry, is not adequate. In the future it will be necessary to develop the kind of industrial infrastructure that will enable foreign and domestic business enterprises to conduct business activities with relative ease.

Harmonize Institutions

In order for the region to achieve sustained economic growth, APEC members must work together based on international standards aimed at harmonization in all the relevant areas of statistics, intellectual property rights, and industrial standards. The objective of this harmonization is to overcome discrepancies in areas that impede the activities of business enterprises, trade, and investment. APEC has already undertaken the task of harmonizing trade statistics, and in the future, the APEC process should promote work on harmonization in a wide range of other areas.

Promote Policy Dialogue

To secure growth in the Asia Pacific, APEC members should promote ongoing dialogue on current and future critical issues in the region. These issues should include identifying options and making recommendations for approaches to trade liberalization in the region, promoting policy dialogue in the region, and exchanging information for a common understanding of economic conditions. It is vital that APEC members make active use of occasions such as future APEC meetings and other relevant fora to serve this purpose.

Expand Trans-Pacific Transactions

In recent years, the interdependent relationship in areas such as trade, investment, and human resources across and around the Pacific has increased rapidly and has become a driving force for economic development in the region. In order to continue their sustained economic growth in the years ahead, it is important not only to promote transactions within what is commonly referred to as the Asia Pacific region, that is, North America, Asia, and Oceania, but also to further promote the transactions throughout the broader Pacific Rim.

VI

NEW DIRECTIONS FOR THE FUTURE

21

Future Directions for Pacific Cooperation

Monica Gruder Drake

It is daunting to ponder future directions for Pacific cooperation. Other chapters in this book have explored in detail the origins, nature, scope, and evolution of cooperation in the Pacific region. Here, I will endeavor to speculate on the role the region might play in the new world order that is building. I will begin with a glance at the present context of global international relations, proceed to an examination of what is unique about Pacific cooperation, then review how cohesiveness in the Pacific can be enhanced, before concluding with some thoughts about the model that Pacific regionalism offers for shaping the new world order.

PRESENT CONTEXT OF INTERNATIONAL RELATIONS

The salient feature of today's international relations is the implosion of Soviet communism. This cataclysmic event has shaken the post-1945 world order to its very foundations. The end of the Cold War occasioned by the disintegration of the Soviet Union itself and the breakup of the former Eastern bloc and the reunification of Germany have dramatically altered the global landscape.

Although this upheaval is unsettling, it also provides a unique opportunity to create a new world order or, in other words, a new basis on which nation-states structure their political, economic, and security relationships with one another. To be viable in the twenty-first century, the new system must be predicated on a reevaluation of what constitutes not only the touchstone for interaction among polities but also the scope and methods for such interaction.

The primacy of the sovereign nation-state as *the* single organizing principle for international relations is being acutely tested by the need to accommodate realities that transcend national borders. These include metaphysical factors affecting relationships among human beings, such as religious beliefs, ethnic links, migration, and changing demographics and physical factors such as global warming, atmospheric and oceanic pollution, vector-spread diseases (for example, malaria), and others. The Secretary General of the United Nations Boutros Boutros-Ghali, has acknowledged in his far-sighted 1992 report entitled *An Agenda for Peace*[1] that the machinery built up since the end of World War II to contain or manage conflict by forging consensus among sovereign and equal nations is not totally suited to the realities of today's world. He proposes a shift away from the traditional UN premise of neutrality in conflict and norms of consensus building toward greater engagement in preventive diplomacy and deployment of forces. He also spells out an activist role for the United Nations in post-conflict peace building and peace enforcement. Even these radical suggestions, however, do not hint at any viable alternative to the nation-state as the foundation stone for international peace and security.

Are there other models for effective international relations being tested or used that might serve the needs of the global community of the future? Scanning the landscape does not reveal many likely sources for viable ideas but highlights instead many disheartening examples of how badly things often turn out.

Europe is likely to remain preoccupied for some time with the problems of bringing its western and eastern parts into viable relationship and with the implications of its impotence in the face of appalling tribal warfare in the former Yugoslavia. In addition, the resurgence of ethnic nationalism in the so-called Commonwealth of Independent States is making a mockery of the very concept of "commonwealth." Although the Middle East appears on the verge of a breakthrough by its leaders, old animosities and deep tensions are far from being resolved and remain a serious obstacle to genuine peace. The Moslem countries of the Maghreb and elsewhere are grappling with the threats posed to their economic and political stability by pan-Islamic fundamentalism. Sub-Saharan Africa remains mired in a kind of oblivion, although the transformation of South Africa's political landscape gives reason for some cautious optimism for the future. The Indian subcontinent is rent with ethno-religious strife that continues to act as a damper on socio-economic progress.

In this bleak landscape, a few bright spots are visible. One is the Americas: in the southern part of the continent, significant domestic economic and political transformations are underway that are improving people's lives. The most dramatic of these appear to be occurring in those countries that, perhaps not coincidentally, have Pacific Ocean shorelines, most notably, Chile. In the northern part of the continent, major economic restructuring is taking place under the stimulus (threat?) of the North American Free Trade Agreement among the

United States, Canada, and Mexico. However, the light shimmering brightest is that of the Asia Pacific region.

THE PACIFIC'S OPEN REGIONALISM: A MODEL FOR TOMORROW?

So, the search for innovative approaches to shaping a new world order brings us to examine what is occurring, and why, in the region defined geographically by its contiguity with the Pacific Ocean, which links the landmasses of Asia and the Americas and contains the Antipodes as well as islands of various sizes.

It should be noted here that it has proven difficult over the years to arrive at a commonly accepted definition of what is and is not included in shorthand phrases like the Pacific, Pacific region, Pacific Basin, Pacific Rim, Asia Pacific, or Asia and the Pacific. The connotation varies broadly, depending not only on the context in which the term is used but also on the point of view of the user.

It is an empirically demonstrated fact that the Asia Pacific region has experienced rapid economic growth over the past quarter century. The factors driving that growth have included domestic economic development and export-oriented restructuring in the less developed and newly industrialized economies of the region and trade within and beyond the region. Today, the region is widely described by experts as the most economically dynamic in the world.

Moreover, forecasts for the sustainability of this dynamism are generally optimistic. Thus, the Pacific Economic Cooperation Council's (PECC) *Pacific Economic Outlook 1992–1993*,[2] and its related *Pacific Economic Outlook Update 1993–1994* point out that the region as a whole survived the recessionary cyclical downswing that occurred between 1989 and 1991 rather well and is now poised for another period of robust growth. Economic experts have concluded that there are no inherent barriers to sustaining development over the longer run while cautioning that structural changes in the process of growth are very likely.

Clearly, economic dynamism has been the foundation stone on which the generally stable political relationships among the region's members have been built since approximately the late 1970s. However, it is the contention of this chapter that the manner in which this dynamism was stimulated is as significant as the dynamism itself and offers a model that could be emulated in the creation of a new world order.

Indeed, the economic success of the region has been achieved not by pursuing either of the negotiated forms of economic integration — a free-trade area or a customs union — but by relying on the initiative of business enterprise to catalyze export-led growth, globalization of markets, and liberal investment and information flows.

The Accompanying Statement of the San Francisco Declaration issued by the PECC at its Ninth General Meeting in September 1992 emphasizes the point this way:

> The fact that the (Pacific) region is increasingly open is generally seen as the reason for its dynamism, its flexibility, and its record-setting growth rates. These are the achievements of business leaders and their enterprises whose initiatives created the region — a process supported by government officials, analyzed by academics, and elaborated by journalists.

In other words, Pacific cooperation in the pursuit of economic dynamism and integration has grown from the bottom up and not been imposed from the top down. The institutional framework that has evolved since the mid-1960s is long on dedicated individuals who volunteer their time in the name of the Pacific Community and short on big bureaucracies staffed by officials who interact mainly with other bureaucrats.

The alphabet soup of Pacific institutions, which the uninitiated tend to find both indecipherable and indigestible, is thick with acronyms for ponderously named groups like the Association of Southeast Asian Nations — ASEAN, the Pacific Basin Economic Council — PBEC, the Pacific Trade and Development Conference — PAFTAD, the Pacific Economic Cooperation Council — PECC, and Asia Pacific Economic Cooperation — APEC. These homegrown bodies make major contributions to sustaining the economic dynamism of the region. What is more, they manage, for the most part, to do so without expending massive amounts of financial and human resources. They draw, instead, on inspired leadership as well as dedication by the rank-and-file volunteers to conduct the regular activities of their various task forces, study groups, and committees. In their gatherings, they largely succeed in fostering an atmosphere of informality and collegiality that is conducive not only to nurturing personal rapport and trust but also to promoting genuine debate and consensus building on many issues, including sensitive ones. Ideas articulated in this neutral fashion frequently end up being incorporated into official policy by the governments concerned — precisely the goal of international cooperation.

ENHANCING PACIFIC REGIONAL COHESIVENESS IN THE FUTURE

All its successes to date notwithstanding, the Pacific region cannot afford to rest on its collective laurels. It, too, must avoid complacency and stay in step with the times, especially if it wants to retain its leading position at the head of the pack.

Like the world at large, the region is evolving in a context of rapid, virtually uncontrollable change that, in turn, is affecting interaction between and among its member countries. Among the trends emerging in the region that warrant close monitoring for their potentially destabilizing effects are accelerating environmental depredation, shifting patterns in the arms trade, substantial internal pressures from the growing and increasingly prosperous middle classes in some countries for greater political liberalization, and ever-widening access to uncensored global information media via modern telecommunications. To illustrate this last point, one need only recall that the world's awareness of the events on Tiananmen Square in June 1989 was shaped in large measure by the presence in the Chinese capital of the global news media, who happened to be there, video cameras in hand, to cover the historic visit of then-Soviet leader Mikhail Gorbachev.

Another critical factor to take into account when pondering the future is technology and the enormous impact it has on people and processes. Indeed, technology is emerging today as the new line of demarcation between the haves and the have-nots of the global community. Although telecommuting to the workplace via a modem-enabled computer in one's home may soon become commonplace in the United States and Canada, the fact remains that most people in rural Asia — who far outnumber their city kin — and elsewhere do not yet have reliable access to basic electricity, let alone to sophisticated telephone and computer equipment.

Given this context, it is especially important that the region's existing and emerging institutions and cooperative mechanisms be designed for maximum flexibility and adaptability to changing conditions. Under the guidance of visionary leadership, this can be achieved in a way that validates, rather than obviates, the fundamental openness from which the region has derived so much strength and dynamism up to now.

To be more specific, the institutional framework now being elaborated to give concrete expression to the concept of "Asia Pacific economic cooperation" should be flexible enough to permit expanding economies the agenda for regular ministerial-level consultation. Top among the additional issues for broader consideration would be political, strategic, security, and environmental issues. Encouraging signs of willingness to broaden the cooperative agenda can be found in the very fact that the political leaders of the APEC member countries met at their first summit in November 1993 in Seattle and that APEC environment ministers followed suit in March 1994 in Vancouver.

If the Pacific institutions can demonstrate their effectiveness in finding workable, cooperative solutions to these intractable problems on a regional scale, their credibility as essential building blocks for the new world order would be greatly enhanced. Moreover, their chances of doing so successfully would be improved if the governmental and nongovernmental institutions were to limit their competitiveness with each other and to recognize more explicitly that the overall process of cooperation benefits from their collective presence in the policy-making arena.

In addition to expanding their agendas of common concerns, institutions in the Pacific region must endeavor to expand the base of popular support for their efforts to promote effective intraregional and international cooperation. Perhaps a creative way could be found to harness the converging information and broadcasting technologies for this purpose, as part of an overall effort to guard against an unbridgeable widening of the technology gap.

For example, powerful information-collecting and dissemination tools already widely available in information age countries could be marshaled to help increase public information and awareness throughout the region via sophisticated educational materials, which themselves would be cooperatively conceived and produced.

It also would be beneficial to find ways to demystify the process of formal and informal international relations and make their practices and practitioners more readily accessible to interested nonexperts. Secondary- and tertiary-level educational curricula throughout the region could be enriched by inclusion of learning modules on the practical aspects of regional and international cooperation. This could help foster development of a new generation of internationally minded young people. In addition, writings by and about people and programs in international cooperation could be disseminated more widely to a broader audience beyond the usual decision-making elites.

SHAPING THE NEW WORLD ORDER

With the locus of economic dynamism having shifted from the Atlantic to the Pacific Rim as the twenty-first century approaches, the architectural features of that region's cooperative institutions such as the Pacific Basin Economic Council, PECC, and the Asia Pacific Economic Cooperation reflect the successful synergy among business people, entrepreneurs, intellectuals, academics, political leaders, and public policy makers. These bodies have demonstrated that grappling with major problems on a regional rather than national basis can pare these down to manageable size and make them easier to handle.

It is this chapter's contention that the cooperative mechanisms developed in the Pacific region can serve as a paradigm for international geopolitical relations in the future. If it is replicated successfully, one can envisage a model for global cooperation that is not pyramid shaped, with the United Nations at its apex and regional and other groupings subordinate to it, but spherical, with overlapping and interlinked circles representing regions. Each group tackles its own sets of problems and then discusses with the other groups which of the regional solutions have global applicability. Those that do could then be promulgated under the auspices of a revamped, strengthened United

Nations, which would have the power, both moral and military, to enforce adherence to the agreed-upon solutions. Such a structure would harmonize with the line of thinking elucidated in the United Nations' *An Agenda for Peace*.

If sufficient vision, will, and commitment can be mobilized in support of this approach, then a strong and viable New World Order can be built on the rubble of the old system. Provided it can maintain its own momentum successfully into the next century, the Pacific region can stake its claim now to leading the construction effort.

NOTES

1. Boutros Boutros-Ghali. *An Agenda for Peace: Preventive Diplomacy, Peacemaking and Peacekeeping* (New York: United Nations Publications, 1992), p. DPI/1247.
2. Pacific Economic Cooperation Council. *Pacific Economic Outlook 1992–1993* (Singapore: Pacific Economic Cooperation Council); Pacific Economic Cooperation Council. *Pacific Economic Outlook 1993–1994* (Singapore: Pacific Economic Cooperation Council).

22

A New Democracy for the Pacific Rim Region and the World

Yoriko Kishimoto

The Asia Pacific region will be the stage where critical directions of the world economy, technological development, world democracy and market systems, and world environmental issues will be decided over the next century. This will be true whether the countries work together in some common framework or whether they simply continue independently, each in its own way. This chapter will explore (and raise) issues concerning these areas, with a particular emphasis on the United States and Japan.

In the twentieth century, the world has been operating largely on an agenda set by the countries of the West — one that was framed by the industrial revolution, economic and technological development and competition, the Cold War, the forces of democracy and free markets, human rights, and, today, the environmental movement as well. Countries were forced to join the game, whether they liked it or not.

Today a number of Asia Pacific countries — Japan, Korea, and Taiwan, among others — are in a position where, as they reach the upper echelon of the old hierarchy of economic and technological competition, the rules of the game are themselves beginning to change. The countries and citizens of the Asia Pacific region are able to shape the new values and priorities of the world and regional systems and are in a position of strength to decide what their own societies and economies will look like 50 or 100 years from now. For decades, and in some cases, for centuries, we must appreciate the degree to which the various Asian countries have submerged questions related to their ideal society, culture, and economy in deference to the treadmill of global economic competition and survival. Each country, I believe, must go through a wrenching reexamination of its mission and self-identity, given the realities and possibilities of the new century. In the case of the United States, I discussed dilemmas and possibilities facing us in *The Third Century: America's Resurgence in the Asian Era*,[1] a book I co-authored with Joel Kotkin.

In that book, we addressed the question of the future of the United States at a time when Asian countries seemed to have achieved an unstoppable momentum and were undermining U.S. confidence in U.S. economic competitiveness and raised questions as to whether our open system model based on democracy and free markets was becoming obsolete in a changing world environment. In other words, as the boat seemingly begins to sink, people start to throw things out — for example, political freedoms or, in the case of the United States, discussion of banning all immigration or saying we cannot afford free markets any more. It is important to stop and think about what is indeed dispensable and what we should guard above all.

The conclusion of *The Third Century* was that the greatest strength of the United States lay not in any one ethnic group, nor any one religion or industry, but in the integrity and robustness of our open systems themselves — our open social system and open economic system. We envisioned the world moving in the direction of democracy and market economies. The United States should see that the pain and costs it has paid and is still paying today — in the Civil Rights movement and the more recent Rodney King incidents — are costs that every major nation in the world will eventually have to face. It is just paying these costs early.

The Third Century placed great faith in the forces of democracy and market mechanisms. However, as one country after another seems to embrace these institutions and philosophies, doubt begins to arise as to what the consequences are if and when they have "converted" most major countries of the world. What does all the globalization and free market competition mean for our sense of local community? Is harsh competition and the "market"-ization of all our institutions acceptable and desirable? Churches and schools in the United States are forced to resort to marketing campaigns and revamping their programs in order to compete for markets. Couples often sign prenuptial agreements before marriage. People are judged too much by how much they earn and what they own, as economics and quantifiable factors emerge as perhaps the only common language. Is this the society we want other countries around the world to adopt? Is this not what globalization of market economy trends will inevitably lead to?

Many have shed blood and given their lives under the banner of spreading democracy and free markets around the world. Now that greater democratization and marketization of the world's economies is being realized, we seem to be unable to create a richer vision for this new world. The forces of market and democracy, at least as they exist today, seem inadequate to address the crises of poverty, the environment, racial conflicts. They seem unable to address the human need for emotional warmth and love or the need for the comforting stability of traditional communities and families. Not only do these forces fail to address our most human needs but also they seem in danger of corrupting human nature. Moreover, the forces of democracy and free markets are relatively new to the world in general and are even newer to the countries of the Asia Pacific region. Especially in non-Western countries, leaders will begin to question whether the secular and materialistic values that seem to accompany "modern" societies are ones they desire for their own communities.

ENVIRONMENTALISM AS PRECURSOR TO THE NEXT GENERATION OF DEMOCRACY AND FREE MARKET SYSTEMS

I would argue that although the environmental movement is still very "foreign" to most Asians and Asian countries, it is helping people around the world create a larger and more comprehensive framework necessary for a sustainable world economy and society.

Let us reflect, very roughly, on how the environmental movement has evolved. In the first phase, some people noticed water becoming contaminated and people becoming sick. It was viewed as local pollution, and the solution seemed to be antipollution laws, development of antipollution technologies, and a matter of creating fiscal policies to encourage manufacturers to invest in necessary capital equipment. In the second phase, entire species began disappearing, and quick fixes were no longer adequate. These were regional environmental issues, and people struggled with new concepts such as "ecosystems," airsheds and watersheds, and "pollution prevention." In the third phase, signs of global climate changes emerged and we were confronted with an environmental version of the atomic bomb, slowly exploding. This latter stage is one of global environmentalism. We are struggling for the right response this very day.

Environment is: the aggregate of surrounding things, conditions, influences; act of environing; or state of being environed. Environing, includes forming a circle or ring around, surrounding, or enveloping. Thus, an environmentalist could be interpreted to be one who is aware and acts with the aggregate, or "large picture," in his or her mind, and environmentalism may be seen as having arisen because the circle has closed. In this respect, I have long believed that environmentalism is a most natural step in the overall process of globalization and one that will then lead to what could be called the next stage of "comprehensive environmentalism." This comprehensive environmentalism would integrate concerns about our social/cultural and natural environment with concerns about our economic environment.

An analogy can be drawn between the evolution of the environmental movement to the United States' and the West's struggle to deal with "the rise of Asia." In the first phase, people began to notice textiles, radios, TVs, then steel and automobiles being imported from a country they did not understand. It was seen as a trade problem, and the solution seemed to lie in developing new trade laws and new technologies to stay ahead in the game. In the second phase, entire industries began disappearing, and quick fixes were clearly no longer adequate.

Americans remain stuck somewhere between the first phase and second phase. Most Americans still see Asia in terms of "trade problems." We have not yet evolved in our consciousness from a negative antipollution campaign to positive environmentalism, that is, from dealing with trade frictions to a positive regional and global consciousness about our economic and social environment. Most of the countries of Asia also have failed to look past the frenetic economic competition to conceptualize the kind of national, regional, and world community they would like to shape for the future.

A SUSTAINABLE PACIFIC RIM COMMUNITY

In the third phase of "global environmentalism," or developing a comprehensive framework for our economic, social, and natural environment, I believe the market system and democracy must continue to evolve and change, sometimes in dramatic ways.

New democracy must operate under conditions of:

new technologies for communications, including advancements in telecommunications, the advent of the Cable News Network, and computers;

many new cultures, including cultures very different from those of Western civilization;

a seeming change from a bipolar, hierarchical world to a flatter, "network" environment of equals;

a widespread crisis of confidence in public officials and government in general; and

conditions of no, or almost no, new physical growth. (The United States has depended too much on an exponential growth in incomes and exploitation of natural resources to mask deficiencies in our system. We do not know how much the success of the U.S. experiment in democracy has been dependent on the nation's material wealth, natural resources, abundant land, and significant leadership position in world economic, technological, and military terms.)

The market must also develop a capacity to carry much more complex information and transactions than it can today — in other words, it must become a more "intelligent" market. The market exchange mechanism will be more multimedia and broad-banded, to borrow some jargon from the computer and telecommunications fields.

Let me illustrate by sharing an anecdote. A friend had spent two weeks in China, teaching plant managers about management, marketing, and technology development. He expressed amazement that the Chinese had no concept of the market or marketing, because the state had always been there to tell them what to make and also to buy the goods they produced. According to him, the Chinese had been operating in a vacuum unfathomable in our society.

I can imagine a future when a person will be similarly amazed when reading about our era, characterized as a time when people and managers operated unconnected and oblivious to a potentially much more sophisticated market that is sensitive to environmental and social, as well as economic, costs of human action.

This new sophistication level will be made possible partially by technological progress. For example, Germany has laws that require manufacturers to take back packaging for purposes of recycling. As new materials and processes are developed, it becomes much more complex to keep track of how a part was made and what materials were used. The more that is known about the product, the more effectively it can be recycled or reused. Also, cost allocation and transmittal can be done more accurately by allowing consumers and intermediary processors to make more intelligent decisions, based on true cost and resource use as well as utility. Use of bar code-like technology and interactive communication systems may make this more feasible.

Along with loading products and services with environmental information, I believe that we will witness increased demand for social information. In other words, the new consciousness about the natural environment will open up a welcome Pandora's box of other issues. Once consumers, workers, and citizens in general become aware that the absorption capability of the natural environment is, in fact, limited, they are more open to understanding that the absorption capability of the social environment also has limits. The world has become smaller due to technology, war, and population growth. Just as one can no longer throw chlorofluorocarbons into the atmosphere without long-term consequences, neither can one ignore half of the world without inevitable consequences.

We are experiencing a need for old institutions to recreate themselves and for new groups and institutions to arise. In the ultimate world of a globalized society, the role and strength of local and regional entities will be greater, not lesser. However, each institution must go through a process of deeply reconsidering its past and its most basic mission, endeavoring to understand the demands and possibilities of the new world environment, in order to survive and prosper. All local communities and various groups, such as labor unions, must be helped to see the whole picture and to think for themselves how they must change. More importantly, this process will help each institution regain confidence in the aspects of itself that it wishes to preserve and protect above all else. Ironically, the more sophisticated our global and regional systems become, the greater is the value placed on the ultimate source of legitimacy in a democracy, namely, individual citizens and the groups and organizations with which they voluntarily choose to associate.

To reach such a sustainable community, a quantum jump in public education is called for. Education and participation in decision making have always been the cornerstone of democracy. Many difficult public and private decisions will have to be made over the next decades, and paralysis will prevail without broad public support of a common future. Today, every major issue or trade off will have environmental and cross-cultural issues to contend with, of which the average citizen has little understanding.

Chinese families are well-known for working and saving for the future of their children and the longevity and prosperity of the extended family unit. Japanese corporations and families also have been respected for planning and saving for the future, responding to both positive and negative incentives. This inward orientation of protecting and nurturing those inside their circles has helped these particular ethnic groups. The challenge of drawing this allegiance to a larger circle, which includes diverse groups and the environment, will depend upon two forces.

One is the issue of broad inclusion and participation in the larger world society. Japan, to oversimplify, has always felt alone psychologically and without true friends in the world. It has a history and reputation of looking down upon and exploiting its Asian neighbors and exhibits an inferiority complex toward the countries of the West. China has a politically isolated government and a large and economically frustrated population. Both countries are well-known for their historical tradition of treasuring nature and fostering very strong cultural traditions but have had to sacrifice them for the goal of self-determination.

To bring Japan, China, and the United States into the same common circle, we have to create a common future together. This requires breakthroughs in both cross-cultural cooperation and communications and new, comprehensive security issues. Americans and others must understand the magnitude and increasing significance of intercultural differences and strive to build a framework robust enough to accommodate the differences without breaking down.

Americans, in particular, do not realize the degree to which the world has revolved around them for the past half century and the extent to which others are accommodating to them. In a situation where Americans constitute 5 percent of the population of the new world democracy, we will be entering a world where modernization is not equivalent to Westernization. Most Americans do not realize that the environmental movement as it has existed so far has been largely a Western movement. For it to take root successfully around the world, each group will have to recreate its relationship with the environment, given its own history and cultures, its own strengths and weaknesses.

In order to sustain regional and world community, we will need to create a common "tool box" or, at least, an understanding of the differences among the languages and the cultures represented by regions and subregions. In addition, we must also put regional and world safeguards in place to guarantee the minimal dignity, self-determination, and military, food, energy, and other measures for comprehensive security.

The other major factor involved in drawing all nations into a common circle is a successful decentralized market system and independent nonprofit sector. A free market is respected as an apolitical, objective judge of economic efficiency and entrepreneurial excellence and the way to harness the free and innovative energy and talents of a very diverse and democratic population. A strong independent nongovernmental organization sector is the nonprofit counterpart to the free market for businesses. A vital nonprofit sector provides diverse and cross-sector channels for individuals around the world to form linkages and work together in fields ranging from environmental education to multimedia art.

The overall picture that comes into focus is of a world transforming itself from a bipolar, hierarchical system with most of the linkages among nations carried out through national governments and large corporations to a flatter and more decentralized network of equals, with diverse linkages among small and large businesses, between nongovernmental organizations, between citizen groups, and between governments. To give an example from my own San Francisco Bay area, it is said that the inability of this metropolitan area to create effective regional policies and infrastructure, such as for public transit, results from the fact that most members of the regional bodies are composed of locally elected officials. Similarly, most members of international entities are representatives of national bodies. We need a way to break local ties and allow people gradually to build identities as members of international environmental groups, international entrepreneurs' groups, international multimedia pioneers, and so forth, in addition to maintaining their identities as members of their country, companies, and families.

The challenge consists not only in designing regional institutions as part of a complex of local, regional, and worldwide institutions but also in forming regional markets, regional values, and caring for regional natural environments. In the process of forging these new bonds, we must realize that cross-cultural barriers are potentially 10 feet or 20 feet tall, not 2 feet — a revelation that may be painful, especially for people who are not used to accommodating to others on terms different from their own. Thus, I believe that social and cultural issues, which have long been relegated to the periphery of our economics-based society, will come to loom as large on our horizons as the environmental issues. The common lesson to be learned from environmentalism and democracy is that whatever we throw into the ocean, we are destined to get back, washed up against our front door.

The Asia Pacific region will be the stage where critical future directions of the world are decided. With high growth rates, huge populations, and both highly developed and industrially undeveloped economies of very large sizes, the pressures on the environment and the trade offs between immediate economic survival and long-term "sustainable development" planning are nowhere more graphic or painful. The penalty for failing to face up to these newly revealed environmental and cross-cultural challenges will be increasing Balkanization and paralysis. The reward will be a second generation of a more robust and humane world democracy and market system.

Let me conclude with an illustration of the difference between first and second generation democracy and free markets by examining the U.S. politicians' image of a "level playing field" between United States and Japanese companies. When you think about it, a flat, featureless type of field is not a very appealing picture of a society or economy's landscape, but it is probably a necessary intermediary stage for two cultures and economies so different from one another, to build trust and common ground slowly. In the long term, I would much rather see a rich landscape of rolling green hills, streams, mountaintops, and hidden valleys. Diversity is our reward, and in turn, will be our strength, as we transform the borders between our countries from flat, demilitarized zones into a richer maze of country roads, walking trails, and little bridges.

NOTE

1. Kotkin, Joel and Yoriko Kishimoto. *The Third Century: America's Resurgence in the Asian Era*. New York: Crown Publishers, 1988.

23

From Silk Road to Silicon Road: Managing the Challenges of Success during the 1990s

Stephen Cass and Peter Schwartz

Tiananmen Square and the Bubble Burst aside, it has become conventional wisdom in the business world that for Asia, the only way is up. Most of the region is in no hurry to dispel that notion, but can Asia manage the challenges created by its own success? A look at the key driving forces shaping Asia over the next decade suggests that there are three plausible futures for the region, each defining a different type of response and outcome to the challenges of success.

This chapter will outline the possible paths along which the Asia Pacific may develop during the 1990s. To do this, we will first define those key driving forces that will most significantly shape the development of the Asia Pacific region over the next decade. Having done so, we will then suggest three possible directions for the future Asia Pacific.

ASIA PACIFIC DRIVING FORCES

Looking at the future of the Asia Pacific over the next decade, six driving forces emerge as potentially the most significant factors in Asia's development during this period.

The *overseas Chinese network* controls significant portions of regional economies and has international ties to capital and trade flow. In Indonesia, ethnic Chinese account for only 4 percent of the population but control 17 of the 25 biggest business groups and own 70–75 percent of the assets other than those owned by the government or foreigners. In Thailand, about 10 percent of the population are ethnic Chinese who control over half of the country's capital. In Malaysia, only one-third of the population are ethnic Chinese, but they control approximately three-fourths of the economy.

The *strains of growth* may create bottlenecks in labor, urbanization, energy, and the environment. Anticipating a doubling in size of its regional economy over the next decade, Asia will confront limitations in its ability to create a sufficiently skilled and numerous workforce, its ability to overcome urban crowding (65 percent growth in Asia's urban populations is anticipated this decade), its ability to meet demands of energy- and electricity-thirsty industries and consumers, and its ability to halt the deterioration of air and water that has already created severe health problems from Korea to Indonesia. (It is estimated, for example, that up to 20 percent of China's water supply is unpotable.)

Rapidly expanding *intraregional trade and capital flows* are helping Asia to develop as an economic bloc similar to the European Community (EC) and the North American Free Trade Agreement (NAFTA). These trade flows, growing at over 10 percent per year, have already created a more independent Asian trading region in which 46 percent of total exports are traded with other Asian countries. Booming capital flows have developed around high regional savings rates of 30–40 percent in most countries, the massive pool of Chinese expatriate capital now flowing back to the mainland and peripheral economies, and the increasingly regional focus of Japanese foreign investment. This has been accompanied by a massive shift in global bank reserves over the past decade. In 1992, the seven leading East Asian econo-mies held 41 percent of global bank reserves, compared with 17 percent in 1980. Asia will likely have privileged access to a tight global pool of capital.

Increase *subregional development*, with Asian hub cities providing the technology, capital, and management expertise for poorer surrounding areas. Singapore, Bangkok, Hong Kong, and Tokyo/Seoul have emerged as the hubs to Asian subregions, creating economies of scale and the pooling of resources and talent in pursuit of more efficient markets.

Uncertain *regional security arrangements* threaten the long-term stability of Asia while encouraging the United States to maintain a regional presence. Perceptions of U.S. withdrawal combined with a post–Cold War "going-out-of-business" arms sale have led Asian nations to increase defense spending at the fastest rate in the world. China, for one, has embarked on a purchasing and modernization campaign that may enable it to project power far beyond its borders. And with this campaign it is as if the Chinese are saying that they are not prepared to let the Indian Ocean become India's ocean.

A dominant Asian capitalist model of *monolithic capitalism* promotes economic rationality at the possible expense of intangibles such as civil rights, the environment, and welfare. Asian countries have opted for a soft authoritarianism in which one predominant party or charismatic leader — be it China's Communist Party or Indonesia's

Suharto — exercises predominant power, rejecting the chaos and costs of U.S. and European forms of capitalism. Asia's leaders and entrepreneurs are opting for a quasi-authoritarianism out of the conviction that the combination of authoritarianism and a market economy will produce tremendous growth throughout Asia.

REGIONALISM, SUBREGIONALISM, OR CHAOS?

Shaped by the above driving forces, the Asia Pacific may develop in three plausible directions over the next decade. Which course Asia follows will be determined by which of the driving forces proves to have the greatest influence over Asian development and, of course, on the state of the global economy, particularly its ability to resist the rise of protectionism.

These three plausible futures suggest three levels of regional organization and cooperation: a regionally integrated, a subregionally integrated, and a disintegrated Asia Pacific. What might these worlds look like?

A Regionally Integrated Asia Pacific

In the first plausible future, the dominant driving forces of the overseas Chinese networks and growing intraregional trade and capital flows combine in an open global economic environment to produce a remarkably high-growth, highly integrated Asia Pacific. Globally, regional trading blocs such as NAFTA and the EC resist protectionist pressures and become "building blocs" to an even more integrated global economy.

These Chinese populations practice a form of capitalism never seen in the West: an authoritarian, Confucian-influenced capitalism that cherishes economic freedom but neglects democracy despite the liberalizing impact of a growing middle class — and that proves to be the most dynamic and successful form of capitalism in the supposedly nonideological 1990s.

A key factor in the success of the Chinese network during this period is investment from unleashed Chinese savings and "mattress money" brought back into the system (in 1992, amounting to over $350 billion total: $200 billion of foreign exchange reserves in China, Taiwan, Hong Kong, and Singapore; approximately $150 billion in savings accounts within China; and an estimated $30–50 billion in "mattress money" within China). However, none of these vast sums of capital would have made a difference without the simultaneous development of smoothly functioning capital markets, helped by the relaxing of Chinese capital flow and currency controls by the end of the decade. A successful Chinese economic reform process bears fruit amidst rapid growth and explosive infrastructural (particularly telecom) needs.

However, this new style of capitalism would have accomplished little without the accompanying telecommunications explosion that occurs throughout Asia during the decade, and it is the Chinese, a diaspora separated by great distances, who most successfully seize on the importance of telecommunications in a global information economy. In China itself, a country with a per capita income of less than $500, 180,000 people in Shenzhen are using pagers by 1991, out of a total population of 2 million. In 1990, data traffic in Hong Kong grows by an amazing 80 percent annually. It is this expanding web of telecommunications that provides the final connection to the overseas Chinese network, touching off the China boom decade of the 1990s and the highest sustained economic growth rates that the world has ever seen. By 2000, the Chinese diaspora economy spans the Pacific, from Beijing to San Francisco to Toronto, and beyond.

The growing power of the Chinese does not go unresisted. Asian states, Singapore and South Korea in particular, continue to insist that the United States remain a political/military power in the region to counterbalance the growing power of China and to forestall Japanese rearmament. The end political result is a fairly stable U.S.-Japanese-Chinese triad in the Asia Pacific region, with Japan mediating the U.S.-Chinese relationship and the United States helping to mediate Japanese and Chinese relations with other Asian states.

In the political affairs of the region, a key potential constraint to growth, the Asian political transitions that are to take place during the late 1990s, proves to be less of a threat than had been anticipated by Asia specialists. Although the post–World War II generation of leaders, the Asian gerontocracy, begins to pass away, a new generation of leaders has emerged in Asia, with little or no memories of the war and the political rivalries from which it erupted. These new leaders understand the economic basis of Asia's power, they recognize the debilitating effects of political infighting and conflict in the former Eastern bloc and Soviet Union, and they realize that regional cooperation and continued economic growth are the paths to greater prominence in global affairs. In the development of this cooperation and economic growth the Asia Pacific Economic Cooperation (APEC) plays an increasingly important role.

Although APEC's initial role in managing Asia Pacific political relations is fairly limited, the institution gradually takes on more roles: becoming a forum for resolving intra-APEC disputes such as those over intellectual property rights, becoming a clearinghouse for regional economic and political information, even taking on a mediation role in emerging disputes such as those in the mid-1990s over resource development in the South China Sea. By 2000, the term "Pacific Community" has come into common use as a way of describing APEC, and by 2005, an economic grouping, formally called the "Pacific Community," emerges. By the close of the 1990s, intra-APEC trade is now 80 percent of total APEC exports (up from 65 percent in 1991) and still climbing.

However, what enables Asia to sustain the high growth rates of the 1990s is a shift to more efficient "green" technologies (helped along by ongoing U.S-Japanese research into nanotechnology) that are both extremely profitable for technology producers — such as Japan and the United States — and extremely conducive to increased efficiency and productivity. This new range of technology is used, first of all, to burn fuel more efficiently, particularly the coal pollution that shrouded Chinese cities during the early 1990s. The technology is then applied to industrial and manufacturing processes, where, despite the high initial costs, the manufacturing and environmental efficiencies achieved help to avert the potential bottlenecks of labor supply constraints and environmental and health degradation.

One mutually beneficial way of structuring this environmental cooperation with the rest of Asia is through overseas development assistance that targets environmental problems — helping to ease the problems, promote economic development, and create markets for Japanese environmental technologies and products.

Sustainable growth becomes the central concept of Japanese economic development because it is the only way of guaranteeing the long-term viability of Asian development and Japan's financial stake in that development.

In this open, regionally integrated economy, Asia's economy expands rapidly — over 8 percent average regional gross national product (GNP) growth per year — as the regional integration of trade and capital accelerates in a robust global economy. Economic success is paralleled by a booming Asian pride and cultural identity that is driven by the increasingly successful Chinese communities around the globe.

A Subregionally Integrated Asia Pacific

However, what if the driving forces of subregional development and a weak regional security structure are the dominant driving forces? Given the highly diverse levels of economic development throughout the Asia Pacific, it may be that Asia rejects regional integration for a more localized approach to development and cooperation. In this world, Asia develops into four subregions, including, from north to south,

a Sea of Japan zone, centered on the massive, $30 billion Tumen River Area Development Program project, incorporating a trading area of the two Koreas, northeast China, Siberia, and Japan;

a Greater China zone, incorporating south China's provinces of Guangdong, Fujian, Guanxi, and Hainan Island, with Taiwan and Hong Kong;

an Indochina zone, centered on Thailand and incorporating the three Indochina countries of Vietnam, Laos, and Cambodia plus Burma, the southwestern Chinese province of Yunnan, and, possibly, Singapore; and

an Insular Southeast Asia zone, centered on the growth triangle of Singapore, the southern Malaysian state of Johore, and Indonesia's Batam Island plus Brunei, the rest of Indonesia, and Papua New Guinea.

These new subregional blocs, however, have little in common with the trading blocs that began to emerge in the early 1990s. These new economic areas prove to be the building blocks of a new Asian economy — a critical stage in the economic development of the region into the twenty-first century. Four key factors conspire to bring about this new, subregional model of development: hub cities' need for cheap resources and labor, the drive for supranational economies of scale, the desire to maximize the advantage of geographic proximity in an Asia highly dependent on manufactured goods, and the maintenance of political legitimacy by focusing more closely on the development of local populations and markets.

Politically, there is no clear regional leader in this world, and a continued U.S. presence proves critical to maintaining stability. Indeed, as the Chinese outward-looking defense doctrine of "peripheral defense" increasingly overlaps with China's need to secure resources and trade routes for a booming economy, Chinese movements into the South China Sea appear ever more threatening. It is only through U.S. naval cooperation and patrols with the Association of Southeast Asian nations (ASEAN) and Vietnam (the newest member of ASEAN) that the Chinese ultimately realize the significant costs to their economic reforms of a hard-line stance on this issue — but not without protests and sabre rattling.

This initial cooperation and the growing fear of China has a particularly important political implication. It leads ASEAN to become a significant political, as well as economic, force in the region. Military cooperation is continued, at the behest of Singapore in particular, and arms sales into Southeast Asia increase at a rate that outpaces the rest of the Asia Pacific. These are the states that feel most threatened by China and, yet, remain suspicious of giving Japan too great a role in the political/security management of the region because of historical experience. A new ASEAN-based security alliance begins to emerge in the region to balance the power of both China and Japan.

To the north, Korean reunification is a direct result of the subregionalization of economic development in the Sea of Japan zone. Having witnessed the messy and expensive German reunification process of the early 1990s, South Korea is in no hurry to tie itself to the inefficient, poor economy to the north. Pursuing a strategy of development before unification, South Korea invests heavily in North Korea, particularly in the most crucial areas of transportation and telecommunications infrastructures. South Korea also invests aggressively in the Tumen project in neighboring northern China and as far away as Siberia. All of this investment is designed to develop markets and resources (and political allies) for the newly unified Korea. By the turn of the century, a new, and even more powerful, player is thrown into the Asian balance: a united Korea.

In the economic sphere, the subregionalization of Asian economies begins to have an important impact as growth rates begin to diverge significantly between hub areas. In Greater China, for example, the average GNP growth rate for the second half of the decade reaches 7.6 percent, as compared with 6.4 percent for Indochina, 4.6 percent for the Sea of Japan, and 6.6 percent for Southeast Asia. The wide differences in growth rates reflect the high growth rates in the dynamic Greater China zone and the fact that Japan and South Korea are mature industrial economies on a par with — no longer catching up to — the West.

In the world economy as a whole, however, economic growth is less robust. Disappointed by dwindling returns on European and North American investments and seeing the continued growth of Asian economies, Asian investors begin to bring their money and industries home — at first in relatively limited numbers. Later in the decade these numbers grow as:

Investment opportunities in Asia become ever more appealing when compared with the West. At 7.5 percent, Asian GNP growth runs at roughly double the rate of the United States and the EC.

Asian investors increasingly feel unwelcome and unappreciated in countries such as Canada and the United States for both racial and economic reasons.

An uncertain global environment forces Asian investors to focus on what they know best: their own backyards. The Japanese foreign real estate and takeover debacle are a well-learned lesson to stick to basics. The result is increasing investment in countries' backyards.

Formerly threatening political transitions in Asia pass peacefully (particularly in Hong Kong, Indonesia, and China), creating a more secure business climate.

However, the expansion of crossborder trade and contacts at a subregional level has its price. In Indochina, HIV cases reach 4 million. In Thailand, the *mai pen rai* (don't worry/have fun) attitude is impervious to government efforts to change sexual behavior, and these efforts are downplayed for fear of the potentially damaging effects on tourism. All in all, however, subregionally organized Asia Pacific promises fairly high levels of growth and a perhaps more even and stable process of Asian development, if the potential political rivalries and social problems can be managed.

A Disintegrating Asia

"The only way" may not be "up" for Asia. Our driving forces suggest that there is yet another plausible future, one in which Asia fails to manage the challenges of success: in an increasingly protectionist world economy, the Asia Pacific economy slows as the challenges of growth — workforce creation, overcentralization/urbanization, energy bottlenecks, and environmental degradation — are not dealt with effectively and become constraints to sustained growth. The social result is rising Asian nationalism and militarism, as the economic glue that had held these countries and societies together begins to break down and monolithic capitalism leads economic tensions to fester into political frictions.

The signs of economic disintegration are first seen in Japan. The Japanese economy continues to drift as productivity stagnates, the workforce ages and shrinks in size, and other countries, particularly Chinese competitors, begin to catch up with Japan. Japan responds to economic crisis by slashing consumption (and, therefore, imports) and by trying to export its way out of trouble. The effects are damaging for the global trade environment. As Japanese imports fall, U.S. and EC exports to Japan decline, widening the Japanese trade surplus with those areas and stirring up protectionist initiatives in the EC and the emerging NAFTA. Trade blocs become a significant irritant and constraint to trade. U.S. capital shifts from Asia to Latin America. European capital gravitates to eastern Europe and the former Soviet republics. Asian capital comes home to compete in an Asian economic "hothouse."

The structural constraint of slowing productivity proves to be a formidable economic problem throughout Asia. By 1995, the newly industrialized countries begin to experience what was formerly only a European and North American bottleneck: the existing large capital stock proves an impediment to the introduction of newer technologies, and productivity growth slows at a time when the growth of skilled workers in the labor force has also become a bottleneck to economic development and the move to higher value-added manufacturing.

As Asian economies slowdown, investment in infrastructure steadily declines. Indeed, infrastructural investment had been weak before the economic slowdown. During the days of heavy capital investment in manufacturing, returns on investment were rapid and of a high level: 80 percent of Japanese investment in Asia during the late 1980s produced a return within two years. However, investments in such intangibles as infrastructure and the environment did not produce similar gains and were largely ignored by Asian investors looking for a high return on investment. By the late 1990s, the repercussions of these investment decisions are felt throughout the region but particularly in South and Southeast Asia, where living standards have been lower.

Urban overcrowding and environmental degradation pose critical health and economic problems.

In this context, economic problems begin to generate political frictions. The new ideological conflict and nationalism arising from the global competition of divergent models of capitalism generates protectionism as Americans reach the breaking point with Asian economies that refuse to play by the rules. Europeans raise protectionist walls to halt immigration and to preserve their much cherished social welfare state. Asians are confused and angered by the European and U.S. insistence on openness, the environment, workers' rights, intellectual property, and a host of other intangibles with high costs to Asian business.

Fueled by the slowing regional economy, China's political relations also suffer. Chinese heavy-handed "independent" foreign policy and a security vacuum within Asia feed on each other in a downward spiral of intraregional political tensions. China moves to fill the vacuum in Southeast Asia created by U.S. and European isolationism; its navy now dominates the South and East China Seas and has its sights set on the Indian Ocean. Japan, for its part, increases its military role in Indochina, to secure both markets and resources.

Soon China is perceived by other Asian countries as an arrogant power, out for regional hegemony. South Korea, Japan, and Singapore lead efforts to counter Chinese expansion in the region, but they are hindered by their own social and economic problems. While China reaches out to the South China Sea, the Senkakus, and as far away as the Indian Ocean for resources, environmental confrontation increases in Asia over growing carbon dioxide and water supply problems.

Hong Kong is a victim of the unrest. Junior naval officers, with little direction from Beijing, continually harass Hong Kong's Coast Guard and commercial traffic. Democratic protests led by Martin Lee take place in Hong Kong shortly after the transfer. The Chinese move swiftly to halt the unrest, but the unrest is not limited to Hong Kong. South Chinese business sympathizes and sides with Hong Kong for fear of losing profits (Chinese affiliates of Hong Kong firms employ 2 million workers in south China in 1992 and some 4.5 million by 1997 — a substantial support base). The ensuing unrest sours the business climate and puts a halt to what had appeared to be the growing "Chinese Miracle" of the 1990s.

In the global context, no international or regional political leader emerges with sufficient vision to bring competing states together. In Asia, "lifeboat" ethics and a get-rich-quick mentality prevail. Having fractured into trade blocs, the global economy can no longer provide and sustain the high growth rates that Asia became accustomed to in the 1980s.

CONCLUSION

Can the Asia Pacific region cooperate to manage the challenges of its own success? Our analysis of driving forces suggests three possible answers. In the first future, the growing cooperation of the Chinese diaspora and booming intraregional trade and capital flows are the driving forces behind a highly integrated Asia Pacific. In the second future, Asia is guided by its history of entrepôt city-states, an uncertain regional security environment, and modern economic rationalization to manage growth and cooperation through a series of economic and political subregions. In the third plausible future, the bottlenecks created by success and a form of capitalism that neglects externalities vital to economic growth combine in a world lacking sufficient political vision and leadership to put a halt to the Asian miracle.

What this analysis suggests is that the economic success of Asia has created challenges that will not be resolved in the marketplace alone. Astute political management in Asia and abroad, an open global political environment, and a heightened sense of social costs will prove vital to sustaining Asia's growth. Only by meeting these challenges will the Asian Decade become the Asian Century.

Selected Bibliography

Alagappa, Muthiah. "Regionalism and the Quest for Security: ASEAN and the Cambodian Conflict." *Journal of International Affairs* 46(2) (Winter 1993).

Alves, Dora, ed. *Evolving Pacific Basin Strategies.* Washington, D.C.: National Defense University Press, 1990.

America's Role in Asia: Interests and Policies. Report of a working group co-chaired by Robert Scalapino and Lewis Coleman, The Asia Foundation's Center for Asian Pacific Affairs, January 1993.

"APEC: Looking for a Leading Role in Asia's Future." Hudson Briefing Paper No. 144, September 1992.

Arndt, H. W. "Anatomy of Regionalism." San Francisco, Calif.: Center for Pacific Basin Monetary and Economic Studies, Federal Reserve Bank of San Francisco.

Aveling, Harry. "Perencanaan dan Kebi jakan Bahasi di Malaysia." *Kritis* 5(2) (October 1990): 20–35.

Baker, James A. "America in Asia: Emerging Architecture for a Pacific Community." *Foreign Affairs Quarterly* 70 (5) (Winter 1991–92): 1–18.

Benjamin, Roger, and Robert T. Kudrle. *The Industrial Future of the Pacific Basin.* Boulder, Colo.: Westview Press, 1984.

Bergsten, C. Fed. "Sunrise in Seattle." *International Economic Insights* 5(1) (January/February 1994).

Borthwick, Mark. *Pacific Century: The Emergence of Modern Pacific Asia.* Boulder, Colo.: Westview Press, 1992.

Boutros-Ghali, Boutros. *New Dimensions of Arms Reduction and Disarmament in the Post–Cold War Era: Report of the Secretary-General.* E93.IX.8, A/C 1/47/7. New York: United Nations Publications, 1993.

____. *An Agenda for Peace: Preventive Diplomacy, Peacemaking and Peacekeeping.* E.DPI/1247. New York: United Nations Publications, 1992.

Chan, Steve. *East Asian Dynamism: Growth, Order, and Security in the Pacific Region.* Boulder, Colo.: Westview Press, 1990.

Committee for Economic Development, Research and Development. *The United States in the New Global Economy: A Rallier of Nations*. New York: Committee for Economic Development, 1992.

"Cooperation, Conflict in U.S.-Japan Environmental Relations." *Japan Economic Institute Report*, May 28, 1993.

Dam, Kenneth W. *The GATT: Law and the International Economic Organization*. Chicago, Ill.: University of Chicago Press, 1978.

Drobnick, Richard. *Economic Integration in the Pacific Region*. OECD Technical Paper No. 66. Paris: OECD Development Center, 1992.

____. "U.S. Security Leverage in Asian Trade Policy." *Pacific Economic Review* 1 (Spring 1993): 3.

Drysdale, Peter. *International Economic Pluralism: Economic Policy in East Asia and the Pacific*. Sydney: Allen & University of Australia, 1988.

____. "Open Regionalism: A Key to East Asia's Economic Future." *Pacific Economic Papers*, No. 197, Canberra, Australia-Japan Research Center, July 1991.

Earle, M. Mark, Jr. *PECC IX Executive Summary*. Washington, D.C.: U.S. National Committee for Pacific Economic Cooperation, 1992.

"Economic Indicators, Selected Asian Countries." *Far Eastern Economic Review*, June 10, 1993, pp. 72–73.

Elegant, Robert. *Pacific Destiny: Inside Asia Today*. New York: Crown Publishers, 1990.

Elek, Andrew. "Trade Policy Options for the Asia-Pacific Region in the 1990s: The Potential of Open Regionalism." *The American Economic Review* 82 (1992): pp. 74–78.

Far Eastern Economic Review. *Asia 1993 Yearbook*. Hong Kong: Review Publishing, 1993.

Frankel, Jeffrey A. "An Economist's Thoughts on International Economic Issues in Pacific Asia and Their Implications for U.S. National Security." In *NBR Analysis*. Seattle, Wash.: National Bureau of Asian Research, 1993.

____. "Is Japan Creating a Yen Bloc in East Asia and the Pacific?" In *Regionalism and Rivalry: Japan and the U.S. in Pacific Asia*, edited by Jeff Frankel and Miles Kahler. Chicago, Ill.: University of Chicago Press, 1993.

Frankel, Jeffrey A., and Shang-Jin Wei. "Yen Bloc or Dollar Bloc? Exchange Rate Policies of the East Asian Economies," Working Paper No. 93-01, Center for Pacific Basin Monetary and Economic Studies, Federal Reserve Bank of San Francisco. In *Third Annual NBER East Asia Seminar on Economics*, edited by Takahoshi Ito and Anne Krieger. Chicago, Ill.: University of Chicago Press.

Greenhouse, Steven. "New Tally of World's Economies Catapults China into Third Place." *New York Times*, May 20, 1993, pp. A1, A6.

Hardt, John P. and Young C. Kim. *Economic Cooperation in the Asia-Pacific Region*. Boulder, Colo.: Westview Press, 1990.

Harris, Stuart. "Varieties of Pacific Economic Cooperation." *Pacific Review* 4 (1991).

Higgot, Richard A., Andrew Fenton Cooper, and Jenelle Bonner. "Asia-Pacific Economic Cooperation: An Evolving Case-Study in Leadership and Cooperation Building." *International Journal* 45 (Autumn 1990): 823–66.

Indorf, Hans H. *Linkage or Bondage: U.S. Economic Relations with the ASEAN Region*. Washington, D.C.: National Planning Association, 1988.

"Industrial Policy Revisited." *International Economic Insights*, Institute for International Economics, March/April 1993.

International Monetary Fund. *World Economic Outlook*. Washington, D.C.: International Monetary Fund, 1992.

Jackson, Karl, Sukhumbhand Paribatra, and J. Soedjati Djiwandono, eds. *ASEAN in Regional and Global Context*. Berkeley, University of California, Institute of East Asian Studies, 1986.

Jackson, Karl D., and M. Hadi Soesastro. *ASEAN Security and Economic Development*. Berkeley: University of California, Institute of East Asian Studies, 1984.

Keohane, Robert O. "Multilateralism: An Agenda for Research." *International Journal* 65(4) (Autumn 1970): 733–36.

Kim, Roy, and Hilary Conroy, eds. *New Tides in the Pacific: Pacific Basin Cooperation and the Big Four (Japan, PRC, USA, USSR)*. Westport, Conn.: Greenwood Press, 1987.

Kojima, Kiyoshi. "Economic Cooperation in a Pacific Community." *Asia Pacific Community* 12 (Spring 1981): 1–10.

____. *Japan and a Pacific Free Trade Area*. Berkeley: University of California Press, 1971.

Kotkin, Joel, and Yoriko Kishimoto. *The Third Century: America's Resurgence in the Asian Era*. New York: Crown Publishers, 1988.

Kozmetsky, George, Hiroshi Matsumoto, and Raymond Smilor, eds. *Pacific Cooperation and Development*. New York Praeger, 1988.

Krause, Lawrence B. "The North American Free Trade Area and Asia-Pacific Economic Cooperation." Graduate School of International Relations and Pacific Studies, University of California, San Diego, 1992.

____. "Pacific Economic Regionalism and the United States." In *Impact of Recent Economic Development on US-Korean Relations and the Pacific Basin*. Washington, D.C.: Korea Economic Institute, 1991.

Krause, Lawrence B., and Kim Kihwan, eds. *Liberalization in the Process of Economic Development*. Berkeley: University of California Press, 1991.

Krause, Lawrence B., and Sueo Sekiguchi, eds. *Economic Interaction in the Pacific Basin*. Washington, D.C.: The Brookings Institution, 1980.

Lee, Kuan Yew. "Asia-Pacific Region in the New Geopolitical Context." Keynote address at the Informal Gathering of World Economic Leaders, Congress House, Davos, Switzerland, February 4, 1990.

____. "Asia Pacific: A Bullish Sceario Relies on Partnership," *Inernational Herald Tribune*, June 24, 1991.

Linder, Staffan Burenstam. *The Pacific Century: Economic and Political Consequences of Asian-Pacific Dynamism*. Stanford, Calif.: Stanford University Press, 1986.

Martin, L. G., ed. *The ASEAN Success Story: Social, Economic and Political Dimensions*. Honolulu: University of Hawaii Press, 1987.

McCord, William. *The Dawn of the Pacific Century*. New Brunswick, N.J.: Transaction Publishers, 1991.

"Ministers Call for Global Cooperation to Strengthen Growth Prospects." *International Monetary Fund Survey*, May 17, 1993.

Naya, Seiji. *Pacific Economic Cooperation in a Global Context*. Honolulu, Hawaii: East-West Center, 1989.

Ohmae, Kenichi. "The Rise of the Region State." *Foreign Affairs*, (Spring 1993): 78–87.

____. *The Borderless World*. New York: HarperCollins, 1990.

Pacific Economic Cooperation Council. *Pacific Economic Outlook 1993–1994*. Singapore: Pacific Economic Cooperation Council, 1993.

____. "Pacific Economic Development Report 1992–1993." Singapore: Pacific Economic Cooperation Council, 1992.

Preeg, Ernest H. *The Quest for Asia-Pacific Economic Cooperation: Rationale, Objectives, and Modalities*. Washington, D.C.: Center for Strategic and International Studies, 1990.

"Preparing for the Pacific Century." Papers of a conference to explore the potential for Pacific Basin economic cooperation, sponsored by the Commission on U.S.-Japan Relations for the Twenty-First Century, Washington, D.C., July 1991.

Rieger, Hans Christoph. "Regional Economic Cooperation in the Asia-Pacific Region." *Asian-Pacific Economic Literature* 3, September 1989.

Rostow, W. W. *The United States and the Regional Organization of Asia and the Pacific, 1965–1985*. Austin: University of Texas Press, 1986.

Ruggie, John Gerard. "Multilateralism: The Anatomy of an Institution." *International Organization* 46 (Summer 1992): 561.

Scalapino, Robert A. *The Politics of Development: Perspectives on Twentieth Century Asia*. Cambridge, Mass.: Harvard University Press, 1989.

Scalapino, Robert A., and Gennady Chufrin, eds. *Asia in the 1990's: American and Soviet Perspectives*. Berkeley: University of California, Institute of East Asian Studies, 1991.

Scalapino, Robert A., and Masatako Kosaka, eds. *Peace, Politics and Economics in Asia: The Challenge to Cooperate*. McLean, Va.: Pergamon-Brasseys Publishers, 1988.

Scalapino, Robert A., Sezaburo Sato, Jusuf Wanandi, and Sung-joo Han, eds. *Asia and the Major Powers: Domestic Politics and Foreign Policy*. Berkeley: University of California, Institute of East Asian Studies, 1989.

Shibusawa, Masahide, Haji Ahmad, and Brian Bridges. *Pacific Asia in the 1990's*. London: Routledge, 1992.

Soesastro, Hadi, and Han Sung-joo, eds. *Pacific Economic Cooperation: The Next Phase*. Jakarta: Center for Strategic and International Studies, 1983.

Sopiee, Noordin. "ASEAN and the Pacific Basin Concept: Four Questions and Five Imperatives." In "Day after Tomorrow in the Pacific Region." *Asia Society and World View* 24 (1981): 35–36.

Suh, J. W., and J. B. Ro, eds. *Asia-Pacific Economic Cooperation: The Way Ahead*. Seoul: Institute for International Economic Policy, 1990.

Taylor, Paul. "Regionalism: The Thought and the Deed." In *Framework for International Relations*, edited by A.J.R. Groom and Paul Taylor. New York: St. Martin's Press, 1990.

"Thailand: Expanding ASEAN," in "Regional Briefing." *Far Eastern Economic Review*, March 4, 1993, p. 14.

The 1993 Information Please Almanac. Boston: Houghton Mifflin, 1993.

United Nations Development Program. *Human Development Report 1992*. New York: Oxford University Press, 1992.

"United States and China Relations at a Crossroads." The Atlantic Council of the United States and National Committee on United States-China Relations, February 1993.

Van Horn, Mike. *Pacific Rim Trade: The Definitive Guide to Exporting and Investment*. New York: AMACOM, 1989.

West, Philip, and Frans A. M. Alting von Geusau, eds. *The Pacific Rim and the Western World: Strategic, Economic, and Cultural Perspectives*. Boulder, Colo.: Westview Press, 1987.

Whalley, John. "The Uruguay Round and GATT: Whither the Global System?" Paper presented at the 20th Pacific Trade and Development Conference, Washington, D.C., September 10–12, 1992.

Widenbaum, Murray. "Greater China: The Next Economic Superpower?" *Contemporary Issues*, Series 57, February 1993, pp. 2–3.

Wijkman, Per Magnus. "The Existing Bloc Expanded? The European Community, EFTA, Eastern Europe, and the CIS." Paper presented at the 20th Pacific Trade and Development Conference, Washington, D.C., September 10–12, 1992.

World Bank. *World Development Report 1992*. New York: Oxford University Press, 1992.

Young, Soogil. "Globalism and Regionalism: Complements of Competitors?" Paper presented at the 20th Pacific Trade and Development Conference, Washington, D.C., September 10–12, 1992.

___. "East Asia as a Regional Force for Globalism." Paper presented at the Workshop on Regionalism and the Global Trading System, Geneva, September 3–5, 1992.

Index

About the Contributors

Barbara K. Bundy is Executive Director of the Center for the Pacific Rim and Masters Program in Asian Studies at the University of San Francisco.

Stephen D. Burns is a specialist in analysis and implementation of Asia Pacific economic cooperation issues and is currently pursuing an advanced degree in public administration at George Washington University.

Hector Cardenas is Director General for the Pacific in the Ministry of Foreign Affairs of Mexico.

Stephen Cass is Project Coordinator of the Asia Pacific Scenarios Project conducted by Global Business Network.

Allen C. Choate is Executive Vice President of The Asia Foundation and is a Fellow at the Harvard University Center for International Affairs.

José Juan de Olloqui y Labastida is currently Ambassador of Mexico to the United Kingdom.

Monica Gruder Drake is head of M. G. Drake & Associates, an international management consulting firm.

Donald K. Emmerson is Professor of Political Science and Southeast Asian Studies at the University of Wisconsin-Madison.

Gareth Evans is Minister for Foreign Affairs of Australia.

Huang Fan-zhang is a Senior Research Fellow and Vice-President of the Economic Research Center of the State Planning Commission, Beijing, People's Republic of China.

Harry Harding is a Senior Fellow in the Foreign Policy Studies Program at The Brookings Institution.

Walter E. Hoadley is Senior Research Fellow at the Hoover Institution, Stanford University.

Vladimir I. Ivanov is Chairman of the Asia Pacific Region Studies Department in the Institute of World Studies and International Relations of the Russian Academy of Sciences.

Kim Kihwan is a Senior Advisor at Kim & Chang, a legal and management consulting firm in Seoul, Korea.

Yoriko Kishimoto is co-founder of and planning director for the Coalition for the Presidio Pacific Center, San Francisco, and principal of Japan Pacific Associates in Palo Alto.

Bih-jaw Lin is Director of the Institute of International Relations at National Chengchi University in Taipei.

Nobuo Matsunaga is president and director of the Japan Institute of International Affairs, an envoy of the Government of Japan, and an advisor to the Minister for Foreign Affairs.

Mahathir bin Mohamad is Prime Minister and Minister of Home Affairs of Malaysia.

Tapan Munroe is Chief Economist for Pacific Gas & Electric Company, San Francisco.

Saburo Okita was the Chairman of the Institute for Domestic and International Policy Studies, Tokyo, at the time of his death in 1992.

R. Sean Randolph is Managing Director of RSR Pacific Group in San Francisco.

Robert A. Scalapino is Robson Research Professor of Government Emeritus at the University of California at Berkeley.

Peter Schwartz is co-founder and President of Global Business Network.

M. Hadi Soesastro is Executive Director of the Centre for Strategic and International Studies in Jakarta, Indonesia.

Kimberly V. Weichel is President of Weichel & Associates, a firm specializing in international trade, marketing, communications, and development.

Ippei Yamazawa is Professor of Economics at Hitotsubashi University.